Rethinking children's care

Edited by
JULIA BRANNEN AND PETER MOSS

OPEN UNIVERSITY PRESS
Buckingham • Philadelphia

For Jack, Barbara and Maureen

Open University Press
Celtic Court
22 Ballmoor
Buckingham
MK18 1XW

email: enquiries@openup.co.uk
world wide web: www.openup.co.uk

and
325 Chestnut Street
Philadelphia, PA 19106, USA

First Published 2003

A catalogue record of this book is available from the British Library

ISBN 0 335 20987 4 (pb) 0 335 20988 2 (hb)

Library of Congress Cataloging-in-Publication Data
Rethinking children's care / edited by Julia Brannen and Peter Moss.
   p. cm.
Includes bibliographical references and index.
ISBN 0-335-20988-2 – ISBN 0-335-20987-4 (pbk.)
    1. Child care—Great Britain.   2. Child care services—Great Britain.
I. Brannen, Julia.   II. Moss, Peter, 1945–

HQ778.7.G7 R48 2002
362.7'0941–dc21   2002025397

Typeset by Graphicraft Limited, Hong Kong
Printed in Great Britain by Biddles Limited, Guildford and Kings Lynn

Contents

Notes on contributors

Both the editors and all the contributors are researchers at Thomas Coram Research Unit, Institute of Education, University of London.

CHAPTER 1

Concepts, relationships and policies

PETER MOSS and JULIA BRANNEN

Introduction

This book connects the subject of care and children with the work of a particular group of researchers. We use the phrase 'care *and* children' rather than 'care *of* children' to reflect certain understandings of children and childhood. The authors in this book view children as being active in care relationships, rather than as passive dependants. As we shall show (for example in Chapter 11), children can be givers, as well as recipients, of care. Children as a group are assumed to have a relationship to care as a moral question and a public issue as well as being a responsibility of parents and other adults. Moreover, children as a social group occupy a number of social statuses. 'Children' are often thought of only in relation to childhood, the first stage of the life course and related to chronological age. But adults also occupy the generalized status of children, being the offspring of parents: in this sense, a 55-year-old can be as much a child as a 5-year-old. Children born in a particular historical period also form a generation, so that for example some may talk about today's young adults as 'Thatcher's children'.

Our exploration of 'care and children' will take a wide view, from very young children placed with childminders by their parents, to grandparents who, as children, provide care for their parents. The book will also explore care in a wide range of settings and involving a wide range of carers, from formal care in group settings by paid workers to informal care by parents or relatives in ordinary homes. Such a wide remit raises the question as to how far care as a concept is meaningful in different settings and in different relationships – and if so, what it means. But before addressing this question, we shall turn to a brief account of the historical background to the research and discussions in this book and to the research setting of the contributors to the book.

Children's care and the history of the Thomas Coram Research Unit

The contributors to this book are all researchers at the Thomas Coram Research Unit (TCRU), a research centre based at the Institute of Education, University of London. TCRU was established in 1973, taking its name from an eighteenth-century pioneer in the public care of children – what we would call today child care or residential care for children and young people. Appalled by the dire, and usually fatal, conditions of the many abandoned children in London, Captain Thomas Coram (1668–1751), a retired sea captain, set about raising money to build an institution that would provide exemplary care. The Coram Foundling Hospital, the first of its kind in Britain, was opened in 1741 in what is now the Bloomsbury area of central London. It continued on this site until the 1920s, when the original hospital was pulled down, and its residential care work transferred outside London until 1953 when the hospital, now in Berkhamsted, finally closed (though Thomas Coram's work continues today in the innovative but non-residential services provided to children and families by the charity Coram Family). In Chapter 3, Christine Oliver provides an account of the care regime at the hospital towards the end of its days during the first half of the twentieth century, as recalled by women and men who were brought up in the hospital's care and shows how institutional care erased the ties of such children with their families.

TCRU has been concerned with children and care from its beginning. The first major work of the unit in the 1970s involved setting up and evaluating two 'children's centres' (the Thomas Coram and Dorothy Gardiner Centres). These demonstration projects were 'early excellence centres' for their time, visionary in combining care for children under 5 years with a variety of other projects, including education, child health and family support, available free of charge to all families living in a local catchment area, defined as within pram-pushing distance.

The centres were the brainchild of TCRU's first director, Professor Jack Tizard. He turned his attentions to early years services in the late 1960s as he became increasingly aware of their great inadequacies: insufficient in number, incoherent in structure, unresponsive to the needs of families with children (for a sample of his cogent critique see J. Tizard et al. 1976). Previously, Jack Tizard had played a major part in the postwar reforms of child care, another part of the story of which is described by Claire Cameron in Chapter 5. Jack's contribution sought to transform residential care for a group then called 'mentally handicapped children' (now called children with learning difficulties). In the 1950s, most of these children who were unable to live at home were consigned to long-stay hospitals, often large and isolated institutions providing for children and adults with learning difficulties. Here they were cared for on wards by nurses and doctors. The conditions in these hospitals were generally bleak and in some cases very poor indeed, becoming in the 1970s the subject of public scandal and official inquiry (for accounts of life for children in long-stay hospitals, see Oswin 1971, 1978).

But well before the 1970s, Jack was questioning the very principle of institutionalizing children with disabilities in this way, comparing their treatment with that of children without disability. In one of these long-stay hospitals, he set up a small experimental unit – Brooklands – where a group of children from the hospital lived under another care regime: the application of 'principles of child care that are today regarded as meeting the needs of normal children deprived of normal home life' (J. Tizard 1964: 85). The results were striking:

> The children in Brooklands changed considerably during the two years of the study. They kept in good physical health and, living much of the time out of doors engaged in gross motor activities, they looked healthy, sun-tanned and alert . . . They were often eager, active and purposeful, and in this way presented a striking contrast to their behaviour on arrival. They became able to play, socially and constructively, at a level approaching that of their mental age. Emotionally they became far less maladjusted . . . They were able to play co-operatively with other children, to take turns with as much grace as comparable normal children, and to share. They were thus affectionate and happy children, usually busy and interested in what they were doing, confident and full of fun.
>
> (J. Tizard 1964: 133–4)

TCRU maintained this interest in the care of children in long-stay hospitals through, for example, the work of Maureen Oswin, remarkable for its depth of insight and profound humanity (Oswin 1971, 1978). The unit also continued Jack's interest in early years services after his death in 1979. It was, for example, a pioneer in the study of childminding (Mayall and Petrie 1977, 1983) and out-of-school care (Petrie and Logan 1986; Petrie 1990), both fields in which the unit still has an active interest (see Chapters 7 and 8 for recent childminding research). Professor Barbara Tizard, the unit's second director and Jack's wife, developed a critical and influential body of research on residential care, foster care and adoption, nurseries, parental involvement in schools, children's intellectual competences, educational disadvantage, and racial identity (for example, B. Tizard 1977; B. Tizard and Hughes 1984; B. Tizard et al. 1988; B. Tizard and Phoenix 1993).

The chapters in this book bring together more recent work by researchers from TCRU on children and care, from the mid-1990s to the present day. But TCRU's background, outlined above, has left its mark, both in a willingness to question and rethink social policy and practice relating to children's care, and the assumptions which underlie these. It is also a constant reminder that we ignore history at our peril. So while this book is focused on contemporary conceptualizations and discussions of care, it also has a strong historical element, illustrating how ideas about care, as well as the language and practices to which they give rise, are produced and reproduced within particular historical times and geographical spaces.

We began this chapter by describing two dimensions which connect the contributions in this book: the broad remit of children and care and a critical mass of researchers who have worked at TCRU since the early 1970s. But contributions to this book also connect around three issues: developments in the conceptualization of care; the relational and power aspects of care; and developments in care as social policy. First, with respect to the concept of care, 'care' is a word much used, especially in policy. But what might it mean? From the understandings that are available, which become influential, even dominant, in discourse? Second, relationships of care. What relationships are involved in care? Between whom and to what effect? Third, care and policy. How is the concept of care understood in policy? What structures, purposes, provisions and practices are produced by particular concepts and discourses of care? How does care relate in policy to other domains such as education and health?

Care as a developing concept

'Care' is one of those words widely used yet rarely defined. As a result 'the concept of care is both ambiguous and contested . . . and has been used in such diverse ways that it is in danger of losing its core meaning' (Daly and Lewis 1999: 6). In Chapter 4, Pat Petrie outlines the diversity of meanings that have been attached to the word 'care' in the English language: anxiety, burden, concern; protection, responsibility; having regard or liking for someone; caring about and taking care of; giving care and receiving care. As this shows, 'care' comes down to us today through the ages bearing many meanings which carry different values.

The conceptualization of care is an historical process in which ideas about what care of children may mean have been subject to changing policies and practices inscribed by the norms and cultures of particular groups, places and historical times. Chapters 2, 3, 4 and 5 examine various instances of this process, with their explorations of the history of 'child care' and 'childcare' policies, provisions and practices. In this book, following the practice in policy documents, 'child care' (two words) is used to refer to social work, residential and other social welfare provisions for children who are 'in need' or 'looked after' and policy for these groups; while 'childcare' (one word) is used to refer to nurseries, childminders and similar provision for children used mainly while parents are at work, and policy for this type of care service. In legislation, the term 'day care' has been used to refer to childcare provisions, and still does so in relation to regulation.

As notions of care (in respect of children) evolve over time through public policy and public discourse, care may be viewed as an *ideological notion*. Care as a concept and its particular contextualized meanings shape our understandings and interpretations of the world and the ways in which we consider how we and others ought, or expect, to act. At the same time, care is a *social scientific concept*, and as such an analytical tool which provides critical, in-depth insights into social phenomena. For example, to take the theme of control and power to which we shall return, through critical analysis of the concept care and its applications we may see how care regimes operating in a variety of systems (childcare, child care, education, health and so on) exercise, in Bernstein's terms, both visible and invisible forms of control (Bernstein 1975, 2000): on the one hand, visible control via authority, organizational hierarchies and structures; and, on the other, invisible or 'symbolic' forms of control. In the latter case, authorship and authority are transferred to children, and regulation is exercised through specialized forms of 'communication' (including knowledge as well as particular modalities of language) which are themselves embedded in social and economic structures (this latter point being crucial).

Ideological notions and social scientific concepts are not, however, distinct and unrelated. It is important to take account of the ways in which both public discourses and social scientific discourses shift and the relationships between the two (Nilsen and Brannen 2002). Concepts and theories in the social sciences are themselves products of historical social processes and social structures: they are not devoid of ideology. Referring again to the work of Bernstein (2000), the 'external languages of description' which conceptualization provides, enable social scientists not only to describe but also to interpret social and historical phenomena – but never from a position of neutral objectivity, always from within particular contexts and with a particular perspective.

Care as a concept has received much attention in recent years in the academic if not in the policy world. Since the 1970s, feminist scholarship has sought to make the work or labour aspect of care visible, to understand the processes and structures through which care is mainly undertaken by women, and to illuminate the consequences of the highly gendered nature of caring for women's access to material resources and social status within families, the labour market and in the wider society. From an initial focus on unpaid, informal care in the family, work on care has expanded to take in paid care work and the relationship between paid and unpaid care work.

One important concept of care to emerge from this work, and in particular from feminist analyses of welfare states, is 'social care'. Three dimensions are particularly important in this concept:

> The first is care as *labour*. This draws attention to the nature of the work involved. But it is important also to make reference to the conditions under which such work is carried out . . . Highlighting the labour aspect in this way emphasises care as a verb and carers as actors. The second dimension of the concept sets care within a *normative framework of obligations and responsibilities*. Care is not like work or other labour because it is often initiated and provided under conditions of social and/or familial responsibility . . . Third we see care as an activity with *costs*, both

financial and emotional . . . We have arrived at our three dimensional approach in which we define social care as the activities involved in meeting the physical and emotional requirements of dependent adults and children, and the normative, cost and social frameworks within which this work is assigned and carried out.

(Daly and Lewis 1999: 6, emphasis added)

The concept of 'social care', it is further argued, transcends conceptual dichotomies: between the public and the private; between formal and informal settings; between paid and unpaid carers; between the state and the family; between the care of children and the care of adults (Daly and Lewis 1999; Kröger 2001). It involves physical, mental and emotional work – caring for and caring about. It involves feeling responsible and taking responsibility. Social care, therefore, involves work that may be undertaken unpaid in the home by family members (usually female), or that may be commodified and undertaken as paid labour by public or private sector workers (usually women) (Ungerson 1997).

This conceptualization of care has great value, not least for its attention to the labour and costs of care, especially for those 'condemned' to care (women), and its recognition of the complexity of care including material, emotional and moral dimensions. But it also raises some difficulties, in particular arising from its transcendental conceptualization of care, with its implication that the activity of care is essentially the same, no matter what the setting, the main issue being where the boundaries are drawn, for example between private and public.

Care, we would agree, always involves labour, costs and responsibility. But care may differ in other important respects in different settings. For example, to take examples from the book, can a mother's care of her child in her home be equated with a childminder's care of that mother's child in the minder's home (Chapters 7 and 8)? Or can either be equated with the care of a group of children by a nursery worker (Chapter 2)? Or with the care given by nurses to children on a hospital ward (Chapter 9)? Childminders, nursery workers and hospital nurses may have taken over some of the labour of care from the mother, but is their practice of care to be understood as mother substitution (that is, with mother care the norm, which other forms aspire to emulate) – or do each of these care relationships have distinctive features?

We would argue that they are distinctive in some important respects, because each is situated within a particular context – a distinctive setting, with particular networks of relationships and particular connections between care and other purposes such as education or health. In Chapter 4, for instance, Pat Petrie explores the theory and practice of pedagogy, widespread in many countries of continental Europe in paid work undertaken with collectivities of children in a range of settings. Not only does pedagogy work with and through the group, but also it adopts a holistic approach to the child, in which caring is understood to be closely linked to learning and socialization or upbringing (indeed she suggests pedagogy might correspond to a concept more familiar to British ears, 'education in its broadest sense'). Studies of contemporary childhood in Nordic countries, where many children are in centres and other formal services from a very early age, have concluded that children quickly appreciate that centre and home are two different types of environment, each with distinctive relationships and requiring distinctive ways of behaviour (Dencik 1989). Referring to the Nordic experience, Mayall (1996: 56) comments that developments in these countries have 'set [the stage] for extracting children out from under the family, conceptually, and thinking about them, not only as individuals, but also, more widely as a social group'.

The conclusion we draw is that there are some transcendent elements in care, but that there are also some elements that are diverse and particular to time and place. Increasing the number of nurseries, for example, may move some labour and costs from mothers to paid workers in the public domain: both operate within a framework of obligations and responsibilities. But a nursery does not replicate the relationship of mother and child, and it requires different forms of caring relationship. The problem with the concept of 'social care' is that it may, unwittingly, reinforce an idea of mother care as normative, and hamper the development of concepts of care relevant to other settings; for example, a group setting for children which provides a public space for a wide range of possible projects and relationships, a space in which care might be understood as part of a wider pedagogical approach.

The moral and ethical dimensions of care

Feminist thinking has also developed the concept of care within ethical frameworks of obligations and responsibilities. As Finch and Mason (1993) have argued, responsibilities for family members are not a matter of applying fixed rules or prescribed moral norms of obligation. Rather, responsibilities are created over time with respect to moral claims, and through negotiation, sometimes explicit but sometimes not. Care responsibilities are, therefore, the product of human agency and are closely linked to gendered moral identities and their construction, for example the identity of daughter, mother or grandmother. Variations – for example, why one sibling does more caring than another – occur because 'responsibilities are a product of interaction between individuals over time' (Finch and Mason 1993: 168). Because of the relational and context specific nature of responsibility, it is mistaken to think that it is possible to 'read off' 'people's likely actions from the beliefs which they express about family relationships, particularly in answer to survey questions' (Finch and Mason 1993: 174).

On the other hand, parental responsibility for non-adult children is not negotiable in the sense that parents have a legal responsibility to care for their children and that young children cannot care for themselves. 'Parents are allocated responsibility for young children . . . [with parent–child relationships] *defined as relationships* in which parents take responsibility for the material and emotional welfare of children' (Finch and Mason 1993: 168, original emphasis). However, even parent–child relationships may be 'located within the framework of "developing commitments", rather than the idea that fixed rules of obligation cover parent–child relationships' (Finch and Mason 1993: 168). For children, even young children, interpret and act upon parents' rules, guidelines and demands, while many parents today do not act towards children in authoritarian ways. Chapter 11 (by Julia Brannen and Ellen Heptinstall) starts from the premise that children make a contribution to family life and shows how children as sentient actors offer their parents emotional support.

While Finch (1989) has developed the concept of care as moral under-standing through social practices via a sociological analysis of people's every-day lives, feminist philosophers have developed more general social theories based on an all-encompassing ethic of care starting from interpersonal rela-tions rather than rights (Leira 2002). Both, however, foreground the ethical nature of relationships and practices of care, and the constitution of these relationships and practices within specific contexts, rather than their neces-sary production in conformity to universal moral codes.

Setting an 'ethics of care' within a normative framework, Tronto (1993: 103) defines caring as 'a species activity that includes everything that we do to maintain, continue and repair our "world" so we can live in it as well as possible'. Care, she says, consists of a number of elements – caring about, caring for and care receiving. An ethics of care is about 'a practice rather than a set of rules or principles . . . It involves particular acts of caring and a "general habit of mind" to care that should inform all aspects of moral life' (Tronto 1993: 127). An ethics of care attaches particular value to responsibil-ity, competence, responsiveness and integrity.

The ethics of care approach is broad, in some ways more transcendental than 'social care'; it applies to all social relationships, so connecting discus-sions of care not only to the personal but also to the environment, armed conflicts and indeed the global economy. Yet the way care is framed in this approach – as a social practice including a general habit of mind – also makes it easier, in a service context, to envisage how care might relate to specific service domains, such as child care, education or nursing. Rather than being a distinctive field of work itself ('social care' or 'child care' work), care can be understood as a dimension of working, which can be incor-porated into many fields. Work in particular and distinctive fields – such as child care, education, nursing, pedagogy – can bear a caring dimension, or not. Workers can adopt caring practices and habits of mind, or not. The teacher or nurse or nursery worker or childminder can apply an ethic of care – be caring in their nursery, teaching, pedagogy to a lesser or greater extent.

Sevenhuijsen (1999a) captures this sense of care as a practice that can permeate many fields when she writes:

> The notion of 'care as social practice' can provide useful points of depar-ture, provided the practice of care is not exclusively sought in that

which is generally thought of as care: the relations between 'caring' and 'dependent' people in situations of child-rearing, sickness and social need. In fact *practically all human behaviour carries aspects or dimensions of care*, even though there is certainly not always an official vocabulary for expressing this . . . Even horse-riding and bio-chemical research can be carried out with greater or lesser degrees of care.

(Sevenhuijsen 1999a: 23, emphasis added)

Several contributors to this book (for example Peter Moss in Chapter 2 and Claire Cameron in Chapter 5) use the concept of an ethics of care in their analysis of particular services for children – childcare in the former case, child care in the latter. But this concept is more than an analytical instrument. It poses a challenge to all involved in services for children. For it opens up the idea that these services have an important ethical dimension, involving practitioners in a process of ongoing and often complex decisions about what is the 'right thing' to do. This can be at odds with technical and managerial approaches which have been a feature of the resurgence of liberal government since the 1980s (Rose 1999), and the importance they attach to instrumental values and universal rules. Wærness (1999), speaking of recent developments in Norwegian services for elderly people, highlights this contrast:

Rather than transferring the instrumental business approach to public care services, which is what has happened to an increasing extent during the last decade, a new approach based on an understanding that good care is a moral issue where neither the client nor the care worker can be treated as objects is needed. This approach does not suggest new 'outcomes-oriented' principles for organizing the services. Instead we have to learn there is no way to shield care workers from the burdens connected to providing care in difficult and ambiguous situations.

(Wærness 1999: 225)

Wærness here raises a further way of conceptualizing care, care not as ethic but as business. While there may have been a recent turn to privatized provision in many service areas, in particular those providing for elderly people, in many areas of children's care this 'business approach' is not new. In Chapter 5, Claire Cameron describes the 'baby farming' prevalent in the nineteenth century, while long-term public neglect of childcare provision has meant that services have mostly been provided through the private market, in particular by self-employed childminders and for-profit nurseries. While the post-1997 Labour government has for the first time since 1945 given public policy prominence to childcare, it has opted to work through the private market, intervening only in cases of 'market failure'.

The concept of care as commodity and business views paid care work as a series of discrete activities which can be defined, regulated, packaged and priced, then traded as products in a marketplace. Care when commodified is brought within an instrumental and calculable rationality, with the various actors recast as buyers and sellers, purchasers and providers, seeking information to strike the best deal and enmeshed in contracts to ensure the deal is adhered to. Chapters 7 and 8, by June Statham and Ann Mooney respectively, illustrate some of the tensions that arise in childminding between care and money, with parents and childminders often reluctant to assume their allotted role of traders bargaining over costs in an assumed market: both may find this marketized concept at odds with a non-instrumental concept of care which foregrounds trust relationships. Yet, at the same time, childminders, as self-employed service providers, place themselves at a disadvantage by their unwillingness to be 'business like', sustaining their own poor pay and conditions. In Bernstein's (2000) terms, childminders exercise invisible or symbolic control in the regulation of their relations with parents. However, such modes of control are increasingly located in the visible or explicit negotiations demanded by business and private markets, which childminders find difficult to reconcile with the implicit ways in which they communicate with parents.

Our discussion of the conceptualization of care by no means exhausts the possibilities. As Leira (2002) suggests, the right to care and the right to be cared for are in some contexts and societies part of the social rights of citizenship and may be encompassed within the term 'inclusive citizenship' (Knijn and Kremer 1997). While the rights of carers especially of parents (mainly mothers) to care for their children have been attended to if only partially in Britain, the rights of children to (non-parental) care and to care of a high quality remains a novel idea. In Chapter 9 on nursing care, Helen Chalmers and Peter Aggleton raise the possibility that nursing care for children might be developed within the UN declaration on children's rights.

Care relations and power

Care is typically analysed dyadically and as a relationship between unequals – between those who 'need' care and those with a duty to give care. The care-giver is conceptualized as independent and active and the recipient by definition as passive and dependent. Rather than only focusing on a dyadic mother–child relationship, we can understand childhood and the care of children as lived and located to a greater or lesser extent in a network of relationships, made up of family members but also other children and adults. Children, for example, have always lived part of their lives outside the home, and this remains true today, even if there may be an historical shift from time outside the home spent in informal situations (for example, playing outside with friends) to time outside the home spent in more organized or formal settings (for example, nurseries, playgroups, out-of-school centres). These non-familial relationships play an influential part in children's lives.

While we would not wish to deny that children 'need' care, we would also want to suggest a more dynamic and complex picture than active carer, passive child. Within their networks of relationships, children give as well as receive care – not only to and from adults but also with other children. In Chapter 11, for example, Julia Brannen and Ellen Heptinstall refer to children being care-givers as well as care-receivers. Children are conceptualized as active agents, co-constructors of relationships and identities, and able to contribute to their families (and other settings) in a variety of ways including providing care.

Understanding care relationships means not simply looking at relationships in the here and now. It means taking a dynamic view of care relationships and the ways in which people (women) repay care over the course of the life course and across family generations, as in Chapter 10 (by Julia Brannen, Peter Moss and Ann Mooney) which is concerned with care in four-generation families. In this chapter we may observe instances of reciprocity of care-giving and care-receiving between different female family members over time. A grandmother giving care to her grandchild and to her own elderly parent today is likely to have been a recipient of care 25 years earlier, when she was herself a parent with a young child, and she will receive care again in due course, when she enters frail old age: in this way, over her life course, she will have both received and given care in her social position of child. In a different way, support given by parents to their children during the transition to adulthood may be reciprocated by the next generation providing similar support to their own young people rather than providing direct reciprocity to their parents. This transmission of care may, moreover, constitute part of a wider pattern of intergenerational transfers, including money and other material resources.

Care relationships may also involve transfers across geographical space. They are increasingly part of processes of globalization. Hochschild (2000) has written about 'global care chains', which she defines as

> a series of personal links between people across the globe based on the paid or unpaid work of caring . . . One common form of such a chain is: (1) an older daughter from a poor family who cares for her siblings while (2) her mother works as a nanny caring for the children of a migrating nanny who, in turn, (3) cares for the child of a family in a rich country.
>
> (Hochschild 2000: 131)

While Hochschild draws her examples from the United States, we can find more examples of these global flows in western Europe – for example, domestic workers and carers, employed by affluent families, who are drawn from central and eastern Europe and beyond (Andersen 2000), or nurses and teachers recruited to Britain from throughout the world. These transfers lead to a drain upon the much needed resources of the source countries. Another facet of globalization, the provision of services by overseas companies, is nurtured by increasing privatization and marketization of services and the World Trade Organization's General Agreement on Trade in Services (GATS) which facilitates greater marketization of public services.

> For the private health care providers of the USA, the glittering prize remains the public health sector in other OECD [Organization for Economic Cooperation and Development] countries, which have remained substantially closed to private sector competition from foreign corporations. The prospect of public services coming under threat from GATS in this way has roused a storm of protest from countries which value the public provision of basic services such as health and education.
>
> (Hilary 2001: 17, 37–8)

We have moved into dangerous terrain. Here, care relationships not only involve love, responsibility and attentiveness, but also contribute to inequalities and exploitation between individuals, groups and polities. Gender is a key issue here; as many of the chapters suggest, caring (both formal and informal) remains largely women's responsibility. Even when men enter the care workforce, as Chapter 6 shows, men may feel constrained by dominant models of masculinity and feel excluded from informal networks among the women. Power also enters via divisions of social class, ethnicity, nationality and emerging forms of capitalist enterprise within processes of globalization.

For at the heart of care relationships is the issue of power. Indeed, it is striking how often the issue of power – or control as it is often expressed – emerges in the chapters in this book, illuminating how care carries risks as well as possibilities. What do we mean by power?

Many recent British policy initiatives in the field of care (for example, an emphasis on children's rights and participation, 'cash for care' in adult care) cast themselves in the guise of seeking to 'empower' those who are cared for. This represents a particular view of power as the attribute of *persons* notably bureaucrats and professionals who provide services. Empowerment discourses aim to redistribute power to the recipients and users of care services.

But there are other more complex ideas about power and power relations. Foucault's thinking on this subject is important and relevant. In his view, we can never stand outside power relations. While some persons may have more power than others, power is ever present and all pervasive. It both surrounds people and is wielded by them – we may be subjected to power, but we also exercise power. So while there are structural disparities in power as a resource, all of us are implicated in relations of power:

> in human relations, whatever they are – whether it be a question of communicating verbally ... or a question of a love relationship, an institutional or economic relationship – power is always present: I mean the relationship in which one wishes to direct the behaviour of another.
>
> (Foucault 1987: 11)

Power relations are local and diffuse. Indeed, services for children are important spaces for the exercise and study of power relations. It is important to distinguish the ways in which power regulates and governs, and the extent to which these processes are overt or covert since this has implications for the ways in which those regulated read such messages and hence for their ability to concur with or resist such regulation (Bernstein 2000). One way that power is exerted – in nurseries, schools, hospitals and any other service for children – is through the discourses of professionals and experts which are highly influential in shaping the practices of parents and practitioners. Such discursive regimes or regimes of truth (Foucault 1980: 131) are mechanisms for rendering reality amenable to certain kinds of actions (Miller and Rose 1993). By the same token, they also exclude alternative ways of understanding and interpreting the world. In short, regimes of truth make assumptions and values invisible, turn subjective perspectives and understandings into apparently objective truths, and determine some things are self-evident and realistic while others are dubious and impractical.

When researchers, policy makers and practitioners talk about empowerment, for children or parents, at the same time they are seeking to govern or regulate behaviour, not overtly through diktat ('you must do this or else you will be penalized') but covertly through dominant discourses ('we should do this as this child is "in need" because her development is impaired'). To take two examples discussed in this book (Chapters 2 and 7), both the 'child in need', which permeates child care, and child development, which permeates childcare, can be understood as important concepts within dominant discourses. Both contribute to particular social constructions of children – in the former case, as dependent, weak and poor; in the latter, as an essential being with universal properties and inherent capabilities whose development is viewed as an innate process biologically determined, following general laws. Both generate particular rationalities and practices, through which practitioners and children are governed. Both can be seen as, in fact, disempowering although they may not be seen as such by those involved: for power is not only pervasive but also often invisible, it being a feature of dominant discourses that they are taken for granted.

Power is not just about governing behaviour. It is also implicated in the construction of identity, including the shaping of care identities – those of carers and those of the cared for. In his later work, Foucault pays particular attention to the construction of subjectivity. He explores how the forces of power and knowledge act upon people to shape this process, and so to constitute the self. But Foucault does not confine himself to relationships between people. He also speaks of care involving a relationship with the self and speaks of 'care of the self'. This is not about discovering our 'true' self, but is rather a matter of whether and how we choose to constitute ourselves ('invent, not discover, who we are': Bernauer and Mahon 1994: 147), and by so doing resist the forces of power and knowledge that otherwise fashion our subjectivity.

Returning to our earlier discussion of ethics, Foucault understands ethics as the 'practice of an intellectual freedom that is transgression of modern knowledge-power-subjectivity relationships . . . which seeks to open the possibilities for new relations to self and events in the world' (Bernauer and Mahon 1994: 152–3). Rather than an abstract normative code, ethics is a mode of self-formation and the way we fashion our freedom; it 'requires him to act upon himself, to monitor, test, improve and transform himself' (Foucault 1986: 28). In Chapter 10, Julia Brannen, Peter Moss and Ann Mooney discuss a critical case of a grandmother who, understood from a Foucauldian point of view, has struggled successfully to define her own subjectivity through rejecting an identity constructed around care-giving. Christine Oliver in Chapter 3 describes how the regime in the Foundling Hospital constructed a new identity for cared-for children as 'foundlings' – and how many struggled in later life to create a different identity.

A closely related danger of power in the care field is the possibility that care relations can smother difference, through trying to make the Other (for example, the child for whom we care) into the same. This danger arises from a long-standing western need 'to know': 'in Western philosophy, when knowledge or theory comprehends the Other, the alterity of the latter vanishes as it becomes part of the same' (Young 1990: 13). Foucault (1983: 19), also concerned with Otherness, speaks of 'how an Other is always pushed aside, marginalized, forcibly homogenized and devalued as [western] cognitive machinery does its work'.

This concern is foregrounded in the ethics of care literature. For Tronto (1993), responsiveness – one of the main values in an ethics of care – involves finding a relation to the Other based on responsibility and the recognition of difference: 'responsiveness suggests a different way to understand the needs of others rather than to put ourselves into their position . . . [O]ne is engaged from the standpoint of the other, but not by presuming that the other is exactly like the self' (Tronto 1993: 135). An important issue for care relationships, therefore, which Peter Moss discusses in Chapter 2 in relation to childcare services, is how to relate to the Other and difference, in a way that is welcoming and respectful, rather than grasping and totalizing. This challenge is exemplified in Chapter 6 where Charlie Owen argues that in encouraging men to participate in paid childcare, the expectation that men should be like women is neither unrealistic nor desirable. Rather in order to change the gendered nature of childcare, there needs to be more than one model of masculinity to guide men's performance.

The issue then is not to do away with power relations in general, or to remove them from care relations, which is impossible. Nor can any of us – policy makers or practitioners, researchers or other experts, parents or other relatives – stand outside power, occupying some objective position from which we can discern the truth and act in a neutral way. From this perspective, 'empowerment' may increase the ability of children or adults to care for the self – but only to a limited extent. For the rhetoric of 'empowerment' which focuses upon the individual ignores the social and relational nature of power, failing to address the ways in which power flows in different directions through a complex web of relationships.

Indeed, as the three-dimensional model of power developed by Lukes (1974) suggests, discourses of empowerment may render the exercise of power invisible.

[I]s it not the supreme and most insidious exercise of power to prevent people, to whatever degree, from having grievances by shaping their perceptions, cognitions and preferences in such a way that they accept their role in the existing order of things, either because they can see or imagine no alternative to it, or because they see it as natural and unchangeable, or because they value it as divinely ordained and beneficial? To assume that the absence of grievance equals genuine consensus is simply to rule out the possibility of false or manipulated consensus by definitional fiat.

(Lukes 1974: 24)

Power, in Foucault's view, though unavoidable, is not inherently negative or bad. It has positive aspects. It is enabling, productive in the sense that it has creative and generative dimensions. Power may be productive, but it is also dangerous: it cannot be ignored, not least in relationships of care. It should be unmasked, made visible. For only if power is rendered visible can it be recognized, contested and resisted. We need to be aware, sceptical and critical about discourses which claim to be 'the truth' and also about our own part in care relationships. Sevenhuijsen (1999a) captures this complex relationship to power in her discussion of what she terms a 'politically formulated ethics of power', which she argues should not make its objective the elimination of power.

Rather it should work with a multi-faceted understanding of power, which can capture both its restraining and enabling, creative and generative dimensions, and which can also differentiate between power and domination. Such an understanding should make sure that power is recognisable and manageable, and that unfair differences in treatment or arbitrariness cannot take hold of public decision-making. It can also contribute to exposing oppression, repression and systematic forms of dominance and assist in ways of reversing them.

(Sevenhuijsen 1999a: 66)

In dwelling on these perspectives on power, we want to make clear the importance we attach to being attentive to structure as well as agency, including the social and economic structures in which individuals and regimes of truth are located (Bernstein 2000). The cases of identity formation referred to above – the grandmother and the Coram 'foundlings' – involve a dialectical relationship between agency and structure. Both are discussed in their respective chapters from an historical, structural perspective which locates the individuals concerned as living in a particular time and place with particular resources and constraints. Furthermore, Bernstein's work shows how certain linguistic/discursive strategies of control emphasize only the agency or self-regulatory side of the agency/structure divide and can 'result' in the sources of social control or rather control itself becoming invisible (Bernstein 2000). Thus for example childcare policies which emphasize parents' ability to make choices about services may be considered *disempowering* if the structural constraints upon choice are rendered invisible to them.

Children's care and public policy

While public policy in Britain often speaks of 'care', it is rare to find any sustained discussion of the concept of care in policy documents. For example, as Peter Moss shows in Chapter 2, the frequent use of 'childcare' by the current New Labour government is not matched by a depth of enquiry about the meaning of the concept. Or to take another example, the extensive academic literature on the concept of 'social care' does not appear to connect with policy – despite frequent reference to the term 'social care' in policy documents. 'Social care' in English public policy emerges as an umbrella term for describing the wide range of non-health services for which the Department of Health in England is responsible including 'child care'. A similar umbrella function has been noted at a European level: '"social care services" has European-wide acceptance as referring to non-cash care services provided by social workers and other professional groups for user groups such as children and families, elderly people and people with disabilities' (Munday 1998: 4).

Policy relating to care, and the associated discourses and practices, may not be subject to much conceptualization by policy makers. It is, however, subject to major changes of direction. The care of children with learning difficulties in long-stay hospitals, that Jack Tizard helped to change, may seem grotesquely inappropriate today, yet it was deemed quite fit and proper for many years. Government policy today may call for more childcare services, but for many years policy was neutral or hostile to such forms of care. We may wince at the accounts of prewar Foundling Hospital care, yet in its day the Foundling Hospital was seen as a centre of excellence.

We may choose to see such changes as signs of progress. But they can also be seen as signifying how care – policy and practice – is situated within particular temporal, spatial and cultural contexts. What we see as 'best practice' today may not seem so in another generation, nor will it necessarily be viewed as such from the perspectives of those countries and groups who prefer different approaches or who have different traditions. An historical perspective is a reminder of the provisional and contingent status of all policies, and the practices and provisions to which they give rise.

Policies on the care of children are shaped by powerful discourses, in particular around the relationship between individual, family, market and state, and concerning gender. Countries embody particular 'gender regimes', a concept which describes how the state embodies a set of power relationships between men and women, and which includes a gender hierarchy and division of labour (Connell 1990). Adopting a similar focus on the relationship between gender and labour (both paid and unpaid), Lewis (1992, 1997) argues that welfare states are inscribed with gender norms, in particular the extent to which it is assumed by policy makers that women should be dependent on male breadwinners; the corollary of such dependency is an assumption that women should take responsibility for care work. Lewis's typology divides states into three groups: strong male breadwinner (for example, Ireland and Germany), modified male breadwinner (Britain and France) and weak male breadwinner (Scandinavian countries).

Esping-Andersen (1999) applies other criteria to classify welfare states, describing Britain as a *liberal* welfare state characterized by a residual or minimalist approach with targeted, means-tested benefits. Liberal states such as Britain have also been reluctant to pursue 'defamilialization', that is policies, in particular the provision of care services, 'that lessen individuals' reliance on family; that maximise individuals' command of economic resources independently of familial or conjugal reciprocities' (Esping-Andersen 1999: 45). In both respects, liberalism reflects its core values: the private nature of family and caring, and the virtue of individual responsibility.

Recent years have seen the emergence in Britain of views about government and the state which Rose (1999) has termed 'advanced liberalism'. Advanced liberalism brings to bear new ideas about government and new technologies for governing. But it also reasserts the liberal belief in the value of autonomous individuals who are able to accept responsibility for managing their own risks and those of their children and family, and achieving this autonomy through paid work: the family as private sphere is thereby reaffirmed. Accompanying neo-liberal economics value market and instrumental relationships, flexibility and fluidity. In this instrumental rationality, everything can be valued and everything has a predetermined outcome: 'all aspects of social behaviour are now reconceptualised along economic lines – as calculative actions undertaken through the universal human faculty of choice' (Rose 1999: 141).

From these liberal perspectives, children's care is an essentially private concern, allocated to the private sphere of the family. If not able to be practised in the family, then care is viewed as a product or a commodity which the market can provide, the autonomous individual can purchase, and whose value is to be calculated and whose quality is to be assured through various human technologies and managerial methods. In other areas of care notably elder care, another pattern in the commodification of care is evident: the transformation of public to private and marketized care.

This context has a powerful influence on practice as well as policy. Childcare is a product to be purchased by working parents on the market, and the 'consumer' (parent) is supposed to make rational purchasing choices with the benefit of information from various quality control methods: inspections, accreditations and so forth (as illustrated vividly in Chapter 8, which focuses on childminders). Government's role is to step in only where market failure occurs.

An exception to this is the public provision by local social services departments of 'sponsored day care' for 'children in need' (the subject of Chapter 7). The rationale for public intervention in these relatively few cases is a failure of parental responsibility: though even here, the local authorities concerned mainly buy services within a local 'childcare' market. For the same reasons of failed parental responsibility, government assumes responsibility for the residential care of children and young people and other 'child care' services provided through child welfare agencies (the subject of Chapter 5).

This context of advanced liberalism adds to the ambivalence which surrounds the concept of care, not just for children but more generally. The need for care is seen as indicative of deficit: the absence of the normatively prescribed state of individual independence achieved through the status of paid worker, a status highly prioritized in current government policy. As Chapter 2 explores, further tensions are now building between a gender regime which continues to allocate childcare to mothers, and an advanced liberal government which places high value on individual autonomy achieved through employment (as well as on competitiveness in global market capitalism, to be achieved by optimal use of the potential labour force).

What is lacking in British social policy, in our view, is a conceptual language which links citizenship to notions of interdependence, in place of binary and false oppositions between dependence and independence (Brannen 2000). Rather than starting from the notion of the individual and of obligation as deriving from rights – the Third Way approach (Sevenhuijsen 1999b) which is based on masculinist ideas of a desirable norm of the 'autonomous self' (Gilligan 1982) – we would argue for an ethics-based approach to care. This would start from the idea of responsibility and obligation *between* people, and would view the self as a moral subject which derives from and exists in relation to a network of relationships with others (Sevenhuijsen 1999b).

Liberal ideas of care and a particular 'gender regime' work together to create policies concerning the workforce involved in children's care, and indeed the care of adults: childcare and social care workers. Paid care work with children (but also elderly people) is premised on deploying women's supposed 'essential qualities' from the privacy of the home into the public arena of care services. Relying on naturally acquired caring skills (whether biologically or culturally applied is not relevant here), these women are viewed as requiring but limited training for doing care work; by implication this means that most men exclude themselves from such work (Chapter 6). Anything needed in addition to these 'natural' capabilities involves simple low-level technologies, and the application of prescribed procedures and standards, acquired through on-the-job training. The result is a childcare and social care workforce in Britain of over 1.3 million (if we include workers in childcare, residential care for children and young people and eldercare), over 90 per cent of whom are women, with low levels of education and training, and poor pay and other employment conditions (Simon et al. 2002).

So far we have referred on several occasions to terms such as 'childcare', 'childcare services' and 'childcare workforce'. But we acknowledge that it is increasingly difficult to conceptualize, let alone define, a distinct policy entity of 'childcare'. Just as the borders between social care, health and housing are becoming less distinct in policy and provision for elderly people, both in Britain and elsewhere in Europe, so too are borders between care and education (and some would add play and leisure) blurring with respect to children. In England and Scotland, all 'childcare' services are now within the administrative responsibility of education, 'childcare' services for under-5s are given an overtly educational role, while schools are encouraged to become sites for a range of 'childcare' and other services.

So far there have been no reforms of the workforce. But what this might involve can be seen in Sweden. A reform implemented in autumn 2001 has brought the training of school teachers and pre-school and school-age childcare workers (for children from 0 to 18+ years) within one framework, involving a $3^{1}/_{2}$ year higher education course, 18 months of which is shared, with specialization chosen only later on. In the future, all workers trained in this way – whether working in nurseries, schools or free-time centres – will be termed 'teachers'.

Reforms in Britain which seek to bring childcare and education into a new and close relationship raise important and difficult questions about the concept of care and require a rethink about how children's care relates to other fields – not only education, but also health, play and social work.

Rethinking children's care

Care and care work, we would argue, are contestable subjects, in the sense that there are choices to be made – about concepts, relationships and policies of care. There are no self-evident answers to these choices, which are ethical and political. Our title – *Rethinking Children's Care* – is a call for curiosity, provisionality and critical thinking, which is 'a matter of introducing a critical attitude towards those things that are given to our present experience as if they were timeless, natural, unquestionable' (Rose 1999: 20).

The book, and the work of TCRU, also illustrate the value of multiple perspectives in provoking new and different thinking. As already noted, we range over formal and informal care, different kinds of carers and care in different settings. Our perspective is both historical and contemporary. The research at TCRU is informed by several disciplines notably psychology, social policy and sociology. It is influenced by different theoretical perspectives which include feminist theory, a life course and intergenerational family perspective, and developments in the field of childhood studies. Finally, while the book focuses primarily on work undertaken in England (and refers to England unless otherwise stated) the book is strongly influenced by long-standing and wide-ranging cross-national work undertaken at TCRU, both in the minority and majority worlds. Our experience of other societies provides a lens through which to view our own and to see it in a different light.

The chapters in the rest of the book fall into three parts. Chapters 2, 3, 4 and 5 take an historical perspective, and explore different concepts of care of children over time and how these have translated into policies and practices. Chapters 6, 7, 8 and 9 focus on care relationships and care practices in particular formal settings (nurseries, social services, childminders and nursing). Chapters 10 and 11 are concerned with informal care relationships within families; Chapter 10 concerns children's understandings of and their contribution to care in family life, and Chapter 11 looks at care-giving and care relationships as they are negotiated in families over the life course and between women across four family generations. In Chapter 12 we consider briefly some implications of rethinking children's care for policy, practice and research.

References

Andersen, B. (2000) *Doing the Dirty Work? The Global Politics of Domestic Labour.* London: Zed Books.

Bernauer, J. and Mahon, M. (1994) The ethics of Michel Foucault, in G. Gutting (ed.) *The Cambridge Companion to Foucault.* Cambridge: Cambridge University Press.

Bernstein, B. (1975) *Class, Codes and Control,* Vol. III. London: Routledge and Kegan Paul.

Bernstein, B. (2000) *Pedagogy, Symbolic Control and Identity: Theory, Research, Critique.* Boston, MA: Rowman and Littlefield.

Brannen, J. (2000) *Employment, Care and Citizenship, 14th Sinclair House Debate: The Silent Revolution – The Change in Gender Roles.* Bad Homburg: Herbert Quandt Foundation.

Connell, R.W. (1990) The state, gender and sexual politics, *Theory and Society,* 19(5): 507–44.

Daly, M. and Lewis, J. (1999) Introduction: conceptualising social care in the context of welfare state restructuring, in J. Lewis (ed.) *Gender, Social Care and State Restructuring in Europe.* Aldershot: Ashgate.

Dencik, L. (1989) Growing up in the postmodern age: on the child's situation in the modern family and the position of the family in the modern welfare state, *Acta Sociologica,* 32: 155–80.

Esping-Andersen, G. (1999) *Social Foundations of Postindustrial Economies.* Oxford: Oxford University Press.

Finch, J. (1989) *Family Obligations.* Cambridge: Polity.

Finch, J. and Mason, J. (1993) *Negotiating Family Responsibilities.* London: Routledge.

Foucault, M. (1980) *Power/Knowledge: Selected Interviews and Other Writings, 1972–1977.* London: Harvester Wheatsheaf.

Foucault, M. (1983) On the genealogy of ethics, in H. Dreyfus and P. Rabinow (eds) *Michel Foucault: Beyond Structuralism and Hemeneutics,* 2nd edn. Chicago: Chicago University Press.

Foucault, M. (1986) *The Care of the Self.* New York: Pantheon.

Foucault, M. (1987) The ethic of care for the self as a practice of freedom, in J. Bernauer and D. Rasmussen (eds) *The Final Foucault.* Cambridge, MA: MIT Press.

Gilligan, C. (1982) *In a Different Voice: Psychological Theory and Women's Development.* Cambridge, MA: Cambridge University Press.

Hilary, J. (2001) *The Wrong Model: GATS, Trade Liberalisation and Children's Right to Health.* London: Save the Children Fund.

Hochschild, A. (2000) Global care chains and emotional surplus value, in W. Hutton and A. Giddens (eds) *On the Edge: Living with Global Capitalism.* London: Jonathan Cape.

Knijn, T. and Kremer, M. (1997) Gender and the caring dimension of welfare states: towards inclusive citizenship, *Social Politics: International Studies in Gender, State and Society,* 4: 328–62.

Kröger, T. (2001) *Comparative Research on Social Care: The State of the Art*. Brussels: European Commission (available on www.uta.fi/laitokset/sospol/soccare/).

Leira, A. (2002) Care: actors, relationships, contexts, in B. Hobson, J. Lewis and B. Siim (eds) *Contested Concepts in Gender and Social Politics*. Cheltenham: Edward Elgar.

Lewis, J. (1992) Gender and the development of welfare state regimes, *Journal of European Social Policy*, 2: 159–73.

Lewis, J. (1997) Gender and welfare regimes: further thoughts, *Social Politics*: summer, 160–77.

Lukes, S. (1974) *Power: A Radical View*. London: Macmillan.

Mayall, B. (1996) *Children, Health and the Social Order*. Buckingham: Open University Press.

Mayall, B. and Petrie, P. (1977) *Minder, Mother and Child*. London: Institute of Education, University of London.

Mayall, B. and Petrie, P. (1983) *Childminding and Day Nurseries: What Kind of Care?* London: Heinemann.

Miller, P. and Rose, N. (1993) Governing economic life, in M. Gane and T. Johnston (eds) *Foucault's New Domains*. London: Routledge.

Munday, B. (1998) The old and the new: changes in social care in Central and Eastern Europe, in B. Munday and G. Lane (eds) *The Old and the New: Changes in Social Care in Central and Eastern Europe*. Canterbury: European Institute of Social Services, University of Kent.

Nilsen, A. and Brannen, J. (2002) Theorising the individual-structure dynamic, in J. Brannen, S. Lewis, A. Nilsen and J. Smithson (eds) *Young People, Work and Family: Futures in Transition*. London: ESA/Routledge.

Oswin, M. (1971) *The Empty Hours*. London: Allen Lane.

Oswin, M. (1978) *Children Living in Long-stay Hospitals*, SIMP research monographs no. 5. London: Spastics International Medical Publications.

Petrie, P. (1990) School-age childcare and local government in the 1990s, *Local Government Policy Making*, 17(3): 6–10.

Petrie, P. and Logan, P. (1986) *After School and in the Holidays: The Responsibility for Looking after School Children*, Thomas Coram Research Unit working and occasional paper no. 2. London: Institute of Education, University of London.

Rose, N. (1999) *Powers of Freedom: Reframing Political Thought*. Oxford: Oxford University Press.

Sevenhuijsen, S. (1999a) *Citizenship and the Ethics of Care: Feminist Considerations on Justice, Morality and Politics*. London: Routledge.

Sevenhuijsen, S. (1999b) *Caring in the Third Way*. Leeds: Centre for Research on Family, Kinship and Childhood.

Simon, A., Owen, C., Moss, P. and Cameron, C. (2002) *Mapping the Care Workforce: Supporting Joined-Up Thinking. Secondary Analysis of the LFS for Childcare and Social Care Work*. London: Institute of Education.

Tizard, B. (1977) *Adoption: A Second Chance*. London: Open Books.

Tizard, B. and Hughes, M. (1984) *Young Children Learning: Talking and Thinking at Home and at School*. London: Fontana.

Tizard, B. and Phoenix, A. (1993) *Black, White or Mixed Race?* London: Routledge.

Tizard, B., Blatchford, P., Burke, J., Farquhar, C. and Plewis, I. (1988) *Young Children at School in the Inner City*. Hove: Lawrence Erlbaum.

Tizard, J. (1964) *Community Services for Mentally Handicapped Children*. London: Oxford University Press.

Tizard, J., Moss, P. and Perry, J. (1976) *All Our Children*. London: Temple Smith/New Society.

Tronto, J. (1993) *Moral Boundaries: A Political Argument for the Ethics of Care*. London: Routledge.

Ungerson, C. (1997) Social politics and the commodification of care, *Social Politics*, 4: 362–81.

Wærness, K. (1999) The changing 'welfare mix' in childcare and care for the frail elderly in Norway, in J. Lewis (ed.) *Gender, Social Care and State Restructuring in Europe*. Aldershot: Ashgate.

Young, R. (1990) *White Mythologies: Writing History and the West*. London: Routledge.

Care and the development of social policy

C H A P T E R   **2**

Getting beyond childcare: reflections on recent policy and future possibilities

PETER MOSS

Introduction: inclusions and exclusions

'Childcare' is all the rage today, the valued goal of government, employers and parents. England has a National Childcare Strategy, with a Childcare Unit in government to implement the strategy, targets for extra childcare places, and a Childcare Tax Credit to subsidize parents' use of childcare services. But it was not ever so. For many years, 'childcare' was surrounded by public and private hostility or, at least, ambivalence. In this chapter, I tell the short story of 'childcare' policy since the Second World War, provide a framework for understanding that history and examine how 'childcare' has come to be understood. I will argue that it is time to question, indeed discard, the term 'childcare' with respect to policy and provision, and reconsider the meaning and place of 'care' in services for children, especially in relation to education.

I shall focus on 'childcare' not 'child care'. 'Childcare' is part of the vocabulary of the Department for Education and Skills (DfES), but also of other government departments with an interest in 'childcare' and especially its economic role (for example, the Treasury and the Department for Work and Pensions). As noted in Chapter 1, the two-word form is used in relation to social work, residential and other social welfare provisions for children: it is part of the vocabulary of the English Department of Health and local social services departments. During the 1990s, 'child care' has become subsumed into a new public policy concept which has emerged in the social welfare field, and which spans cradle to grave: 'social care'. 'Child care' meets 'childcare' as we shall see in this chapter and in Chapter 7, when 'childcare services' are used for 'child care' purposes, in particular providing a service for children defined by social workers as 'in need'.

'Childcare', the one-word form and the subject of this chapter, refers to services such as nurseries, childminders, nannies and (for older children) out-of-school centres, all mainly used for children while their parents are at work. It is also used to refer to 'informal' arrangements, mainly involving relatives: indeed, relatives remain the most common form of childcare in England (Mooney et al. 2001). Today in public policy, 'childcare' extends to children well into their secondary school years. The National Childcare Strategy, for instance, covers children up to 14 years.

I shall also focus on children below compulsory school age. I shall discuss 'childcare services' rather than informal carers. 'Childcare' provided by relatives (mainly grandmothers) raises other issues which merit separate attention. One issue is the relationship between social class, education, employment and childcare: not only are parents with lower levels of education less likely to be employed full time, but also they are less likely to use 'formal' services for childcare (Mooney et al. 2001). Another issue concerns the current and future relationship between formal and informal childcare. Relatives are the most common form of care in England, but in Sweden, where formal services are widely available and parents are entitled to a place in these services for children over 12 months, less than 5 per cent of children aged 1 to 6 years were cared for by relatives in 1999 compared to 76 per cent who attended centres and childminders (Swedish Ministry of Education and Science 2000).

A final comment on terminology. The terms 'day care' and 'day care services' were used in public policy up to the 1990s, rather than 'childcare' and 'childcare services'. After a few minor roles in the mid-1990s, 'childcare' makes its starring appearance on the public policy stage with the election of a Labour government in 1997 and the launch of the National Childcare Strategy in 1998. This represents, as I shall show, a recognition of public responsibility to support employed parents, 'childcare' having been previously the language of individuals and organizations advocating such support (for example the National Childcare Campaign).

However 'day care', welfare language which defines services in terms of being non-residential rather than in terms of the age group for which they provide, refuses to leave the stage entirely. Regulation of 'childcare services' continues within the legislative framework of the Children Act 1989, which refers to 'day care' services. The new national standards for regulation, introduced in 2001, are for 'the regulation of day care and childminding'. I shall use the term 'childcare' to cover both 'day care' and 'childcare'.

Childcare: a potted postwar history

Childcare was part of the Second World War effort. Nurseries were opened as part of a drive to increase women's employment at a time of national emergency. Once the war ended, policy went into reverse and the government stance for most of the postwar period was spelt out. The Ministry of Health (1945) stated clear disapproval of care for young children in nurseries or indeed other non-maternal care – unless exceptional circumstances made maternal care undesirable or impossible:

> The Ministers concerned accept the view of medical and other authority that, in the interests of the health and development of children no less than for the benefit of the mother, the proper place for a child under two is at home with his [*sic*] mother. They are also of the opinion that, under normal peacetime conditions, the right policy to pursue would be positively to discourage mothers of children under two from going out to work . . . and to regard day nurseries and daily guardians [childminders] as supplements to meet the special needs . . . of children whose mothers are constrained by individual circumstances to go out to work or whose home conditions are in themselves unsatisfactory from the health point of view, or whose mothers are incapable for some good reason of undertaking the full care of their children.
>
> (Ministry of Health 1945)

The limited public role in provision of childcare, with its welfare focus on families deemed not-normal, was reiterated in the 1960s, 1970s and 1980s. A 1968 Ministry of Health Circular limited public provision to a number of defined circumstances, in particular children: with only one parent; who need temporary day care on account of the mother's illness; whose mothers are unable to look after them adequately because they are incapable of giving young children the care they need; for whom day care might prevent the breakdown of the mother or the break-up of the family; whose home conditions constitute a hazard to their health and welfare; whose health and welfare are seriously affected by a lack of opportunity to play with others (Ministry of Health 1968).

Official opposition to mothers of young children working was reflected in these criteria, which provided public support only to employed lone mothers. But the circular also made its opposition explicit. Day care, it said,

> must be looked at in relation to the view of medical and other authority that early and prolonged separation from the mother is detrimental to the child; wherever possible the younger pre-school child should be at home with his mother; and the needs of older pre-school children should be met by part-time attendance at nursery schools and classes.
>
> (Ministry of Health 1968)

The thread of opposition ran through other policy statements. A report from the Department of Health and Social Security (1974) on 'preparation for parenthood' noted that 'a strong theme to emerge from consultations [with professional, voluntary and research organisations] was that mothers of young children in particular should be encouraged to stay at home'. In addition 'a range of medical and nursing opinion was in favour of efforts to dissuade mothers from going out to work' (a feature of all these documents was a resort to legitimacy based on expert, but always anonymous, opinion). The Department of Education and Science (1972) joined in, anxious to ensure that nursery education would not become a Trojan Horse for introducing publicly supported childcare: 'the majority of educationalists regard part-time attendance at school as sufficient, indeed preferable for most children until they reach compulsory school age' (Department of Education and Science 1972).

This statement reflected the conclusions of the influential Plowden Report, published in 1967, which had advocated an expansion of nursery education – as long as it was only part-time (Central Advisory Council for Education 1967). The committee argued that 'our evidence is that it is generally undesirable, except to prevent a greater evil, to separate mother and child for a whole day in a nursery', but went further 'to deplore the increasing tendency of mothers of young children to work'. It made one exception: where mothers had to work because of 'financial need'. Their children were one of several groups who might be eligible for the 15 per cent of full-time nursery education places proposed: but otherwise 'it is no business of the educational service to encourage these mothers'.

The 1980s brought a change of tone politically. Rather than outright castigation of working *mothers*, there was acceptance (at least in public) of working *parents*. To work or not to work was a matter of individual or family choice. The government should not take sides, for example by providing support to working parents.

The Children Act 1989 reaffirmed the principle of public provision of childcare services as a welfare measure for exceptional circumstances. But it refined the principle. Rather than the 1968 circular's shopping list of circumstances, the legislation offered a general concept: 'the child in need'. Section 17(10) of the Act defines a child as being 'in need' if

(a) he [sic] is unlikely to achieve, or maintain, or to have the opportunity of achieving or maintaining, a reasonable standard of health or development without the provision for him of services by a local authority . . . ;
(b) his health or development is likely to be significantly impaired, or further impaired, without the provision for him of such services; or
(c) he is disabled.

A duty is placed on local authorities 'to provide a range and level of services appropriate to the children in their area who are "in need"', and these services include 'day care provision for pre-school and school age children'. (For a fuller discussion of the provision of day care for 'children in need', see Chapter 7.) This new definition closed off the one prospect of public support for childcare for employed mothers (or fathers). The 1968 circular included lone parents needing to work as eligible for this support: the Children Act 1989 definition excluded any reference to parental employment.

The public duty to provide or fund childcare services thus remained carefully circumscribed within a welfare framework. Childcare services otherwise were a private matter, for parents to purchase in the market. There was, however, a long-standing public duty to regulate the private market in childcare services, or most of it (nannies have never been publicly regulated).

The Children Act 1989 not only refined the public duty of provision, but also reformed the system of regulation which was implemented in 1991 (see Chapter 5 for a fuller discussion of the Children Act 1989). More recently, in 2001, the regulatory system has been further overhauled, with new national standards and responsibility for implementation passed from local authority social services departments to the Office for Standards in Education (Ofsted).

First signs of a change in public policy towards childcare for working parents appeared during the mid-1990s. Tentative steps were taken along the road of state support. The Conservative government introduced two modest measures: a subsidy to low income working parents called the 'childcare disregard' (1994) and modest short-term support for new 'school age childcare' services, the 'Out of School Childcare Initiative' (OOSCI) (1993). Neither measure emanated from the Department of Health, which until then had sole responsibility for 'day care' services. The childcare disregard fell to the Department for Social Security, the OOSCI to the Employment Department (from where it transferred in 1995 into the newly formed Department for Education and Employment (DfEE)).

The return to power of a Labour government in 1997 heralded a second turning point in postwar public policy on childcare. It took two major steps. First, responsibility for 'day care services' was transferred from the welfare to the education system. The Department of Health was left with 'children in need', and the use of 'day care' for these children. But responsibility for 'day care services', including their regulation, passed to the DfEE. Second, for the first time since the Second World War, and in contrast to the previous government's tentative moves, the Labour government offered wholehearted public policy support to working parents, especially mothers: 'the Government welcomes women's greater involvement and equality in the workplace and wants to ensure that all those women who wish to can take up these opportunities' (DfEE 1998: para. 1.6). Statutory leave entitlements (maternity and parental leave) were improved and extended. But above all, there was to be more 'childcare' (the term 'childcare' now replaced 'day care' in government discourse). Under the heading 'a new approach to childcare' in the key policy document *Meeting the Childcare Challenge*, the change in public policy was spelt out:

> It is up to parents to decide what sort of childcare they want for their children. This is not a matter for the government. But it is the Government's responsibility to ensure that parents have access to services to enable them to make genuine choices. The National Childcare Strategy will deliver this . . . Our aim is to ensure quality affordable childcare for children aged 0 to 14 in every neighbourhood, including both formal childcare and support for informal arrangements.
>
> (DfEE 1998: para. 1.26)

The state's role of regulation continued, as did the central role of private providers in delivering services through a childcare market. But now, the state committed itself to making childcare more accessible by stimulating an expansion of places (the current target is a net increase of places for 1 million children from 0 to 14 years, by 2004); establishing new structures to plan and oversee this expansion in each local authority area (Early Years Development and Childcare Partnerships); and making childcare more 'affordable' by public funding, mainly through a childcare tax credit to subsidize costs for low and middle income parents (introduced in 1999), but also through a plethora of over 40 funding streams. Right at the end of the twentieth century, 'childcare for working parents' had become a major policy goal and government responsibility: 'day care for children in need', the previous focus of public policy, was now marginal.

To finish this potted history requires a return to the relationship between childcare and nursery education. In the early 1970s, government and others were seeking to prevent an unseemly intimate relationship developing between the two. Over the years, however, the relationship has got closer. An increasingly influential expert discourse has emphasized the inseparability of care and education, and policy has followed. By the late 1980s, government had accepted that education can and should take place in childcare settings. The 1991 Guidance on the implementation of the Children Act 1989 has a section on 'education in day care settings', the aim being 'to offer 3 and 4 year olds in day care settings experiences comparable in quality with those offered to children attending school' (Department of Health 1991: para. 6.40). The expansion of education for 3- and 4-year-olds, initiated in the mid-1990s by the Conservative government with their 'nursery vouchers' strategy (introduced on a pilot basis in 1996), and followed by Labour (but without vouchers), is premised on education being delivered and funded in a range of settings, both schools and childcare services.

Meeting the Childcare Challenge goes further, insisting 'there is no sensible distinction between good early education and care: both enhance children's social and intellectual development' (DfEE 1998: para. 1.4). The Early Excellence Centre programme, begun in 1998, is intended to provide model services which 'will demonstrate what can be achieved through integrated services . . . typically [offering] integrated childcare and education provision' (DfEE 1998: para. 2.15). The Foundation Stage provides a curriculum for children between 3 and 6 in all services (schools or childcare) that are funded by government to provide early education (Qualifications and Curriculum Authority (QCA) 1999, 2000). Not only has responsibility for 'day care' moved from the Department of Health to the Department for Education and Skills, but also within the Department for Education, since 2001, the previously separate Early Years Division (dealing with pre-school education) and Childcare Unit (focusing on provision for children aged 0 to 14 with working parents) have merged into one unit. And from 2001, as already noted, regulation of 'day care services' now comes within the remit of Ofsted, the schools regulator.

At the same time, government is showing increased awareness of the potential of schools for providing childcare. There is a policy interest in 'extended schools' (England) and 'community schools' (Scotland). These schools can provide a range of services, including childcare, to pupils, pupils' families and the wider community (see DfES 2001).

So we finish this short history with childcare receiving public policy plaudits, and in bed with education – even if the future union of the two remains uncertain.

Influences on childcare policy: national survival, liberalism and maternalism

Before considering how 'childcare' has been understood during postwar years, I shall outline a framework for interpreting the history of policy over this period. The framework has three main components, which interlock but are also in tension. The trick for government is to keep them tensed and thereby mutually supportive while avoiding the tension reaching breaking point.

The first component has been a norm of individualized care within the family, a discourse typical of a liberal society (Randall 2000). The liberal orientation foregrounds the distinction between public and private spheres, locating family and care within the latter. In his original analysis of welfare state typologies, Esping-Andersen (1990) argued that liberal welfare states such as Britain were characterized by a residual or minimalist approach with targeted, means-tested benefits. More recently he has argued that liberal welfare states have not followed 'defamilialization' policies (as has been the case in the Scandinavian, 'social democratic' welfare regimes), which 'lessen individuals' reliance on the family; that maximize individuals' command of economic resources independently of familial or conjugal reciprocities' (Esping-Andersen 1999: 45).

The second component is gender. Liberal ideas intersect with ideas about gender to shape concepts and practices of care. Connell (1990) uses the term 'gender regimes' to describe the way in which the state embodies a set of power relationships between men and women: the gender regime includes a gender hierarchy and a gender division of labour. Randall (2000) concludes that one important aspect of the British state's gender regime has been a powerful 'ideology of motherhood' or maternalism, which still exercises considerable informal influence:

> [T]he 'maternalist' assumption that the mother's primary and natural duty is to look after her child, and that as an extension childcare is and should be a 'women's' issue, has been literally embodied in the political process, through a gender division of labour running virtually up to the top.
>
> (Randall 2000: 183)

Liberal theory places children within the private, family sphere. Maternalism further defines childcare as 'women's work'. Hence the many (and continuing) references to 'mothers' in public policy.

The third component is the broader, socio-economic imperatives of national policy. The state's commitment to 'childcare for working mothers' in the early 1940s was driven by wartime production needs. The current commitment to 'childcare for working parents' is driven by a cluster of government concerns: the eradication of poverty; commitments to gender equality; the need for a competitive workforce (HM Treasury 2000).

The labour market too has changed. For many years after the Second World War, the economy did not need to employ most women with young children. For years the employment rate among this group was around 20 to 25 per cent. Most of these mothers worked part-time, often very short hours. But since the late 1980s, there has been a rapid growth of employment among this group. Women have increasingly returned to work after maternity leave without taking a break from the labour market while their children are young. Moreover, this growth has mainly occurred among women with higher levels of education in higher status occupations (Brannen and Moss 1998). Not only does the economy have increasing need of women with young children, but also the employment expectations and practices of women are changing. Childcare is a growing political demand of 'work rich' families at one end of the social spectrum, and a growing political need of government to reduce the number of 'work poor' families at the other end.

As the political imperative has moved to favour childcare, the question facing government is how to reconcile this apparent move to a more public and collective form of child-rearing with liberalism and maternalism. The dilemma confronting a liberal and gendered state is not only how to rationalize the intrusion of the public in the private sphere, but also how to avoid undermining the responsibility of the family and the individual parent (in fact, the mother) for children.

First and foremost, it should be recognized that the liberal state has long understood that it cannot leave the private entirely private. The family has always been understood to be far too important to be actually left to its own devices. To address this dilemma, 'a whole range of technologies were invented that would enable the family to do its public duty without destroying its private authority' (Rose 1999: 74).

Government involvement in childcare can be seen in this light. There is a long history of welfare interventions in which 'day care' acts as a technology, providing a means of prevention, protection or 'family support' where families or mothers are unable to provide normative care. In the 1990s, as government has come to emphasize the central importance of employment, another important justification for intervention has emerged: 'market failure' preventing families assuming their private responsibility for making childcare arrangements. Initiatives like childcare tax credit and Neighbourhood Nurseries have been justified on the grounds that the market in childcare services is inaccessible for lower income families and fails to operate at all in poor areas.

But there is also a third *raison d'état* increasingly deployed as a rationale for extended state intervention: childcare has an important role to play not only in employment but also in education. Governments have become increasingly convinced of the need to extend the provision of education, long recognized as an area requiring state intervention, to older pre-school children (3- and 4-year-olds). The rationale behind this is that 'early education' provides a technology which can enhance later school performance and that families cannot by themselves provide adequate early education. This is particularly true for families who function less well and for whom early interventions, it is argued, can contribute to breaking a presumed cycle of disadvantage.

The liberal state now finds itself intervening to an unparalleled extent in the private world of family and children. How does it manage the tensions this creates? How does it (to quote Rose 1999) 'enable the family to do its public duty without destroying its private authority'?

In the welfare field, a study of the workings of 'day care for children in need', the subject of Chapter 7, found that day care services were mostly provided as short-term crisis support rather than as part of a long-term practice of child-rearing:

> The majority of placements were offered on a part-time and short-term basis . . . Their function was to meet a particular need which often involved working with parents, after which sponsorship would be withdrawn: day care was not intended to provide an ongoing service.
>
> (Moss et al. 2000: 246)

Used thus, 'day care for children in need' can be viewed as a response to the breakdown of normative care, with the purpose of enabling the resumption of that care. Childcare services are a short-term welfare technology to re-establish private, maternal care, not part of a longer-term child-rearing practice. The number of children involved is also small – less than 2 per cent of the pre-school population. But what about the much larger growth area of 'childcare for working parents'?

The account by Rose of the development in Britain of public interventions involving the family and the child describes how government exerts influence not only directly, but also indirectly:

> The modern private family remains intensively governed, it is linked in so many ways with social, economic and political objectives. But government here acts not through mechanisms of social control and social subordination of the will, but through the promotion of subjectivities, the construction of pleasures and ambitions, and the activation of guilt, anxiety, envy and disappointment . . . The autonomous responsible family stands as the emblem of a new form of government of the soul.
>
> (Rose 1990: 208)

The new discourse of policy now tells parents that childcare is not just acceptable, but positively to be desired. I have already noted the admission during the 1990s of childcare services as providers of early education for 3- and 4-year-olds. But the educational benefits of childcare are now held to be even wider, applying to all ages: 'There is clear evidence that good quality day care in the earliest years has long-term benefits for children's social and intellectual development' (DfEE 1998: para. 2.2). *Meeting the Childcare Challenge* goes still further:

> Good childcare is not just something parents need when they go out to work or study. It is good for children. It can help them to grow up happy and confident. It can introduce them to the joys of play and the love of books. Young children who are used to playing with other children find starting school easier.
>
> (DfEE 1998: 2)

The two 'tests of success' for the National Childcare Strategy are more parents able to work or study and 'better outcomes for children, including readiness to learn by the time they start school' (DfEE 1998: para. 1.29).

A new public discourse is therefore emerging which presents childcare services as a good and normal thing, neither abnormal nor detrimental. From this perspective, 'childcare' is not a necessary evil. It is a benefit that can deliver more good outcomes than the family alone. We have moved from the discourse of the possible harm to children of non-parental care to the discourse of the possible constraints on children's development of parental care.

As well as desires, subjectivities are worked on. In the old discourse, exemplified by the Plowden Report, mothers with young children who also worked were to be deplored (Central Advisory Council for Education 1967). In the new public discourse, the 'good parent' is socially constructed as a user of childcare services – or at the very least, it is possible to use childcare services and still consider yourself a good parent.

Nor does using childcare services require rethinking the parent–child relationship. The greater the amount of non-parental care for young children, the greater the emphasis in public policy on the primacy of parents and the private family domain. The Children Act 1989 set the scene by devoting Part One to a discussion of 'parental responsibility for children'. Public policy and a mass of communications by a burgeoning family and parenting industry seek to assure 'parents' (who are now ungendered) that really little has altered. The first paragraph in *Meeting the Childcare Challenge*, a document which envisages a major expansion of non-parental care, starts by centring parents and the parent–child relationship:

> Good parenting is the key to ensuring that children grow up happy and well-prepared for adult life. Parents are the first and often the greatest influence on their children's development and education. They will always have the primary responsibility for the care and well-being of children.
>
> (DfEE 1998: para. 1.1)

Families, childhood and employment may be changing in complex and uncertain ways. But parents remain 'key', 'first', 'greatest', 'primary'.

Government policy itself is clear. 'Childcare' is now the subject of public policy, but responsibility and practice remain in the private domain. It is understood as a market commodity, to be purchased by parents exercising choice as consumers: government intervention focuses on regulation of the market and rectifying 'market failures'. Children in this market scenario remain objects of their parents' private purchasing decisions.

What about maternalism – how does that adapt to the age of non-maternal childcare and the rhetoric of 'parents'? Mothers increasingly are no longer available to do all the caring, but children remain primarily a maternal responsibility. Making 'childcare arrangements' is still mainly down to mothers, and childcare continues to be viewed as a financial charge on mothers' earnings (Himmelweit and Sigala 2001). Childcare services themselves are constructed as providing substitute maternal care through an 'attachment pedagogy' – a term used by Singer (1993) to express the idea that mother care is needed for secure development and that, in its absence, non-maternal care requires to be modelled on a dyadic mother–child relationship.

We can see various indications of this. Most obviously, it is apparent in the childcare workforce, overwhelmingly composed of women, with poor pay and conditions and most of whom have low levels of qualifications (Cameron et al. 2001; Mooney et al. 2001). The rationale for this situation is the linkage between motherhood and childcare work, through which the gender regime is perpetuated in new conditions:

> The predominant ideology of motherhood has informed and shaped understandings of how caring work in early childhood services is constituted . . . Early childhood services have to a greater or lesser extent been seen as offering mothering substitutes, and an obvious demonstration of this is the virtually all female workforce; women are the visible carers and women proxy mothers.
>
> (Cameron et al. 1999: 165–6)

Comparing nurseries in England, Italy and Spain, Penn (1997) argues that childcare services in England (unlike the other two countries) emphasize a quasi-maternal model of care, foregrounding the dependency of children, nurturing and one-to-one relationships. Similar ideas appear in the welfare field with respect to 'day care for children in need' (see Chapter 7 for a fuller discussion).

The 'care' in 'childcare'

'Childcare' has become associated, in policy and the public mind, with enabling mothers to work in paid employment, and 'childcare services' with providing this function, a function which is commodified, to be sold in the private market and bought by mothers acting as consumers. The idea is to provide substitution for normative care, in the home by mothers. In this broader context, how might we understand the 'care' in 'childcare'?

Understandings of 'care' in the case of young children frequently centre on a dyadic adult–child relationship. As Tronto (1993) observes, too often, care is described and defined as a necessary relationship between two individuals, most often a mother and child. As others have noted such a dyadic understanding often leads to a romanticization of mother and child, so that they become like a romantic couple in contemporary Western discourse. The dyadic understanding also presumes that caring is naturally individualistic, though in fact few societies in the world have ever conceived of child rearing . . . as the responsibility of the birth mother.

(Tronto 1993: 103)

Not only is care understood in dyadic and individualistic terms, but also the adult is autonomous and the child dependent. The care in 'childcare' means the adult (the mother or her substitute) cares for the child.

What does this 'care' consist of in the current policy discourse? There seem to be two main elements. First, there is a physical side: the adult helping with the activities of everyday life (washing, feeding and so on) and providing a safe environment (a major concern of regulation). Second, there is an emotional side:

The National Childcare Strategy is not just about providing safe places for children to wait until their parents come to collect them. Children, especially the younger ones, need the emotional security of warm, loving carers who take a close and consistent interest in their happiness and well-being. Good quality childcare must promote children's development.

(DfEE 1998: para. 2.1)

This last sentence alerts us to another feature of 'care' in the new childcare discourse: its active relationship with education and development. Government has bought in fully to an expert discourse of the inseparability of 'care' and 'education'. Whereas for many years it was a case of care *or* education, now all the talk is of care *and* education.

But the relationship between the two is not clearly articulated and is somewhat confusing. The National Childcare Strategy asserts that 'there is no sensible distinction between good early education and care: both enhance children's social and intellectual development' (DfEE 1998: para. 1.4). The statement is ambiguous. Does it mean that 'care' and 'early education' are conceptually synonymous? Or does it mean that they are conceptually separate, but are both necessary conditions for enhancing development? This seems implied by the comment that 'children need to be happy and emotionally secure, and to have ample opportunities for constructive play' (DfEE 1998: para. 1.4). 'Care', as understood here, takes us back to the idea of safety and security, while 'education' is associated with 'constructive play'.

Getting beyond childcare

It may seem perverse to argue that now is the time to drop the term and concept of 'childcare' – just when its time seems to have come. However, I want to make the case for doing so, for getting beyond childcare. My conten-tion is that 'childcare' is understood, both in the public mind and in public policy, in a narrow and highly instrumental way. This impedes rethinking and restructuring the provisions we make for children and families, as well as thinking critically about the concept of care and about the relationship of care to other concepts, most obviously education.

The narrow, instrumental and dominant understanding is that 'childcare' is a necessary condition for mothers to undertake paid work. This under-standing focuses attention on one function – providing an alternative to maternal care while mothers are employed. While some may take a few 'children in need' paid for by local welfare departments, 'childcare services' are provided predominantly for children with working parents They are therefore oriented towards children whose parents have higher incomes and levels of education (who are both more likely to be employed and to use 'formal' childcare services rather than informal care by relatives). Childcare services operate apart from other services for young children: welfare services (such as family centres) specifically for less advantaged families on the one hand, and predominantly 'education' services (for example playgroups and nursery classes), not geared to the needs of working parents on the other. The resulting situation is fragmented and divisive.

The constant use of terms like 'childcare' and 'childcare services' – linked to a narrow idea of 'childcare for working parents' – inhibits the con-ceptualization and realization of early childhood services as complex and inclusive institutions offering a wide range of possibilities for *all* local chil-dren and parents (whether or not employed). The idea of a 'children's centre' for each community, providing a wide range of services for local children and families, has been recommended by various groups (The Childcare Com-mission 2001; Holtermann 2001). Examples have been around for some time, certainly as far back as the 1970s when a number of 'combined centres', such as the Thomas Coram Children's Centre, were established. Since 1999, the government's programme for Early Excellence Centres (EECs) has pro-vided yet more examples. In addition to childcare and education, many of these centres provide or host a range of other services, geared to all children and families in their locality. But these EECs, fewer than 50 at present, to be extended to 100 by 2004, are drops in the ocean compared, for example, to the 8000 plus private day nurseries whose business is primarily providing 'childcare for working parents'.

The narrow, instrumental and dominant understanding of childcare also focuses attention on one relationship – between mother and child. Preoccu-pation with this dyadic relationship distracts attention from the possibility that early childhood services are not, and need not be, like home: instead, they offer opportunities for different relationships. They question the liberal assumption that the proper and normal place for young children is located in the family and private sphere, as dependants of their parents. Instead, early childhood services offer another possibility: that young children might be viewed as active subjects with rights and voice, members of a social group and located both in the family and in the wider society. Rather than a centred and exclusive parent/mother–child relationship, the child might be understood to be situated in a dense and complex network of relationships connecting people, environments and activities.

Dahlberg et al. (1999) explore the concept of the early childhood institution as a forum or public space in which children and adults can participate together in many projects of social, cultural, political and economic significance. They locate this forum in civil society – not as part of the state or the economy, and not as part of the private domain. They propose that it is characterized by particular relationships suited to a public space:

> It is not to be understood as a substitute home. Young children – both under and over 3 years of age – are seen to be able to manage, and indeed to desire and thrive on, relationships with small groups of other children and adults without risking either their own well-being or their relationship with their parents . . . If we approach early childhood institutions as forums in civil society, the concept of closeness and intimacy becomes problematic. It can turn public situations and institutions private . . . [I]t hinders the ability of the institution to realize its own social life and relationships and devalues or trivializes the idea of a public space. To abandon ideas of intimacy, closeness and cosiness . . . does not mean being uncaring. Instead, Ziehe (1989) offers a contrasting concept to closeness, the concept of intensity of relationships implying a complex and dense web or network connecting people, environments and activities which open up many opportunities for the young child.
>
> (Dahlberg et al. 1999: 81–2)

This idea of an environment and relationships qualitatively different to the home is expressed by Loris Malaguzzi, first director of the early childhood services in the northern Italian town of Reggio Emilia. The services in Reggio place great emphasis on the role of parents and on the relationship between children, parents and services. But Malaguzzi saw children living their lives in different places, marked by different relationships and different possibilities:

> The children in Reggio understood sooner than expected that their adventures in life could flow between two places. [Through early childhood institutions] they could express their previously overlooked desire to be with their peers and find in them points of reference, understanding, surprises, affective ties and merriment that could dispel shadows and uneasiness. For the children and their families there now opened up the possibility of a very long and continuous period of [children] living together [with each other], 5 or 6 years of reciprocal trust and work.
>
> (Malaguzzi 1993: 55)

Institutions that offer many possibilities for all children and families and which offer environments and relationships quite different from the home, are a far cry from 'childcare for working mothers'. But childcare also inhibits our thinking about the place of care in early childhood services. In the

British childcare discourse, 'care' is a tradable commodity, consisting of the performance of certain physical and emotional tasks. Initially placed in opposition to another function, 'education', it is increasingly treated as complementary – as a necessary condition for educating young children.

But 'care' can be understood quite differently – as an ethic. Understood in this way, it forms a different relationship to education, and the many other projects that are possible within the early childhood institution viewed as a forum in civil society. As elaborated by Tronto (1993: 127), an ethics of care is about 'a practice rather than a set of rules or principles . . . It involves particular acts of caring and a "general habit of mind" to care that should inform all aspects of moral life'. She defines caring as 'a species activity that includes everything that we do to maintain, continue and repair our "world" so we can live in it as well as possible' (Tronto 1993: 103).

Care itself consists of four elements – caring about, taking care of, caregiving and care-receiving. The ethics of care has a further four elements – responsibility, competence, responsiveness and integrity. Responsiveness for Tronto involves finding a relation to the Other based on responsibility and the recognition of difference:

> responsiveness suggests a different way to understand the needs of others rather than to put ourselves into their position . . . [O]ne is engaged from the standpoint of the other, but not by presuming that the other is exactly like the self.
>
> (Tronto 1993: 135)

The ethics of care provides a different way of thinking about 'care' in early childhood institutions. If, as suggested above, we conceptualize the early childhood institution as a forum or public space in civil society – then, we can reposition 'care' as one possible ethical approach (there could be others) to work with children and families in a forum or public space. It would foreground responsibility, competence, integrity and responsiveness to the Other. What are some of the implications?

Care as ethic moves us from care as a task performed by adults on children. Rather care is inscribed in all relationships – not only between adults and children (understood as an interactive and reciprocal relationship), but also between adults (parents, workers and others) and between children themselves. Adults *and* children care, and express this care in all relationships in the early childhood institution (as Chapter 11 shows, the same is often true of families, in which children are active carers, not dependent objects of care).

Care as ethic also permeates all the projects of the institution – including education if that is deemed a project. Care and education may be closely linked, but not as parallel projects. Rather care, as an ethic, has an important influence on how the project of education is conceptualized and practised. The corollary is that the theory and practice of education is not self-evident: there are different understandings and possibilities, not all of which are compatible with an ethic of care.

Readings (1996) proposes an understanding of education which is entirely compatible. For him 'teaching and learning are sites of obligation, loci of ethical practices and not means of transmission of knowledge' (Readings 1996: 155). The educational relationship must embody responsiveness to otherness, through 'listening to thought':

> The condition of pedagogical practice is an infinite attention to the other . . . it is to think beside each other and ourselves to explore an open network of obligation that keeps the question of meaning open as a locus for debate . . . [For] doing justice to thought means trying to hear that which cannot be said but which tries to make itself heard . . . This is a process incompatible with the production of even relatively stable and exchangeable knowledge.
>
> (Readings 1996: 165)

Care as ethic raises questions not only about the meaning of education, but also about the concept of 'development'. Child development figures strongly in current discourse about 'childcare' (that is, good quality childcare promotes development). It has become a central discipline in the early childhood field. It has, however, been subject to criticism (see Dahlberg et al. 1999). Through a system of concepts and classifications, it has shown a propensity to order, regulate and normalize: 'the emergence of developmental psychology was prompted by concerns to classify, measure and regulate . . . [it is] a paradigmatically modern discipline arising at a time of commitments to narratives of truth, objectivity, science and reason' (Burman 1994: 35). With its universal and totalizing account of the child, development can become a means for governing the child:

> normalization operates through the discourse of developmentality when the generalizations that stipulate normal development are held to be defined and desirable, and all departures from that circumscribed stipulation are held to be not-normal or deviant. The generalization serves as the norm, and the lives of children are evaluated with reference to that norm.
>
> (Fendler 2001: 128)

Dahlberg, like Fendler, views child development as providing a means for controlling children. It is a totalizing and objectifying practice that attempts to grasp the child, making the child into the Same:

> the so called autonomous child is still governed through the normalizing gaze of the classifications and categorizations of psychology . . . To put everything which one encounters into categories and classifications implies that we make the Other into the Same as everything which doesn't fit into these categories, which is unfamiliar and not taken-for-given, has to be overcome.
>
> (Dahlberg 2001: 5)

Dahlberg is very influenced by the work on ethics of Emmanuel Levinas, who conceives ethics in terms of relationships, in particular how we relate to the Other. 'The ethics of an encounter' emanates from respect for each individual, and recognition of the challenges posed by difference and multiplicity. How can we relate to the Other without trying to make the Other into the same as us? How can we move from grasping the other to respecting the Other? This ethical relationship, Levinas argues, is characterized by a relationship of infinite responsibility and responsivity to the Other and a consequent rejection of instrumentality, an obligation to the Other without expectation of recompense or exchange.

In their approach to otherness, the ethics of an encounter and the ethics of care have much in common. To adopt an ethical approach which foregrounds otherness raises profound issues for practice and relationships in early childhood services:

> In the face-to-face relation the other is absolutely other and I have to take responsibility for the other and this relation is a welcoming. I hear the call of the other and this call is an ungraspable call as the other is absolutely other . . . To think an other whom I cannot grasp is an important shift and it challenges the whole scene of pedagogy . . . To have the capacity to relate to absolute alterity one needs to interrupt totalizing practices . . . It presupposes that we dare to open up for the unexpected, for the coming . . . From this perspective, teaching and learning starts with ethics. It starts with receiving, welcoming and hospitality.
>
> (Dahlberg 2001: 7–8)

Conclusion: taking a critical approach

I have tried to show how 'childcare' policy and provision have been the product of certain understandings and assumptions, the consequence being a system of divided and divisive services and a workforce that suffers low training, pay and status. I have argued that the concept of 'childcare' has become a liability, closing down rather than opening up new possibilities. At some future date we might want to reintroduce 'childcare': but for the moment, I contend, it needs to be erased.

One consequence of such erasure could be to provoke a critical approach to how we understand early childhood institutions, the work and relationships within them, and concepts such as 'care', 'education' and 'development'. A critical approach is 'a matter of introducing a kind of awkwardness into the fabric of one's experience, of interrupting the fluency of the narratives that encode that experience and making them stutter' (Rose 1999: 20). It means making the familiar strange and appreciating that things offered as timeless, natural and unquestionable are not. Taking a critical approach opens up the possibility that there are other ways to think and practise, and therefore choices to be made.

'Care as an ethic' then becomes one choice for how we understand care, a choice which carries implications for thinking about and practising education, for whether and how we decide to use 'development' as both theory and technology, and for the conduct of relationships among and between children and adults.

References

Brannen, J. and Moss, P. (1998) The polarisation and intensification of parental employment in Britain: consequences for children, families and the community, *Community, Work and Family*, 1(3): 229–47.

Burman, E. (1994) *Deconstructing Developmental Psychology*. London: Routledge.

Cameron, C., Moss, P. and Owen, C. (1999) *Men in the Nursery: Gender and Caring Work*. London: Paul Chapman.

Cameron, C., Owen, C. and Moss, P. (2001) *Entry, Retention and Loss: A Study of Childcare Students and Workers*, Department for Education and Skills (DfES) research report no. 275. London: DfES.

Central Advisory Council for Education (1967) *Children and their Primary Schools* (Plowden Report). London: HMSO.

Childcare Commission, The (2001) *Working to the Future for Children and Families*. London: Kids' Clubs Network.

Connell, R.W. (1990) The state, gender and sexual politics, *Theory and Society*, 19(5): 507–44.

Dahlberg, G. (2001) We are responsible for the other: reflections on early childhood pedagogy as an ethical practice. Unpublished paper.

Dahlberg, G., Moss, P. and Pence, A. (1999) *Beyond Quality in Early Childhood Education and Care; Postmodern Perspectives*. London: Falmer.

Department for Education and Employment (DfEE) (1998) *Meeting the Childcare Challenge*. London: Stationery Office.

Department for Education and Skills (DfES) (2001) *Schools: Achieving Success*. London: DfES.

Department of Education and Science (1972) *Education: A Framework for Expansion*. London: HMSO.

Department of Health (1991) *The Children Act 1989 Guidance and Regulations, Vol. 2: Family Support, Day Care and Educational Provision for Young Children*. London: HMSO.

Department of Health and Social Security (1974) *The Family in Society: Preparation for Parenthood*. London: HMSO.

Esping-Andersen, G. (1990) *The Three Worlds of Welfare Capitalism*. Cambridge: Polity.

Esping-Andersen, G. (1999) *Social Foundations of Postindustrial Economies*. Oxford: Oxford University Press.

Fendler, L. (2001) Flexible desire: the construction of an educated subject through developmentality and interaction, in K. Hultqvist and G. Dahlberg (eds) *Governing the Child in the New Millennium*. London: Routledge Falmer.

Himmelweit and Sigala (2001) The welfare implications of mothers' decisions about work and childcare. Paper presented to the European Sociological Association Conference, Helsinki, August.

HM Treasury (2000) *Budget 2000: Prudent for a Purpose, Working for a Stronger and Fairer Britain*. London: Stationery Office.

Holtermann, S. (2001) *Children's Centres: Exploring the Costs and Delivery of a National Scheme*. London: Daycare Trust.

Malaguzzi, L. (1993) History, ideas and basic philosophy, in C. Edwards, L. Gandini and G. Forman (eds) *The Hundred Languages of Children*. Norwood, NJ: Ablex.

Ministry of Health (1945) *Circular 221/45*.

Ministry of Health (1968) *Circular 37/68*.

Mooney, A., Knight, A., Moss, P. and Owen, C. (2001) *Who Cares? Childminding in the 1990s*. London: Family Policy Studies Centre, in association with the Joseph Rowntree Foundation.

Moss, P., Dillon, J. and Statham, J. (2000) The 'child in need' and 'the rich child': discourses, constructions and practices, *Critical Social Policy*, 20(2): 233–54.

Penn, H. (1997) *Comparing Nurseries*. London: Paul Chapman.

Qualifications and Curriculum Authority (QCA) (1999) *Early Learning Goals*. London: QCA.

Qualifications and Curriculum Authority (QCA) (2000) *Curriculum Guidance for the Foundation Stage*. London: QCA.

Randall, V. (2000) *The Politics of Child Daycare in Britain*. Oxford: Oxford University Press.

Readings, B. (1996) *The University in Ruins*. Cambridge, MA: Harvard University Press.

Rose, N. (1990) *Governing the Soul: The Shaping of the Private Self*. London: Routledge.

Rose, N. (1999) *Powers of Freedom: Reframing Political Thought*. Oxford: Oxford University Press.

Singer, E. (1993) Shared care for children, *Theory and Psychology*, 3(4): 429–49.

Swedish Ministry of Education and Science (2000) *Maximum Fees and Universal Pre-school*, fact sheet UOO.017. Stockholm: Swedish Ministry of Education and Science.

Tronto, J. (1993) *Moral Boundaries: A Political Argument for the Ethics of Care*. London: Routledge.

Ziehe, T. (1989) *Kulturanalyser: Ungdom, Utbildning, Modernitet* (Cultural Analysis: Youngsters, Education and Modernity). Stockholm: Norstedts Forlac.

CHAPTER 3

The care of the illegitimate child: the Coram experience 1900–45

CHRISTINE OLIVER

Introduction

Historical sociology reminds us that concepts of care, in addition to being influenced by broad social categories such as age, class and gender, change over time and according to place. In acknowledging the importance of social and historical context to debates concerning the concept of care and its associated practices, this chapter takes as its subject the care of the illegitimate child during a specific time (1900–45) and a particular institutional setting (the Foundling Hospital). It examines the care policies and practices of the Foundling Hospital, former pupils' accounts of being cared for as a foundling, and relates both of these to the overarching concept of illegitimacy, during the first half of the twentieth century.

We now live at a time when diverse family structures and relationships are acknowledged and reflected in social policy and public provision, for example, in relation to family support and child care. Yet, some family forms, such as the single parent family, continue to attract adverse comment. To a certain extent, these criticisms echo the social condemnation of families that did not conform to the bourgeois ideal of marriage and family life in the nineteenth and early twentieth centuries. This model privileged marriage, and the hegemony of fathers within the family. Consequently, social exclusion was felt most acutely by families without fathers, particularly unmarried mothers and their illegitimate children. Until the 1960s, the stigma attached to illegitimacy functioned as a powerful means of social control of women and children. This was reflected in, and reinforced by, laws that discriminated against illegitimate children (Jeger 1951; Commission on the Status of Women 1971).

This chapter begins with an investigation into the historical origins of the Foundling Hospital, and the development of its distinctive and enduring care regime. This is followed by a discussion of the ways in which the traditional pattern of care provided by the Foundling Hospital may have been influenced by the social stigma of illegitimacy. The accounts of former pupils of the Foundling Hospital are then investigated to explore the impact of illegitimacy upon their childhoods and adult lives.

The hypothesis is advanced that the care provided by the Foundling Hospital was influenced by the social stigma of illegitimacy to the extent that it was underpinned by the principle of separation (of the illegitimate child from the mother, from foster families, and from wider family and community networks). The Foundling Hospital's care might be interpreted as benevolent in protecting the illegitimate child from social rejection; but it also protected society from the illegitimate child, and his or her potentially contaminating effects.

On an individual level, interviews with former pupils suggest that their experience of growing up in an institutional setting influenced their identity, and their sense of belonging to the wider society. The very word 'foundling' suggests their uncomfortable status as a free-floating individual, existing outside of the networks of relationships that constituted the family, the basic building-block of society. For many respondents, their lifetime 'quest' was reported as a need to re-establish a sense of belonging, and to 'put their past behind them', by marrying and having a family of their own. Thus, illegitimacy, and the ideology of the family, appears to have functioned as a powerful source of social exclusion during former pupils' childhood years, but also as a potential refuge from the stigma of illegitimacy in later adult life.

Care policies and practices of the Foundling Hospital

The Foundling Hospital was established in the early eighteenth century by Captain Thomas Coram, with the assistance of many distinguished artists and musicians of the day, such as Hogarth, Handel, Gainsborough and Reynolds (McClure 1981). When it first opened in 1741, the Foundling Hospital's purpose was to provide care for the many babies who, at that time, were abandoned and left to die on the streets of London. Thereafter, demand for places consistently outstripped the Foundling Hospital's resources. In the 1830s, a Royal Commission was established to investigate ways of regulating the charitable support provided by the Foundling Hospital. In 1836, Parliament laid down the criteria that would henceforth govern admission to the Foundling Hospital.

The Foundling Hospital's admission criteria concerned the marital status of the mother, her reputation, the age of her child, and the willingness of the father to accept financial responsibility for his child (Nichols and Wray 1935). As a charitable institution, it was distinctive in restricting its benevolence to illegitimate children. Other charities cared for a wider range of children, including those termed 'waifs and strays' (Ward 1990). Prior to admission, the board of governors also investigated the mother's character and sexual morality (or lack thereof). Attempts were made to ascertain whether her predicament was due to an uncharacteristic slipping from grace, or the result of having fallen victim to a false promise of marriage. Only women of 'good character' were considered eligible. As far as the illegitimate child was concerned, only babies (up to 12 months old) were accepted into care.

The Foundling Hospital was also unusual in including the circumstances of the putative father in its investigations. It would appear that issues of financial and moral responsibility (rather than specifically *sexual* morality) were emphasized. Where at all possible, attempts were made to locate errant fathers to persuade them to acknowledge their financial obligation to the mother and her child. Only failure in this regard would qualify a child for admission into the Foundling Hospital.

The Coram care regime

During the eighteenth century, the Foundling Hospital evolved a phased system of care, linked to the age of the child and their perceived care needs. This system of care remained largely unchanged until the 1940s.

Having an admissions policy that was restricted to young babies meant that the Foundling Hospital was obligated to provide a high level of individual care and attention for its charges during their early years. The Foundling Hospital had learned from its early history that caring for large numbers of babies in one setting was labour intensive, costly, and risky in terms of infant ill-health and mortality (McClure 1981). Over time, the Foundling Hospital had developed the practice of placing babies with selected foster families in a small number of villages outside London.

From the first few weeks or months of life, until the age of 5 or 6 years, the men and women interviewed were fostered with a working-class family in rural Kent, Surrey or Essex. (In the nineteenth century, some children were placed further afield.) This arrangement meant that children could be cared for at a relatively low cost and in circumstances which, while at arm's length from the Foundling Hospital itself, were sufficiently restricted geographically to allow for some monitoring of the child's care and well-being. The arrangement also provided a source of income for working-class families in these villages.

Once Coram's children reached school age, they were separated from their foster family and (until 1926) were admitted into the Foundling Hospital in London. In 1926, the Foundling Hospital was temporarily relocated to Redhill (1926–34) before moving to new and permanent premises on the outskirts of Berkhamsted (1934–53). Children lived in one of the Coram schools until the age of 14, when pupils were 'placed out' into service (military for the boys, domestic for the girls). A small number, usually those deemed unfit for military service, were found apprenticeships. All Coram young people remained under the official guardianship of the charity until they were 21 years old.

Care and illegitimacy

To what extent was the care provided by the Foundling Hospital influenced by the child's status as illegitimate? At the point of admission, the Foundling Hospital contracted to accept responsibility for the care and upbringing of the illegitimate child from infancy. Thus, the Foundling Hospital's care policies might be interpreted as aiming to save the mother and the child from any lengthy exposure to the potentially damaging effects of illegitimacy.

Separation

The Foundling Hospital also attempted to contain the negative effects of illegitimacy by ensuring a complete and (almost) irrevocable separation of the mother from her child. Once accepted into care, each child was baptized and given a new name. A mother entered into a contract with the Foundling Hospital not to contact her child, although letters of enquiry concerning the child's general well-being were permitted. However, mothers received only the most general of responses and letters, and any gifts or tokens of affection were never passed directly to the child. Only in a very small number of cases were children allowed to be 'reclaimed' by their mothers, and only then after a very thorough investigation into her circumstances.

This arrangement facilitated the rehabilitation of the mother's reputation and social status. As one respondent put it, 'the Foundling Hospital took over care of me and my mother departed for pastures new and a new life'. However, in effect, this arrangement, while restoring respectability to the mother, passed the burden of the social stigma of illegitimacy to the child. It was the *child* who was separated from the wider community, and what might have been perceived as their morally polluted origins.

Nevertheless, there were aspects of the Coram care regime that provided for a degree of social integration for illegitimate children during their early years. While they were in foster care, it is likely that Coram children were a feature of village and family life across the generations, and that this practice provided a relatively accepting social environment. Children were frequently brought up alongside the biological children of their foster mothers, and with other foster children. The Coram care regime thus gave children an experience of family life during their early and, some might argue, most significant years, in terms of individual development. Their experiences during these years may indeed have acted as a kind of innoculation against the relative bleakness of later school life.

However, it is probably significant that the transition from foster care to institutional care occurred when children reached school age. Indeed, one respondent had happily begun to attend her local primary school. But this was an exception and not the rule. The pattern of care followed by the Foundling Hospital prevented illegitimate children from mixing with their peers in the community once they reached school age. Thus the theme of separation (initially from the birth mother, and subsequently the foster family) represented an important feature in the care of Coram children.

Growing up as a 'foundling'

Having explored some of the characteristics of the care provided by the Foundling Hospital, we now move to an investigation of what it was like to grow up as a Coram pupil during the first half of the twentieth century. The following discussion draws upon an analysis of 25 interviews with former pupils (13 women, 12 men), aged between 58 and 94 years. Questions were asked about early memories of being in foster care, the transition to residential care, life at school (from the age of 5 to 14 years). Other issues explored included relationships with staff members, school routines and rules, what constituted the high and low points of school life, and the transition from school to work and independent living. Finally, views were elicited about how the experience of growing up in the Foundling Hospital's care influenced adult life. The names of the respondents have been changed to protect their identity and ensure confidentiality.

Foster care

The placing of children in foster families and within a network of familial and community relationships during their early years, produced many accounts of happy, almost idyllic, childhoods. Narratives of an ecology of childhood emerged, where life followed the seasons and its rituals. Their language was evocative of physical and emotional expansiveness; they talked about 'blossoming', and of a sense of belonging.

> *My earliest remembrance is of a big pram for the baby and saucepans and that, and we were all going off to the hop gardens. The hop gardens in Kent were fantastic . . . Memories of happiness, yes. Bill was my sort of guiding light and I went everywhere on his shoulders. And they had an allotment and I'd spend time at the allotment . . . I just remember being there all the time and always with my mother. And I can see myself now, holding on to this black skirt she had on. Happiness, that's the main thing I remember. And I remember the summer, not the winter.*

(May, 72)

However, respondents were not aware during these early years that they were 'foster' children. As far as they were concerned, they were living with their 'real' mother. Consequently, children were not prepared for their abrupt removal to the Foundling Hospital once they reached school age.

Transition into institutional care

The separation of Coram children from their foster parents was often described as the first, and one of the most significant experiences of loss. Children were separated from their foster mothers and siblings with no explanation or preparation.

> All the time at the back of your mind, you were thinking 'what's happened to me? Where did I come from? Where am I going?' you know. And this is the traumatic part really about it all. You feel that you're in a situation where you've foster people and they've left you. Nobody tells you why it happened, you know? ... so when I went to bed and you were on your own, you'd think what have I done? and begin to feel guilty that you'd done something to cause it.
>
> (Jack, 79)

So uniform and so emotionally traumatic were men's and women's memories of their first day of admission to the Foundling Hospital that they appear to represent a symbolic initiation into a wholly different social order. Their hair was cut severely short (some said 'shaved'), their clothes were removed, they were bathed and given their school uniform. Grief at the separation from their foster mothers was common, as was fear and shock at their new circumstances. Some described the group of children they were admitted with as being completely silent. Others described a room full of naked, crying children.

> And the next memory after all that was getting to Redhill and this very big building and having all our hair shaved off ... I remember Bill saying to me 'Don't cry'. I had this in my mind. Don't cry. I can remember this big stone room that had iron beds and there were two bed heads put together like that. And there was a little boy in the other bed and he was crying all the time: 'I want my mummy. I want my mummy.' And I remember putting my hand through and holding his hand and thinking I must not cry. I had promised Bill I wouldn't cry.
>
> (May, 72)

Admission to the Foundling Hospital represented a pivotal point of transition between two types of care: familial and institutional. In the accounts of former pupils, one type of care was necessarily defined in relation to the other. Familial care was often described, not just in emotional or symbolic terms – of a sense of being 'made a fuss of', of having smart and clean clothes, well-polished shoes and nourishing food – but also in terms of the absence of fear of physical punishment.

Upon entering the Foundling Hospital, children experienced a fundamental change in the nature of the care they received; they moved from receiving individual attention to being just one of a large number who, on the whole, were reported as being treated the same. The nice dresses, smart socks and long tresses of which many respondents were so proud, represented symbols of individual care. These were exchanged for a school uniform that represented sameness, utility and convenience. The quality of the relationship between children and their carers also changed from one of emotional warmth to emotional distance.

> *It wasn't the care we had at home. It was military style. It was 'Here is a job I've got to do, get on with it'. We had a nurse, as we called them who looked after the infants, and her favourite sort of trick – she would get hold of this sponge and slap it in your face like this with great joy. So the staff were not unkind, but certainly not loving. They didn't want to know if you had a problem really. They'd got a job to do.*
>
> (Ronald, 75)

Care and identity

These changes in the nature of the care received and the quality of the relationship with their carers emerged as playing a fundamental part in the reconstruction of the child's new identity as a 'foundling'. Familial care was described as having been encouraging of individuality. By contrast, former pupils described their first day at the Foundling Hospital as the occasion when they lost individuality and a sense of intimate connection with others. They reported feeling that they had become just one of a large anonymous group.

> *You couldn't say anything. You sort of went along with everything . . . you just go along, there was no alternative. And I think I just – you just sort of clam up . . . I was free before and I could – I was finding that I could think for myself. I was starting to express myself and then you went to school and you lost that. So you clammed up.*
>
> (Patricia, 70)

Foster mothers represented the child's sole link with their former life and relationships. For some former pupils, they also functioned as an important source of information or support as they made their transition to institutional care. Sometimes children found out about the meaning of 'foster' mother, brother or sister from their foster mothers when they returned to visit on 'mother's days', which were held on several occasions through the year. Foster mothers also brought toys, chocolates and news of their foster families. On these days, foster mothers and children had an opportunity to meet each other and exchange news. One respondent discovered that she was the last of 26 children cared for by one foster mother. However, some reported that they never saw their foster parents again and that they did not dare to ask questions about their identity, either of staff or of other children. Their curiosity gradually died away, only to re-emerge in adult life.

The regulation of care: space, time and activity

From their first day in the Foundling Hospital, children's lives were dominated by a system and ethos of control made manifest in the regulation of their physical appearance, movement, bodily functions, and of their time and space. Over 400 children were washed, dressed, fed, exercised and given a basic education to a strict daily routine.

Separation and containment

In terms of space, children experienced separation on a macro level (from the local community), through their containment in the school building and grounds, and on a micro level, in relation to the strictly gender-segregated spheres within the school. With the exception of the six-week summer camps and visits to the theatre or circus at Christmas time, children were contained within the premises of the Foundling Hospital during their school-age years.

It was a notable development in the school's history that following the closure of the London Foundling Hospital in 1926, the school moved from an urban to a rural environment. Thus, children experienced a greater degree of isolation from local communities. In London, children were not allowed to stand within six feet of the school gates, but children and passers by were able to observe each other, albeit from a distance. Members of the public, benefactors and school governors came into the school on Sundays to hear the choir in the chapel, view the picture gallery, and sometimes to watch children eating their lunch. However, at the Redhill and Berkhamsted schools, governors visited only occasionally, and members of the public did not enter the school grounds at all. Children were taken for Sunday afternoon walks in the local countryside, but on routes which took them away from the local village. One respondent recalled that the people of Berkhamsted were so concerned at never seeing the children, they wrote letters of complaint to the school. As a result, she recalled being asked to walk along the perimeter of the school grounds in front of members of the local community.

Unlike their peers living in the community, Coram pupils were subject to a high, if not constant, level of adult surveillance. One man recalled the feeling of being watched during every moment, awake or asleep. For one woman, this theme was linked very vividly with the trappings of Christianity:

> *And I remember the playroom had written up . . . 'eschew evil, and do good' . . . and the other was, 'the eyes of the Lord are in every place, beholding the evil and the good'. And fancy somebody watching me the whole of the time. I didn't like the sound of that. But of course, that was before I knew anything about the Bible. I just felt I was being watched.*
>
> (Mary, 90)

Within the Foundling Hospital, separate spheres were created according to age and gender divisions. After an initial period in a separate building for infants, children moved up into the 'big school'. They then moved through the school, changing dormitories as they got older and taller. Girls were separated from boys, living in what were in effect two different schools created within one building. Each school had its own head teacher and staff. Boys and girls lived in male- or female-dominated worlds, except for the presence of female teachers and nurses in the boys' infants' school and first years in the 'big school'. Men intervened more intermittently in the girls' lives: the chaplain for prayers and religious instruction, the choir master for singing lessons and the head master for drill lessons in which they learned to march in military formation. Consequently, although the routine of their lives was identical, girls' and boys' lives were marked by different social and cultural norms.

Care and education: the making of soldiers and servants

In terms of activity, children spent most of their time in lessons. In the Coram care regime, education was not separate from care since it fulfilled a number of important functions. First, lessons provided a means of occupying children for most of the day, a not insignificant priority for an institution caring for a large number of children. Second, education provided the context for instilling discipline. This latter function was related to a third, and equally important function, which was to prepare boys and girls for employment so that they could be self-supporting in adulthood.

While respondents acknowledged that their education was basic, thorough and designed to equip them for a life of service, they did at least acquire sufficient knowledge to enable them to make the transition to working life. Boys and girls were provided with an education in the three Rs (reading, writing and arithmetic), geography, history and literature. The oldest respondent reported that she learned

> *things that it was necessary to know. After all, we weren't going to be wonderful. We were mostly going into service. And you can understand – if you learn the basic of things, when you get older, you learn the rest if you've got any sense at all, gradually.*

> (Amy, 94)

The discipline experienced by children was chiefly determined by gender, not only because boys were perceived as being more unruly than girls, but also because each was being prepared for their eventual station in life. Boys needed to be prepared for a life in the army. Consequently, for all boys, a half-hour period between play and the start of lessons would be spent with the head master on the parade ground. Boys and girls were taught to march but the emphasis upon military life was greater for the boys, for whom parade-ground activities were a feature of daily life. Men recalled being marched into the dining hall, each movement from reaching their seat, to sitting down, eating in silence and then standing up again, being marked by the noise of a gavel.

We were young soldiers in the making, not that we realised it then . . . we used to march up to our places. Stop opposite our plate and our mug. Wait for the next thing [bang of the gavel], turn smartly in, bring our hands together in supplication. Next thing was another clap and then we would say grace. Stay in this position till another [bang], and then smartly to the side again, you see . . . you get over your seat and then sit down. Wait for the next go [bang] and then you could eat.

(Frederick, 87)

For boys, the physical punishment exacted by masters was described as a routine, and relatively accepted feature of school life. Bullying and violence among the boys was also pervasive and in many ways mirrored the behaviour of the masters. Men's accounts of life in the boys' school had a barrack-room flavour to them; they represented narratives of violence based on a hierarchy of age, size and strength. Once boys left the infants school, their entry into the 'big school' was frequently described as an initiation by a process of brutalization. Most men interviewed described the first day of school and the first few years as their 'low points' which they learned to survive, or which they simply endured until they themselves became one of the 'big boys':

I went from infants into the juniors. Now what they do then – they used to take out one and you had to fight each other and it's like a game of conkers, you know . . . And it was the same with fighting . . . And I had to fight every boy in my year and I won and then I had to fight boys in the year above and then I got beaten. And so that was why . . . I became the leader.

(Raymond, 65)

In comparison with male respondents, women's accounts of school life were characterized by a more ready conformity to minimal discipline; these were useful attributes for future domestic servants. The finely tuned hierarchy and competitiveness that were such important features of boys' relationships were almost entirely absent from accounts of girlhood. Physical punishments were less common and it was commented that a few girls were more likely to be scapegoated for whatever transgressions were committed. Only one or two girls were described as bullies. The overall impression given by these accounts was that girls tended to opt for the safety of conformity to school rules and regulations.

The body and sexuality

While cleanliness was encouraged as a means of self-care, other aspects of bodily care were overlooked, if not actively suppressed, by the Foundling Hospital, particularly as this related to signs of physical or sexual maturation. The place of the body in relation to concepts of care produced highly gender-differentiated accounts.

Whereas some men commented on sexual behaviour between boys in a very matter-of-fact way, women made no reference to sexual behaviour between girls. Women's accounts focused on their considerable confusion concerning the significance of bodily changes and the onset of menstruation during early adolescence. Indeed, the school went to considerable lengths to prevent girls sharing information about menstruation. Girls who had their periods were called 'infirmary girls' as they were reported as having to wash in the infirmary rather than the main school building. Discussing menstruation was reported as having the status of a serious 'crime' in the school's order of transgressions: 'You got the cane and your name in the Black Book . . . We thought there was something dreadfully wrong with us.' One of the youngest respondents recalled trying to challenge this secrecy and enforced ignorance:

and I'd vaguely heard that babies had to do with all this. So I thought well while I'm in here I'll ask her so I said, 'What about babies and how does –' and she said 'Get out. We're not dealing with that today'. So on the way out all my friends were queuing up and they said to me 'What's it about?' O and I said, 'It's terrible, do you know, you're going to bleed to death' and I ran down the corridor.

(Helen, 60)

Although the suppression of information on the body, sex and sexuality may also have been a common feature of life in contemporary mainstream schools, girls who lived in the confined world of the Foundling Hospital had fewer opportunities for obtaining information from other sources. Sadly, some accounts of former pupils suggested that this censorship increased the vulnerability of Coram girls to sexual abuse and to having an illegitimate child of their own, once they left the confines of the school.

Children's concepts of care

Former pupils were also keen to describe aspects of the Foundling Hospital's care that had a positive impact upon them. These were described as the 'life rafts' that made the monotony of institutional life more bearable.

It is perhaps not surprising that, given the routine and contained life in the Foundling Hospital itself, memories of enjoyment were chiefly linked to the annual 'escape' to the countryside for the summer camping trip. Improved care was associated with greater physical freedom, reduced adult supervision, and consequently a higher degree of personal autonomy.

'Six weeks under canvas' represented a return to the countryside (and possibly unconsciously, to the happiness of their early childhood). In the private language of the children, the summer camp was an event which they 'glished' for months. It was described as a time of 'freedom', of having better food, and pocket money to buy small items – often salt and pepper – in the local village shops. The thick material of the school uniform was exchanged for khaki. Play emerged as important aspect of children's unsupervised time. The men and women interviewed recalled playing in tin baths, sliding down hills, picking wild flowers, and playing in twos and threes, instead of in a big and anonymous crowd as was the practice in the grounds of the Foundling Hospital.

Second in order of importance to the summer camp was the value attached to relationships with caring adults. Significantly, these caring figures were often not teachers but people who fulfilled a pastoral role, such as the chaplain or After Care Superintendent (who was responsible for supporting Coram boys and girls in their first experience of paid employment), or adults who held domestic positions. Although occupying relatively peripheral positions within the school, these figures helped to sustain a network of caring relationships between current and former pupils.

> *Then Mr Stork, the chaplain, absolute gentleman . . . He was the saving grace really . . . Mr Stork went round all the classes and gave us a short scripture lesson and then he would say 'Any questions?' And I never recall anybody asking about St Paul's message or anything of that sort . . . the questions were invariably 'Who do you think is going to win the cricket this year sir?' and things of that nature. And the other thing that was always being asked was 'How are Crompton, Winter and Foxcroft?' Three of my foster brothers. And all the various boys were asking about their foster brothers who were invariably in the army, and Mr Stork always knew.*
> (Frederick, 87)

In terms of gender, a few men stood out as caring figures though, from the point of view of the boys, ineffectual in influencing the more punitive aspects of school life. It was almost as though, in being caring men, they went against a fundamental assumption about what it was to be masculine within the culture of the school. For girls, the nurses working in the infirmary were perceived as an important source of emotional care. One woman recalled how she willed herself to be ill, so that she could experience more of what she described as maternal care and attention.

The legacy of illegitimacy: lies, secrets and silence

Once children reached the age of 14 years, most left the Foundling Hospital as abruptly as they had entered it. The ambivalence of the protection afforded by the Foundling Hospital was then felt with full force. Former pupils were suddenly required to live with 'outsiders' and were thus exposed to questions about their family backgrounds and schooling. Until 1953, when the Foundling Hospital Act allowed for the provision of shortened birth certificates, employers could identify who among their workforce were 'foundlings'. For boys who entered the army, the risk of being exposed as illegitimate may have been compensated for, to some extent, by the camaraderie of the unit. By comparison, girls were more isolated in domestic service, and families employing them as servants would have known about their origins. Indeed, one family, having previously visited the Foundling Hospital, knew about the famous choir and expected their new 'foundling' to sing for them outside their bedroom door on Christmas Eve.

Men and women described their feelings of shame and strategies of concealment as they negotiated the stigma of illegitimacy in the wider society:

> *And you had to tell so many lies in the early days. Nobody knows now really . . . Even on your marriage certificate you had to put your father. And I put farmer because my foster mother's husband was a farmer. Little things. Oh well, where did you live? Which school did you go to? And you had to tell such lies and it's so distressing . . . to tell so many lies. And that gets you for all the rest of your life. Really it does.*
>
> (Ethel, 86)

Marriage and family life: a safe haven?

Men and women found that, as a single person living on the 'outside', their illegitimacy exposed them to the threat of social rejection and condemnation. By comparison, marriage and family life represented a safer haven for many former pupils. With a spouse, children and (possibly) a network of in-laws, men and women found it easier to respond to personal questions and to participate in conversations concerning the 'normal' events of family life, such as mother's days, Christmas and summer holidays.

Nevertheless, the stigma of illegitimacy was not without its impact on marriage and family life. Women in particular discussed the ways in which illegitimacy influenced their choice of partner. Sometimes romances flourished between former pupils who stayed in contact with each other in adulthood. On the one hand, marriage to another 'foundling' meant that former pupils could dispense with the need to divulge or hide their illegitimacy. On the other hand, a partner who had a 'normal' family background and who was accepting of illegitimacy, provided former pupils with a ready-made network of family relationships. One woman recalled weighing up the pros and cons of her 'fatal attraction' to a number of 'old boys' and her decision not to marry one of them:

> *I think a lot of it was we wanted to marry into a family and we knew the boys had no family, so most of us of my age steered clear of making a strong friendship with one of the boys . . . We did so want a family, and I think that's what steered us into a conventional marriage.*
>
> (Susan, 80)

A further dimension to the impact of illegitimacy on adult life concerned former pupils' attempts to break the historic separation of the illegitimate child from his or her mother. During the late 1940s, the Foundling Hospital began to relax its policy of withholding information on former pupils' birth parents. Several respondents reported that they made enquiries about their origins. The timing of their enquiries was often related to their own family circumstances. Becoming a parent necessarily raised questions about their own parentage; three women reported a wish to find out more about their mothers when they themselves became mothers. Others, particularly of the older generation, were more tentative in their efforts and, despite intense personal curiosity of their own, would not pursue information on their origins in the face of family uninterest or opposition. It was not always clear whether this opposition was a result of anger at a former pupil's mother for having given up her child, or because the very process of investigation reawakened the sense that the whole family was tainted by illegitimacy. Some of the men and women interviewed reported not wishing to rock the boat within the family or threaten their hard-won sense of emotional security. For others, however, the interest of their own children was an important impetus.

Before Coram men and women were in a position to obtain information on their birth parents, illegitimacy functioned as a barrier to the transmission of knowledge across the generations. It was not uncommon for the men and women interviewed to have written down their memories and details of their origins for their children and grandchildren as a way of ensuring that their offspring would not feel as 'rootless' as they had felt themselves to be. Finding out about the identity of the family's grandparents (the respondent's own parents) was described as important, even if they were deceased. Until one interviewee found his mother's burial place, he described his family life as 'happy, but not complete'. This sense of completeness, of coming full circle after having had children of one's own, is echoed here:

And when we found it [the mother's burial place] oh we hugged each other and cried . . . Oh I've taken photographs and I sit and look at it sometimes . . . It was just like coming home to a family. Because I've gone to over 70 without thinking I've got anybody and all of a sudden . . . I mean I've started with nothing and I've got all these beautiful children . . . I just sit and look at all of them and there's a wonderful feeling.

(Susan, 80)

Conclusion

This chapter began with the hypothesis that the care regime of the Foundling Hospital was influenced by the social stigma of illegitimacy, which was reflected in and reinforced by, the separation of the illegitimate child from the mother, the mother's family, and the wider community. This separation, while representing a form of social exclusion, was also linked to the ambivalent and problematic notion of protection. The physical separation and containment of illegitimate children within the Foundling Hospital might be interpreted as protecting society from these living reminders of the sin of sex outside marriage; yet it also undoubtedly protected illegitimate children from frequent experiences of social rejection (at least until they were 14 years of age). In the context of the Foundling Hospital therefore, care, in its relationship to protection, emerges as something of a Janus concept (that is, able to face two directions at once).

The complexities and dilemmas posed by the separation (and protection) of Coram children from the wider society produced conflicting views about whether the care provided by the Foundling Hospital was better or worse than that experienced by children in families 'on the outside'. This issue proved difficult for former pupils to assess, since they were relatively well protected from the poverty that was so widespread in the first half of the twentieth century, particularly during the depression of the 1930s. The impact of poverty on working-class children's lives in the interwar period was highlighted in the following interview in which a former pupil shared her childhood memories in the presence of other family members. In this interview, the idea that a Coram pupil had experienced a deprived childhood was roundly rejected by husband and daughter:

JUNE: *We had our own swimming baths, and we used to play netball, cricket. They [the staff] were very good. And they taught us to swim.*

DAUGHTER: *Which Dad's never learned to swim has he. If you compared my mum's years as a child to my dad's, my mum had far more than he did.*

JUNE: *Because our parents –*

HUSBAND: *She did far more things than I ever done. I never went to no circus.*

DAUGHTER: *And he was an only child as well.*

HUSBAND: *Yes, and all the opportunity I suppose of being on the outside. Just mum and dad. But they [pointing to his wife] were doing well, I'll tell you. You had to go out with the dog and catch a rabbit in my time.*

(Interview with June, 83, and her husband and daughter)

In the context of the institutional care provided by the Foundling Hospital, it is perhaps the issue of emotional care that, from the point of view of former pupils, represented the most serious inadequacy. The separation of children from their foster families marked a transition from an experience of care as relational and full of emotional warmth, to care as a series of tasks to be regulated and rationed. In the latter system, the child was positioned as an object, not a subject of care. In general, the scope for forming caring relationships with adults in the Foundling Hospital was limited and largely focused on those occupying a relatively marginal status (such as adults in pastoral or domestic positions). Yet, the impact of these marginal figures should not be underestimated. They helped to sustain a network of caring relationships between adults and children, and between children and their peers. They therefore helped to compensate for a care regime that, from the outset, had the effect of rupturing or weakening emotional ties (for example, between children and their birth and foster mothers, and with foster brothers and sisters).

The concept of care might also be interpreted as involving the preparation of young people for employment and the capacity to be self-supporting. In terms of the education provided by the Foundling Hospital, some evidence suggests that children received a basic education that was superior to that of many working-class children in mainstream schools. For example, four out of five Coram children passed their army entrance exams, compared with only one out of five of other applicants. However, there are also wider considerations at play, beyond the relative merits of the education provided by the Foundling Hospital, compared with other schools.

In the context of institutional care for children growing up outside their families of origin, care, education, and preparation for employment, were necessarily interlinked. Having accepted the responsibility of caring for illegitimate children from infancy to the age of 21, an important object-ive of the Foundling Hospital's governors was to find employment for Coram boys and girls. Directing girls and boys toward domestic and military service proved an ideal solution; there was a consistently high demand for soldiers and servants, and in both occupations, board and lodgings were provided by the employer. These occupations allowed for the baton of care (in terms of the provision of adequate food and shelter) to be passed on to employers. In turn, these destinations influenced the content and standard of education provided by the Foundling Hospital. In this sense, therefore, the care and education provided by the Foundling Hospital might be interpreted as strictly instrumental, at least in terms of the labour market of the time.

Lastly, the concept of care might also be expected to include attention to physical health and well-being. Eminent physicians were commonly rep-resented among the Foundling Hospital's governors and the health care provided by the Foundling Hospital was widely regarded as of a very high standard. This was no small achievement given that the life chances of illegitimate children in the wider community were so much worse than those of legitimate children. For example, in 1918, infant mortality for babies under 12 months old was 91 deaths per thousand for those legitimately born, compared with 186 per thousand for those illegitimately born (Jeger 1951). The Foundling Hospital had its own infirmary. In addition, children were routinely cared for in the various fever hospitals across London in cases of serious illness. Yet, perhaps unsurprisingly, the accounts of former pupils also illustrate the ways in which physical health care was excluded from considerations of physical and sexual maturation, particularly as this related to the reproductive capacities of girls. Indeed, two former pupils suggested that they knew of girls who, having left the Foundling Hospital, had illegit-imate children of their own and that these children were subsequently accepted into the care of the Foundling Hospital. The splitting of care from matters of sex and sexuality represented, and continues to represent, a common theme in the care of children and young people.

It was, perhaps, society's construction of illegitimacy as a source of shame that had the most negative effects on the men and women interviewed. Following the Second World War, social attitudes concerning illegitimacy gradually began to change. To a certain extent, this development might be linked to widespread debates concerning the care of looked after children that emerged after the Second World War, a time when the number of illegitimate births peaked at 9 per cent of all births (Jeger 1951). As psychologists began to have more influence on the development and conceptualization of child care, there was also less enthusiasm for severing the bond between mother and child, whatever the mother's marital status. The Children Act 1948 might be said to have provided an important impetus in this regard, in that it established the principle that children should be separated from the parent(s) only as a last resort, and even then, if at all possible, as a temporary measure.

The Children Act 1948 brought voluntary childcare charities, such as the Foundling Hospital, within a regulatory framework established by central government. In the few years prior to the Act, the Foundling Hospital began to phase out residential care, in favour of a combination of foster care and day school, to which children from 'the outside' were admitted. Thus the principle of separation that had hitherto underpinned the Foundling Hospital's care of illegitimate children began to loosen its hold. However, it was not until several decades later that illegitimacy ceased to function as a source of social stigma and control in the lives of women and children.

References

Commission on the Status of Women (1971) *The Status of the Unmarried Mother: Law and Practice.* New York: United Nations.

Jeger, L.M. (ed.) (1951) *Illegitimate Children and their Parents.* London: National Council for the Unmarried Mother and her Child.

McClure, R. (1981) *Coram's Children: The London Foundling Hospital in the Eighteenth Century.* London: Yale University Press.

Nichols, R.H. and Wray, F. (1935) *The History of the Foundling Hospital.* Oxford: Oxford University Press.

Ward, H. (1990) The charitable relationship: parents, children and the waifs and strays society. Unpublished PhD thesis, University of Bristol.

CHAPTER 4

Social pedagogy: an historical account of care and education as social control

PAT PETRIE

Introduction

This chapter addresses 'care' in the sense of duty and surveillance as one aspect of society's dealings with children. It uses an historical approach, drawing mainly on the nineteenth century, before turning, briefly, to the present day. A central concern will be the long-standing relationship between care and education: two important planks in policy towards children. I shall suggest that this relationship can best be understood in terms of 'social pedagogy', a term employed little in the Anglophone world, meaning socially provided education, using education in the broadest sense of that word (a discussion follows). I shall describe how the duties of care, undertaken by dominant groups in society towards poor people, have been discharged by means of education-in-its-broadest-sense, including, but not confined to, schooling. An exploration of the underlying premises and actions of social pedagogies can clarify the operation of social power and control, especially as these affect poor children. Social pedagogies have been, for the most part, utilitarian and instrumental, subjecting children – and adults – to the needs of the governing classes and the control of the wider society. They have done so by surveillance, by controlling people's time, location and activities, and by attempting to introduce those who are disaffected from society to dominant cultural forms and understandings: whether those of parenting, religion, literacy or 'worthwhile' leisure activities; their aim has often been to produce a compliant workforce.

The chapter concentrates on care as public action, often couched in terms of duty, towards others, especially their surveillance, education (in the broadest sense) and control. Before it turns to history, the first section provides a short discussion of key terms: care and social pedagogy. The second section examines the history of public policy towards poor people, concentrating on the nineteenth century and the part played by social pedagogies in controlling the poor, addressing their 'Want' and their 'Ignorance'. The third section discusses the value bases of social pedagogies, taking as examples two nineteenth-century figures: Robert Owen and Emmeline Pethick, who, using different pedagogical approaches, attempted to confront the dominant values of their society. In conclusion, the fourth section detects the continuing echo of nineteenth-century concerns and strategies in today's public policy towards children, especially poor children, with the power of social pedagogy harnessed to political agendas of control, public order and economic goals.

Care: duty and surveillance

It is perhaps its ambiguity that makes care such a powerful concept. It appeals to duty, has resonances of fondness and regard, while stress and anxiety lurk in its background. From an etymological viewpoint, in Old Teutonic and Old English 'care' (or its cognates) apparently referred to anxiety, burden and concern (compare careworn and carefree).[1] In Middle English, care acquired meanings referring to a charge or duty, having oversight of someone or something, surveillance with a view to protection, preservation or guidance (*Shorter Oxford English Dictionary*). By 1530, the meaning had extended to having regard or liking for someone. It seems that all these meanings still have currency, whether at the personal level or within ethical and legal discourses. As others have said, the terms – having care of, caring about, and caring for – are different processes. They relate to the different meanings that are bundled together in the word's history. As a result, care can be used within legal frameworks, as in 'duty of care' and 'child care', but it can also be a warm, less sharply defined word, so that the meaning of 'I care for you' can be close to 'I love you'. The chapter concentrates especially at care in the sense of a charge or duty, connected with surveillance, with a view to a child's 'protection, preservation or guidance'. It will often be about services which today are seen as providing 'child care' or 'childcare' (see p. 25), but which in other countries might be seen – perhaps additionally to their care function, perhaps distinct from it – as 'pedagogic' services.

In recent British policy, there are ambiguities surrounding the use of the term 'care', and suggestions of dissatisfaction as to its appropriateness. For example, unease about its use in policy towards children has led to 'children in care' becoming, with the Children Act 1989, 'looked-after children': a term that retains, nonetheless, connotations of surveillance. Yet, *child care* (two words) continues to be the policy field relating to looked-after children, as in the charges of the local authority. Somewhat confusingly, *childcare* (one word) is used to denote a different policy field – that referred to in the current government's National Childcare Strategy. This is about provision for children whose parents work and need alternatives to parental care.

Dissatisfaction with the term finds its expression in coinages such as educare, playcare and early years services which seek to broaden the understanding of work with children, beyond responsibility and surveillance, in order to take a more educative perspective.

'Social pedagogy': bringing care and education together

Many of the social interventions described in the chapter have some pedagogic or educational content – we are here using education in its broadest sense, relating to all that is meant by bringing up children, caring for them (having the oversight of their well-being, as constructed by those in charge) and supporting their development. These are duties which, for the upper classes, have always been fulfilled by parents, and by the nannies, governesses, tutors and schools they have employed. The nineteenth century saw society at large undertaking some of the duties involved in the education of the children of the labouring classes – using the term education in its more narrow and in its broader sense. The necessity to indicate whether 'education' is being used in a broad or a narrower sense leads us to a central dilemma for English speakers. It has implications for how they conceptualize provision for children and for their communication with European colleagues: the English language has no single word that can stand for 'education-in-its-broadest-sense' to distinguish it from 'education-associated-with-the academic-curriculum'.

'Pedagogy' is almost equally difficult for English ears and tongues as it is for English minds: should it be pronounced with a soft *g*, analogous to psychology and other 'ologies', or with a hard *g* in keeping with its continental usage? As well as the awkwardness surrounding its pronunciation, 'pedagogy' is largely unused, outside specialist circles. For educationalists it mostly denotes the science of teaching and learning, and relates to the formal curriculum of school, college and university – what many of our European colleagues might refer to as 'didactics', rather than pedagogy. But 'pedagogy' is given a much broader meaning than didactics in much of continental Europe. It is often used to relate to the education of the *whole* person: body, mind, feelings, spirit, creativity and, crucially, the relationship of the individual to others (Petrie 2001; Moss and Petrie 2002). Those who work in the field of pedagogy support the child's development, whether in school, leisure provision or a in variety of other social services, including residential settings for looked after children, family centres and institutions for young offenders. Most of these are seen in current British policy as care settings, and their broader educational content is less emphasized. We should also note that 'pedagogy' may be applicable to services for adults as well as children, and not confined to schooling and other formal settings.

The term social pedagogy (*sozialpädagogik*: strictly, social pedagogic theory) was first defined in 1844 by Mager, the editor of the *Pädogische Revue*, as the 'theory of all the personal, social and moral education in a given society, including the description of what has happened in practice' (cited in Winkler 1988; quoted by Gabriel 2000: 1). The meanings of words do not stand still, nevertheless in Europe social pedagogy often relates to a field of theory, policy and practice concerning children. In English-speaking countries, we have lost this understanding of work with a foot in both education and care. For our European colleagues, both *child care* and *childcare* are social pedagogic provisions, as to their content of the work (the pedagogy) and as to their basis in notions of societal duties towards children (the pedagogy is social, rather than private, or familial). I would suggest that recourse to this concept is helpful in examining public policy towards children (and their parents) and in distinguishing the common values to be found in socially provided care and 'education-in-its-broadest-sense'.

Addressing Want and Ignorance

It is poor children whom, historically speaking, public policy first addressed and has continued to address. It does so alongside concerns for children more generally, as with current child protection legislation (see Chapter 5), and with the provision of universal education – although universal education was originally aimed at the poor and working classes. Poverty is addressed when poor people appear to be a problem: their existence offends the moral sense for reasons of compassion, notions of human rights and equality or, from a different perspective, they threaten the well-being of society. They can be seen as drains on the public purse, as a seedbed for crime and public unrest, non-participants in the workforce, not contributing to the common good. Social and economic forces, connected with developing industrial mass production and its accompanying financial speculation, had brought labourers into the towns. Compared to their earlier position, poor people en masse were now highly visible. Also, they had become more visible to each other so that the threat of mass uprising frightened the affluent classes. Extreme poverty had become offensive and had to be dealt with. Social pedagogy, those actions that straddle care and education, was one means by which the problem of poverty could be addressed.

We start by considering something of the history of care in England, in the sense, especially, of the religious, philanthropic or political duties assumed by individuals or by society for the well-being (nominally, at least) of others. Both the statutory support of poor people, since Elizabethan times, and their charitable support expanded pervasively in the nineteenth century. Monasteries had supplied the hospitals and schools of the Middle Ages, acting in the name of charity and religion. A religious motivation was appealed to, later, by philanthropic individuals and societies. For example, in the preface to a digest of the reports of the Society for Bettering the Condition of the Poor, published in 1809, Sir Thomas Bernard, linking care with education, writes: 'The care and instruction of the poor form the peculiar and beautiful characteristic of the Christian Religion' and later refers to this as a 'benevolent duty' (Bernard [1809] 1970: 1–2).

Other duties were a matter of statute, rather than philanthropy. Thus, the Elizabethan poor laws let the state decide which of the indigent poor were deserving of 'relief', through the levying of local rates. Taxation is rarely popular and the duties undertaken by the state have often been perceived as burdensome by taxpayers. In the nineteenth century, the principle of 'less eligibility' or disincentive was applied to lessen the imposition on the public purse. Sometimes, relief was available only through residence in the workhouse, with all its restrictions and hardships. The social benefits associated with relieving poverty, and the dangers inherent in not doing so, were ongoing, utilitarian themes in contemporary debate. They appear in the following passage from *A Christmas Carol*. Here, Charles Dickens (1843) personifies as children what he sees as the two great social evils of his time, Want and Ignorance:

> They were a boy and a girl. Yellow, meagre, ragged scowling, wolfish; but prostrate, too, in their humility where graceful youth should have filled their features out, and touched them with its freshest tints, a stale and shrivelled hand, like that of old age, had pinched, and twisted them, and pulled them into shreds. Where angels might have sat enthroned, devils lurked, and glared out menacingly. No change, no degradation, no perversion of humanity, in any grade, through all the mysteries of wonderful creation, has monsters half so horrible and so dread . . .
> 'Spirit! Are they yours?' Scrooge could say no more.
> 'They are man's,' said the Spirit, looking down on them. 'And they cling to me, appealing from their fathers. This boy is Ignorance. This girl is Want. Beware them both, and all of their degree, but most of all beware this boy, for on his brow I see that written which is Doom, unless the writing be erased. Deny it!' cried the Spirit, stretching his hand towards the city . . . 'Slander those who tell it ye! . . . And bide the end!'
>
> (Dicken [1843] undated: 55–6)

Why did these personifications appear in the form of children? From a modern perspective, the 'poor child' is doubly marginalized, by their impoverishment and by their minority status. Dickens' writings are full of images of vulnerable children, from Tiny Tim to Little Nell: the adjectives adhering to these children's first names conjure their smallness and evoke the reader's pity. But childlike as they are, Want and Ignorance are also powerful monsters, fearful warnings for the complacent or hard-hearted. The want and, especially, the ignorance of the poor would be a doom, a terrible judgement, on the respectable classes, the taxpaying trades people, the gentry and the aristocracy. The judgement feared was not only a moral but also a political judgement, such as that of the French Revolution, and threatened in the uprisings of the Chartists and other groups.

However, the duties of the prosperous could appear a heavy burden. Earlier in the novel, when asked to make a contribution for the relief of the Want,

Scrooge had responded: 'Are there no prisons . . . and the Union work-houses? . . . Are they still in operation? . . . I help to support the establishments I have mentioned: they cost enough: and those who are badly off must go there' (Dickens [1843] undated: 8–9).

Education as the content of care

The relief of poverty, the protection of society from debtors and criminals – all came from the public purse. The children of indigent parents and orphans were among those whose distress was 'relieved' by the workhouses, where their conditions were often only minimally better than they would have been outside. (They were in some ways a nineteenth-century equivalent of today's grossly disadvantaged looked-after children.) Nevertheless, nineteenth-century legislation was eventually to insist on these children's schooling as well as their maintenance. It was a public duty (a care and an expense) to provide for these children and to oversee their welfare. Their upbringing included training, through apprenticeships, which also furnished some immediate public profit to their employers and to the public purse. Some children were in the charge of orphanages, endowed by charities, such as the Foundling Hospital in London. Again, notions of care, education and apprenticeship come together in these institutions. A copy of the instructions given to Foundling Hospital children, at the expiration of their apprenticeships, began:

> As the recompense for a long period of care and attention to your maintenance, education, and introduction into life, we have now the pleasing and enviable satisfaction of beholding your entering upon your course in this world, with many important advantages.
>
> (Bernard [1809] 1970: 294)[2]

The document goes on to exhort its recipient to be honest, sober, industrious, prudent, kind and forbearing and to avoid what is now known as the slippery slope of petty crime (Bernard [1809] 1970: 298–9). The care or responsibility that the Foundling Hospital exercised was directed, in the first place, at the preservation of the children's lives and the salvation of their souls. They were baptized on their reception into the hospital and, as the document points out, their education had included 'religious and moral education'. It continues: 'with early religious instruction, and with subsequent care and good habits, you have hitherto been preserved through a period when youth and inexperience are most endangered'. The document proposes the 'Governors of this GREAT AND USEFUL CHARITY' as role models who owe their 'affluence and independence to their own exertions and attentions' (Bernard [1809] 1970: 296, 304, capitals in original). The governors were placing before the foundlings the possibility that they might, through their own efforts, become affluent, no longer dependent on the care of others. The responsibility undertaken by the hospital governors was exercised through the surveillance, education and maintenance of the child. (Christine Oliver's account of early-twentieth-century Foundling Hospital orphans in Chapter 3 also points to care as surveillance, and the linking of education with discipline.) The governors' aim was that their charges should assume the dominant social values of the day, both for their own benefit and for that of respectable society. The governors were not alone in this aspiration for the poor, nor in identifying education as the way forward:

> National education is the first thing necessary. Lay but this foundation and the superstructure of prosperity and happiness, which may be erected, will rest upon a rock; lay but this foundation, poverty will be diminished and want will disappear in proportion as the lower classes are instructed in their duties for then only will they understand their true interests.
> (Cowie 1970: 2, quoting *The Quarterly Review* VIII (1812): 354)

This extract from an influential journal concentrates on schooling, a narrower understanding of education than that of the Foundling Hospital governors, but with the same intention. Public and charitable education was education for the poor, known variously as popular or national education. (For more well-to-do people, their children's education was a private responsibility, exercised through tutors, governesses and, in the nineteenth century, by the growing number of so-called public schools and private day schools.) The use of education as a means of social control, and its provision as the duty of those with an established place in society, can be seen throughout its history.

> It has always been reckoned Wizdom and Policy in a Nation to have as few Beggars, and idle Strollers about their streets as possible. And how is this so effectively prevented as by these schools.
> (Hendley 1725, quoted in Silver 1965: 27)

Through education, adults and children could be made 'acceptable' members of society, healthy, knowing their place and fit for employment. The uneducated and alienated poor, whom Dickens later personified as Ignorance, were seen as a source of civil unrest.[3] They had no stake in society:

> in political commotions, the uneducated pauper has neither principle nor motive, to induce him to respect or defend that of society, the benefits whereof he has not been taught to appreciate. He is prepared for any alteration in the state of things, fearless of change, and indifferent as to consequences.
> (Bernard [1809] 1970: 47)

The Sunday school movement was itself, at least in part, a response to the 'unruliness' of young people, not in this case those who were politically motivated, merely those not contained and controlled by employment:

> One day in the year 1780 Mr Raikes decided to go into the lower part of the town in search of a gardener. The man was not in, and Mr Raikes

was waiting about. Nearby in the street a score of boys were playing 'check'. The din was deafening, the oaths were terrible! Mr Raikes was amazed. Turning to a decent looking woman in a doorway, he expressed his surprise and pain at what he had seen. She replied, 'Ah, Sir, that's nothing. We have it so every day. But Sunday is worse. On Sunday the pin factory yonder isn't working, and so there's more children in the street, and, sir, then it's like hell!'

(Wright 1900, quoted in Cowie 1970: 5)

Where a later age would turn to curfews to contain unruly young people, for Raikes, and others, Sunday schools provided some answer. The argument for a national system of education was made on similar instrumental and utilitarian bases, including that it could be a way of avoiding, to some extent, the expense of other forms of care and relief:

My wish is not to get rid of the Poor Laws, but I think by taking proper steps they may become obsolete . . . In the forefront of my plan for the exaltation of the character of the labourer must appear a scheme for general national education.

(Whitbread 1807, quoted in Cowie 1970: 20)

Popular education, that is the education of the people, the labouring classes, as opposed to the gentry, the aristocracy and the developing middle classes, was promoted for the relief of poverty, the avoidance of civil unrest and crime, and the production of a disciplined and skilled workforce. In the form of schooling, it developed throughout the nineteenth century, culminating in the Elementary Education Act 1870, which provided the universally available elementary schooling that was soon to become compulsory and free. The content of popular education was utilitarian, linked directly to aims for the large working-class population. Popular education did not share the aspirations of the governing classes, where a mainly classically based, liberal education was seen as fitting boys for a leading part in society and where 'higher education, such as it was . . . appeared to be a form of vocational training for clergymen, lawyers and doctors, and an ornament of a harmless kind for those who wanted to be "gentlemen"' (Woodward 1954: 456). Popular education concentrated on scripture, reading, writing and arithmetic, and made much use of rote learning. Concerns for children's health – and that of future adults (and soldiers) – led to the general introduction of 'drill' into schools (it had been one element in the infant schools of Robert Owen, early in the century).

However, it would be wrong to suggest that while utilitarian values were pervasive, the nineteenth-century governing classes were without compassion. Woodward draws attention to Cobbett's recognition of a common humanity: 'What is a pauper?' he asked and answered himself: 'Only a very poor man' (Woodward 1954: 435) and a reading of nineteenth-century literature and history brings to light many similar examples of reformers inspired by notions of justice, equality and compassion.

Prominent though it was, children's schooling was only part of the pedagogic response to Ignorance and Want. The incremental development of schooling, throughout the nineteenth century, while meeting some societal and educational aims, left philanthropists dissatisfied. The work of the Ragged School Union suggests something of the close relationship between the relief of want and educational activities:

> There is a Scriptural instruction as the foundation, then secular instruction, industrial classes, street employments, refuges, the feeding schools, adults, mothers and infant classes, clothing and sick funds, saving banks, libraries and reading rooms, magazines and periodicals, prayer meetings, lectures, ragged churches and emigration.
>
> (MacGregor 1852: 22, quoted in Cowie 1970: 37)

For movements such as the Ragged Schools, the relief of both Want and Ignorance was a duty. Their pedagogic activities were not directed solely at children. The Ragged Schools' remit included facilities for adult education, in the broadest sense of the word, such as libraries and reading rooms. The mothers and infants classes, mentioned in the above passage, provide an example of mothers being instructed so that they themselves might provide a 'better' upbringing for their children. The first English 'School for Mothers', an infant welfare centre, which, among other things, instructed mothers on child-rearing and health, was opened in St Pancras in 1907 (Ensor 1936: 519).

Social pedagogy is not confined to practical instruction and formal learning. Writing slightly later than MacGregor in 1860, James Hole observes:

> There are some agencies which, though they cannot be classed as schools, have an educational importance of the most powerful kind. That view of education which limits it to mere scholastic instruction, is narrow and incomplete.
>
> (Hole [1860] 1969: 107)

Hole goes on to speak of music, theatre, literature, libraries, housing, public parks and games.[4] He is writing about the working classes of Leeds, not about the indigent poor. His enthusiasm goes beyond the instrumental: he has a view as to what are proper and valuable experiences. Nevertheless his concluding paragraph appeals to the pocket:

> Tested by utilitarian views alone, that expenditure which is wisely devoted to the education of the people, to their moral, physical, intellectual, and social improvement, is of all outlays the most economical.
>
> (Hole [1860] 1969: 124)

For Hole, education, was about 'improving' people, bringing them into the same cultural framework as the more prosperous members of society – for whom no special measures were seen as necessary. The dominant classes were, after all, the custodians of the dominant cultural forms.

For the prosperous classes, the squalid effects of the industrial revolution, the fear of political unrest, the obvious social alienation of many poor people, seemed to speak of the 'otherness' of the labouring poor. I would like to suggest that popular education and other social pedagogic activities were, and perhaps remain, from the perspective of the governing and middle classes, a means of reducing the otherness – and the threat – of the poor and working classes. Education, in its narrow and in its broader sense, introduced them to the knowledge, the activities and, pre-eminently, the values of their 'betters'. Such education, or social pedagogy, could provide advice on bringing up children, instruction in reading, writing and religion, and extend to recreational activities.[5]

In 1859 the Recreation Ground Act had recommended the need for identifiable space to be set aside in urban areas because:

> Whereas the want of open public grounds for resort and recreation of adults and playgrounds for children and youth is much felt in the metropolis and other popular places in the realm, and by reason of the great and continuous increase in population and extension of towns such evil is seriously increasing and it is desirable to provide a remedy for the same.

The value placed on open space and recreation was reflected in ensuing Acts of Parliament and in the actions of philanthropic movements. While the governors of the Foundling Hospital had taken on the 'care and attention to your maintenance, education, and introduction into life' for a section of the poor, the wider society was now taking on some of these pedagogic duties. The first children's playground opened in 1877 in Birmingham, again an expression of public responsibility for the activities of poor children (the more well to do had parks, or at least gardens, of their own).

As with schooling, such measures met a wide agenda and were concerned with health and crime prevention, but they were also concerned with what was 'fitting' for human life, including childhood, and how that life should be spent. The streets were not seen as fitting sites for childhood and the setting up of what we would now call 'out-of-school services' was an acknowledgement of this. Children were contained and educated for some hours in school, but school alone could not tame the monsters of Ignorance and Want. From the late nineteenth century, there was a movement to promote centres where children could go after school, perhaps have some food and take part in various 'worthwhile' activities – that is in crafts, music, dance, drama, drill and supervised play. These centres were sometimes known as day shelters, counterparts to residential centres for street children founded by philanthropists such as Thomas Barnardo. Janet Trevelyan, a campaigner for children's play and daughter of another famous campaigner, Mary Ward, writes of her mother's work, at the turn of the nineteenth century:

> Every evening there were those lonely hours when school and tea were over, when children used to wander forth into the streets, out of the way

of the hard-worked mother, and had nothing better to do than play in the gutter or run off to the well-lighted thorough-fares some distance away, there to gaze in the shop windows and to form small gangs on the look out for accidents or fights.

(Trevelyan 1920: 3)

Mary Ward had some small success in promoting play centres. Local authorities were empowered to provide 'vacation classes, play centres or means of recreation' during holidays and at other times, by the Education (Administrative Provision) Bill 1907 (Trevelyan 1920: 25). The permission extended to the use of schools for this purpose. A government memorandum states that public grants could be available for these purposes: 'especially for those children . . . whose home conditions are unfavourable to healthy and happy development' (Trevelyan 1920: 57).[6] However, as with play centres and other youth services today, permissory powers do not equate to provision, nor guarantee its stability. A London police magistrate, trying to fend off closures, wrote 'It would be a calamity if the local Centres . . . should have to be closed . . . I have seen some of the work they are doing, and know how it keeps boys and girls out of mischief' (Trevelyan 1920: xviii–xix).

Pedagogies: means of control or of emancipation

So far, this chapter has attempted to present something of the roots of state and philanthropic intervention into children's lives, especially into the lives of poor children. We have looked at these interventions in terms of care – in the sense of the duty towards, and surveillance of, children and their activities – and have seen how such provision served social ends. In particular, we have seen how it aimed at the adaptation of poor children to the dominant norms and values of society, through schooling and other educational means. I have suggested that 'social pedagogy', education-in-its-broadest-sense, socially rather than privately provided, encapsulates both the care and educational content of these services and indicates that provision serves social ends. Further, the social pedagogy of the nineteenth century was a conscious attempt to control the activities of the poor, to lead them away from crime and towards employment, and to provide them with the morality and religion to which the governing and aspirant members of that society at least paid lip service. That schooling delivers social control is not at all a novel view, but the concept 'social pedagogy' brings together a wider variety of educational and care provision than does schooling, and allows a greater tranche of public policy, historical or contemporary, to be viewed and evaluated as a whole.

There are many potential frameworks for the analysis of social pedagogy. Of these, examining social pedagogy as a means of social control is interesting and important, not least because it can make values and aims explicit, as I hope an historical approach has suggested. However, we would do better to begin to speak in terms of 'social pedagogies', rather than using the singular, in recognition that the ethics and politics that inform pedagogies differ from country to country and institution to institution, and over time. All social pedagogies are political in the sense that they have aims and social effects, both intended and unintended, all relate to the systems of power and control that exist in any society. Pedagogies that arise out of these maintain them, modify them or undermine them. Dominant social pedagogies are informed by the dominant discourse, and relate to the values of the more advantaged members of society. These need not be explicit; the political underpinnings of pedagogic policy and practice can be implicit, informed by 'common-sense' understandings and inferred agreement as to, for example, the causes of poverty and how to alleviate it.

Pedagogies do not necessarily reflect and promote a dominant political position, they can also attempt to subvert it. In the nineteenth century, we can find examples of pedagogies that confront the social structures which produce poverty, going beyond the pedagogies of dependency, duty and surveillance that were more current. Two cases may prove helpful, here, as examples of the forces of change that informed some pedagogies: Robert Owen, known to many across the fields of education and social science, working at the beginning of the century and the perhaps less familiar, Emmeline Pethick, working at the end of the century. Owen was a Utopian, with a grand view, seeking to perfect human nature and society, through rational means. Pethick, on the other hand, worked on a smaller scale and aimed to politicize the young women with whom she worked so that, individually, they would assert their rights, in the face of oppressive employers and, collectively, take part in the trade union movement.

Robert Owen

Robert Owen was not an advocate of radical political action on the part of the working classes, although working-class movements built on his vision, for example his active promotion of cooperativism and trade unionism. His type of socialism aimed at the abolition of poverty through more gradual, less chaotic – and anti-rational – measures than those of revolutionary movements. He lectured and wrote essays for rich and poor alike – but the poor, who formed 'nearly three-fourths of the population of the British Islands' (Owen [1813] 1972: 14) were the prime target of his pedagogy:

> The characters of these persons are now permitted to be very generally formed without proper guidance or direction, and, in many cases, under circumstances which directly impel them to a course of extreme vice and misery.
>
> (Owen [1813] 1972: 14)

At the same time, he believed that the advantaged members of society were educated upon the most mistaken principles of human nature, such, indeed as cannot fail to produce a general conduct throughout society, totally unworthy of the character of human beings.

(Owen [1813] 1972: 14)

His final aim was to 'make the governed and the governors happy', because 'the rich and the poor ... have really but one interest' (Owen [1819] 1972: 154), which he saw as the establishment of a rational society, formed on the basis of self-interest. And while he saw the state of the young human being as, initially, passive and, for good or ill, the subject of adult influence, his system of education aimed to equip them for an active role in a society of equals – as may be seen in the following quotation from the constitution of one of his schools:

1 Every pupil shall be encouraged to express his or her opinion.
2 No creed or dogma shall be imposed upon any.
3 Admitted facts alone shall be placed before the pupils, from which they shall be allowed to draw their own conclusions.
4 No distinction what ever shall exist; but all be treated with equal kindness.
5 Neither praise nor blame, merit nor demerit, rewards nor punishments, shall be awarded to any: kindness and love to be the only ruling powers.
6 Both sexes shall have equal opportunities of acquiring useful knowledge.

(quoted in Silver 1965: 182)

The foundation of his pedagogy was a belief in the perfectibility of the human character. In the debate which today we couch in terms of nature or nurture, Owen came down strongly on the side of nurture and, accordingly, his view of education was based on a rational plan for the formation of character. He aimed to set up a 'practical system ... the complete establishment of which shall give happiness to every human being throughout all succeeding generations' (Owen [1816] 1972: 95), as a result, 'ignorance shall be removed; the angry passions will be prevented from gaining any strength; charity and kindness will universally prevail' (Owen [1816] 1972: 113). In this way, the poor would become rational beings and useful and effective members of the state.

This notion of membership of the state (society) goes beyond the more instrumental views expressed by other social reformers who aimed at the relief of ignorance and want. Owen worked on a grand scale. His views coveted many social issues of his time from poor relief to schooling and from industrial reform to the establishment of utopian communities. He wanted the total reorganization of society – the repositioning of social power – and saw education as an essential part of this in so far as it contributed to the rational ordering of human affairs. The education (in its broadest sense) of children was paramount: 'it cannot now be necessary to enter into the details of facts to prove that children can be trained to acquire *"any language, sentiments, belief or bodily habits and manners, not contrary to human nature"'* (Owen [1813] 1972: 16, original emphasis). Education did not stand alone, but was to be part of an overall scheme for social action and change. At New Lanark, an industrial/pedagogic settlement in Scotland, Owen set about reorganizing working practices and conditions in the mills, and bettering the housing and other living conditions of the people. He made strenuous efforts against drunkenness and set out ways for settling disputes between the inhabitants of New Lanark. He did this alongside the provision of education for children and adults. For Owen, education made sense only in the context of a perfected local community, that could itself be replicated, leading eventually to the reorganization and reform of the whole of society, nationally and internationally.

Emmeline Pethick

We turn now to a woman working on a much smaller canvas, that of a neighbourhood 'girls' club' which Emmeline Pethick ran near Euston Road, in London. The club is one example, drawn from hundreds, of what we would now call either youth work or adult education, and in the nineteenth century included university and public school missions and other social settlements.[7] They were all pedagogic, providing instruction and recreation for young working-class men and women, in the local neighbourhood, made possible by the donation of money, time and personal involvement by the more advantaged classes. Will Reason (1898: ix) described them as based on 'the relations of the cultured to the uncultured classes' and points out that at the time he was writing, they had become 'fully established in the four quarters of the world'. The settlements were seen as providing recreation (more wholesome than that provided by the pub) and as centres from which 'neighbourhood spirit and the spirit of brotherhood shall emanate' (Aldin 1898: 27). The timetable of classes at Toynbee Hall included the utilitarian – ambulance drill, first aid for the injured (with separate classes for men and women) – as well as reading parties on the novels of Sir Walter Scott, and lectures on eighteenth-century music (Reason 1898: 70). There are many ways of viewing these activities. Were they extending the 'good things of life' more widely? Or an attempt at reducing the 'otherness' of the poor, by means of introducing them to dominant cultural forms? Do they represent the exercise of power, in order to control the activities of working-class people and to mould them into greater governability?

What makes Emmeline Pethick of especial interest is that she provides a first-hand account of work undertaken by women, for women (the girls' club movement was widespread) and second that her approach is both personal and overtly political, working against dominant commercial interests. Her pedagogy does not share the far-reaching vision of Owen. Hers was a practical, local approach that aimed at supporting the young women with whom she worked. She writes:

> When my friend Mary Neal started the club ... it was with the first idea
> of making the club the home, where all who came would find welcome

and sympathy and companionship as well as interest and amuse-
ment . . . We wanted to put as much happiness as we could into the two
hours spent together, and we hoped to build up in the club human
relationships that would influence and uplift the rest of their life.

(Pethwick 1898: 104)

Pethick's account provides much evidence of this personal approach, but
what started as an act of philanthropy was drawn into overtly political
action:

But we found that we could not close the doors on the world outside,
or forget its facts in the charmed circle about the fireside . . . It became
our business to study the industrial question as it affected the girls'
employments, the hours, the wages, and the conditions. And we had
also to give them a conscious part to take in the battle that is being
fought for the workers, and will not be won until it is loyally fought by
the workers as well.

(Pethick 1898: 104)

At least partly as a result of this experience, Neal and Pethick came to
analyse society in terms of conflict and class struggle and sought to promote
a similar view in the working-class young women with whom they worked.
In this they differed radically from Owen, whose more ideal view held that
rich and poor shared the same interests, if only they could be brought to a
state of rationality that could acknowledge this.

Not only did Neal and Pethick encourage the 'girls' to confront their
employers over poor conditions, but also they promoted their membership
of the trade unions, and saw their collective activity in the club as a preparation for this:

Women's Trade Unions have been hitherto a comparative failure,
for women have never been trained in the discipline of associated
interests, they have never yet had a chance of grasping the idea of
duty that goes beyond the personal demand. But the working girl
of today is unconsciously absorbing broader ideas that may help to
change her attitude to life, as her interests and energies become absorbed
in the club, and her latent faculties become active in working for its
development.

(Pethick 1898: 112)

Finally, with Mary Neal, Pethick set up an experimental garment workshop, with conditions and pay that were much higher than those usually
available:

though it is such a small scheme at present, it may be the thin end of
the wedge which will ultimately lift the intolerable burden from the
shoulders of the working girl. For if one experiment succeed, others will
certainly be tried, and new developments will be made.

(Pethick 1898: 108–9)

Owen, Neal and Pethick provide examples which, by different means and based on different visions, run counter to the dominant social pedagogy of their times. The care – the responsibility for, and oversight of, poor people – which they undertook was based on understandings that sought to modify the locus of power and control within society, by means of the educative actions upon the women, men and children with whom they worked.

Conclusion: social pedagogy today

This chapter has traced something of the story of social and political action concerning children in the nineteenth century, especially the relief of what Dickens saw as 'Want' and 'Ignorance'. Philanthropists and politicians of the nineteenth century would recognize the purpose of many current initiatives and programmes directed at poor children and parents. Care continues to be allied to education in a sense that goes beyond mere schooling, and can be encompassed in 'social pedagogy'. Social pedagogy has been a pervasive and powerful feature of social organization in the industrial and postindustrial world. In England, today, many of the concerns of the nineteenth century continue to be addressed by care and educational provisions that can be brought together, at a conceptual level, as social pedagogy. The twentieth century saw the incremental extension of public sector education that had its roots in nineteenth century movements for popular or national education. For example, higher education now aims at reaching 50 per cent of the population. At the other end of the age range, more and more children attend, as a matter of public policy, nurseries, early years education and out-of-school services. At the same time the responsibilities of parent are emphasized. Whatever the social and individual benefits of provision, a result has been the increased segregation of children and young people from the wider society, not to mention an increase in the formal control and surveillance of their activities and whereabouts. As employment is a means by which the location, activities and time of adults are controlled, so schooling and pedagogic services control children today and prepare them for the control exercised by employment in the future.

Echoes of the nineteenth century can be heard in the call of the UK prime minister, Tony Blair, for 'education, education, education' as a means of solving many of society's ills. In particular, much anti-poverty policy can be seen in terms of social pedagogy. It is believed that many economic and social difficulties may be alleviated, or indeed solved, by the development of a population which is educated, trained and motivated for employment. The argument, rehearsed over the centuries, continues to run that if 'Ignorance' is reduced, then 'Want', unemployment, social exclusion, ill-health and antisocial behaviour will also be reduced. Many UK government initiatives arise from such understandings: the National Childcare Strategy, which promotes childcare in order to get parents into work, the introduction of the literacy and numeracy hours for all children in primary schools, and the introduction of homework for children from the age of 5 years, are examples.

In addition, today, as in earlier times, many social pedagogic initiatives are targeted directly at poor people, rather than at the whole population. As poverty has grown in recent years, this is in order to reduce 'social exclusion' and, in the case of school children, 'disaffectedness'. The Sure Start programmes typify this approach. Sure Start aims to bring disadvantaged groups, and what are known as vulnerable children, more fully into education and eventual employment, and to attach them more securely to civic life and its values. The programmes provide parental support, education for parenting and childcare/education for the youngest children: pedagogic interventions by which children have an early introduction to the activities and values of society. Other social pedagogic initiatives that aim to modify and control behaviour are anti-drugs education and sex education, whether delivered through youth services or in school.

In conclusion, I should like to make two points. First, that social pedagogy, even if it is taken to include formal education, is not powerful enough to tackle the roots of poverty and disaffection. Second, that social pedagogic provision and systems are means of social control and should be analysed as such.

The limited effectiveness of care/education in the face of poverty has been recognized by commentators from the beginning. William Godwin, writing in the eighteenth century, appeals instead to 'political justice':

> Education . . . though in one view an engine of unlimited power, is exceedingly incompetent to the great business of reforming mankind. It performs its task weakly . . . Where can a remedy be found for this fundamental disadvantage? where but in political justice, that all comprehensive scheme, that immediately applies to the removal of counteraction and contagion, that embraces millions in its grasp, and that educates in one school the preceptor and the pupil?
>
> (Godwin 1793: 244, quoted in Silver 1965: 87)

The solutions to the problem of poverty that pedagogic programmes and services appear to offer are illusory, poverty arises at the level of economic structures which pedagogies cannot touch – although pedagogies may improve the economic standing of some individuals. On similar grounds, the actions of philanthropic agencies and individuals – whether acting through pedagogic means or otherwise – can at best offer only partial solutions to poverty. In fact, if there is to be an answer to poverty, it must be a political answer, based on human equality, democratic values and a determination to challenge oppression. In the end, poverty and inequality can be eradicated only by changing social structures and by the sharing of power and advantage.

This brings me to my final point: that care and education – social pedagogic provision and systems – are a means of social control and should be analysed as such. All pedagogies have in mind, as end product, a certain type of individual and a certain type of society. In order to provide a full account of any pedagogy it is necessary to make it transparent, to reveal the values upon which it is based – rather than to focus exclusively on its more explicit aims. It may be easier to evaluate, with hindsight, the pedagogies of Robert Owen, of the Foundling Hospital governors, or of Emily Pethick and Mary Neal, or, indeed, of the Hitler Youth Movement, than it is to look at society's relationship with children and young people today.

Notes

1 Care is not etymologically connected with the Latin *caritas*, or charity, theologically speaking, a religious virtue, in comparison to philanthropy, a more humanist virtue.
2 See Chapter 3 for a fuller discussion of the Foundling Hospital and its history. Perhaps Tatty Coram, in *Little Dorrit*, received these instructions.
3 It must also be said that, for some, the education of the poor was to be feared, on the grounds, that it would make them less satisfied with their station. It was this, in the aftermath of the French Revolution, which caused Pitt seriously to consider introducing a bill for the suppression of Sunday schools (Silver 1965: 17).
4 Hole lamented that when efforts were made to provide, for example concerts and plays, within the reach of the working classes, they were nonetheless taken up disproportionately by those who were rather more affluent.
5 Working-class people did not value formal education to the same extent. 'The radical reform wing of the working class movement had no specific objectives in the field of formal education. Political ignorance, not ignorance was its target' (Silver 1965: 175).
6 Foreshadowing the provision of the Children Act 1989 to provide out-of-school childcare services for children 'in need' with need defined in terms of children's development – a pedagogic concern.
7 Settlements founded in the nineteenth century still exist, for example Toynbee Hall and Oxford House, both in London. Kids Clubs Network, the English advocacy organization for out-of-school services, developed from a project based in the British Association of Settlements and Action Centres and (before moving to its present home) in Oxford House, thus linking early and present-day pedagogic activities.

References

Aldin, P. (1898) Settlements in relation to local administration, in W. Reason (ed.) *University and Social Settlements*. London: Methuen.
Bernard, Sir T. ([1809] 1970) *Of the Education of the Poor, a Digest of the Report of the Society for Bettering the Condition of the Poor*. London: Woburn Books.
Cowie, E. (1970) *Education*. London: Methuen.
Dickens, C. ([1843] undated) *A Christmas Carol*, in *The Christmas Books*, first published 1852. London: Educational Book Company.
Ensor, R.C.K. (1936) *England, 1870–1914*. Oxford: Oxford University Press.
Gabriel, T. (2001) Social pedagogy in Germany, unpublished report. London: Thomas Coram Research Unit.
Godwin, W. (1793) *The Inquiry Concerning Political Justice, Influence on General Virtue and Happiness*.

Hendley, W.A. (1725) *A Defence of the Charity Schools.*

Hole, J. ([1860] 1969) *Light, More Light.* London: Woburn Books.

MacGregor, J. (1852) *Ragged Schools,* in E. Cowie (1970) *Education.* London: Methuen.

Moss, P. and Petrie, P. (2002) *From Children's Services to Children's Spaces.* London: Taylor & Francis.

Owen, R. ([1813] 1972) First Essay, in *A New View of Society and Other Writings,* Everyman edition. Letchworth, Herts: J. Dent and Sons.

Owen, R. ([1816] 1972) An address to the inhabitants of New Lanark, in *A New View of Society and Other Writings,* Everyman edition. Letchworth, Herts: J. Dent and Sons.

Owen, R. ([1819] 1972) An address to the working classes, in *A New View of Society and Other Writings,* Everyman edition. Letchworth, Herts: J. Dent and Sons.

Pethick, E. (1898) Working girls clubs, in W. Reason (ed.) *University and Social Settlements.* London: Methuen.

Petrie, P. (2001) The potential of pedagogy/education for work in the children's sector in the UK, *Social Work in Europe,* 8(3): 23–6.

Reason, W. (ed.) (1898) Preface, in *University and Social Settlements.* London: Methuen.

Silver, H. (1965) *The Concept of Popular Education.* London: MacGibbon and Kee.

Trevelyan, J.P. (1920) *Evening Play Centres for Children.* London: Methuen.

Whitbread, S. (1807) Hansard VIII, in E. Cowie (1970) *Education.* London: Methuen.

Winkler, M. (1988) *Eine Theorie der Sozialpädagogik.* Stuttgart: Klett-Cotta.

Woodward, E.L. (1954) *The Age of Reform, 1815–1870.* London: Oxford University Press.

Wright, J.J. (1900) *The Sunday School, its Origin and Growth.*

C H A P T E R 5

An historical perspective on changing child care policy

CLAIRE CAMERON

Introduction

The 'care' in British child care has been transformed over time.[1] How we understand care as a public responsibility, what it involves, who does the caring and who receives the care, what values are important to it, all these aspects of care are reliant on their historic underpinnings. Analysis of the concepts and themes employed in relevant legislation enacted over time provides one way of marking changes in understanding in childcare policy. Such an analysis also provides a way of understanding changes in the societal status of childhood (Fox Harding 1991).

This chapter will examine four pieces of legislation enacted in Britain between 1872 and 1989 for their use of the term 'care' and related concepts.[2] These pieces of legislation have been chosen because of their emblematic significance: they each mark a defining contribution to the evolving use of the term care in children's public policy at the time. By examining the meaning of care in the legislation I hope to track the changing concerns of childcare policy and to relate them to wider societal preoccupations. First, it is necessary to briefly define 'care'.

Care is a multidimensional concept (see for example, Tronto 1993; Deven et al. 1998). It refers to practices within families and within other relationships that express emotional meaning as well as labour. Care can take place within both hierarchical relations (parenting, employment) and non-hierarchical relationships (peers, lovers, siblings). It is a practice that overlaps with *taking responsibility* for someone or something, with *competence* at providing good care, and with possible *dependency* of the cared-for person on care (Mason 1996). Tronto (1993) distinguished between four elements of care: caring about, taking care of, care-giving and care-receiving. Each element relates to a particular ethical dimension, in turn: attentiveness, responsibility, competence and responsiveness. While Mason's (1996) definition sees care as independent of related concepts, Tronto (1993) identifies these related concepts (responsibility, competence, dependency) as contained within care.

However, analysis of care within public policy for children has focused not on these comprehensive dimensions of care, but on the specific extent to which the state can take responsibility for those children defined as having a special, vulnerable status. Analyses of child care policy have seen *protection* as central to public 'care'. In order to protect children, it has been seen as necessary to *control* the behaviour or environment of a child and/or their family. Most discussion has been about the tension between control/ protection and care (see Cameron 1999). These dimensions of care policy are in marked contrast to the way care is deployed within family relations, where a central concern is the parallel existence of care as control and care as love (Brannen et al. 2000: 3). This chapter has two aims: to draw out what is meant by care in child care legislation in relation to changing public policy environments; and to consider the constraints and possibilities of the use of the term care in selected legislation in terms of Tronto's four elements and dimensions of care.

The legislation

The four pieces of legislation under discussion here are the Infant Life Protection Act 1872 and the Children Acts of 1908, 1948 and 1989. Each marks a particular era in British social and more particularly child welfare history. The 1870s was a period of self-conscious prosperity and witnessed the development of voluntary societies of all kinds, including those concerned with child welfare. The era marked the beginnings of a consciousness around child maltreatment that was eventually addressed by legal measures (Pollock 1983). The early twentieth century saw 'the invention of the social' (Rose 1999: 112) or the regularizing of social lives and moral order by government using myriad methods of mapping. A major concern was public health and pronatalism, and a confidence in the idea of childhood as a special status that required special treatment. Lord Shaftesbury, commenting on the passage of the Children Act 1908, said it represented a 'quickened sense on the part of the community at large of the duty it owes to the children' (*Hansard* 1908: 1251). The Children Act 1948 was part of postwar reconstruction in many areas of social policy (for example, Education Act 1944, National Health Service Act 1946) and saw the final abandonment of the Poor Law. The Children Act 1948, and the ideas about children it contained, promised a closer, more constructive approach to the relationship between neglected children and public care services.

Finally, in 1989 a new 'balance' between the rights and responsibilities of the state and the family in respect of children and their services was sought.

The legislation followed a series of high profile child abuse cases in which children died (for example, Jasmine Beckford in 1982; Kimberley Carlile in 1986: see London Borough of Brent 1985; London Borough of Greenwich 1987) and local authority social workers were said to have been insufficiently alert to the risk these children were exposed to. Then, in the Cleveland cases (Butler-Sloss 1988), agencies were said to have intervened too quickly in response to allegations of sexual abuse. The Children Act 1989 sought to reassert parental rights and redefine the role of the state.

Thus the first three pieces of legislation mark the rise and fall of the 'social state' (Rose 1999). The social state was represented by a marked shift towards regulating the behaviour of individuals through the use of institutions (for training, punishment, education, asylum and so on) combined with a set of moral values about the importance of order and civility, and idealized ways of being 'good servants – good tradesmen – good fathers – good mothers, and respectable citizens' (Stow 1834, quoted in Rose 1999: 104). The aim was a social normalization in favour of essentially middle-class aspirations: or 'government from a social point of view' (Rose 1999: 130). The fourth piece of legislation discussed here marks a new era in which the social is being contested. The focus of the advanced liberal state is on introducing the market into the supply of social services and setting targets for the achievement of desired outcomes (Rose 1999: 146) and in which the citizen is not merely trained, but is active; a consumer, whose participation serves to regulate professional expertise, and whose autonomy is valorized: 'it appears that individuals can best fulfil their political obligations . . . not when they are bound into relations of dependency and obligation, but when they seek to fulfil themselves as free individuals' (Rose 1999: 166).

Other pieces of legislation could have been chosen to exemplify care in child care legislation. One, the Prevention of Cruelty to Children Act 1889, is a good example of emerging protection by the state, and for the first time brought private family life within the scope of legislation. Since this Act did not significantly build on the Infant Life Protection Act 1872 (in terms of its use of the term 'care') and in order to identify how care was used in legislation at the beginning of the child welfare era and trace its continuities, I have elected to focus on the earlier infant protection legislation.

Infant Life Protection Act 1872

As stated, the mid to late nineteenth century saw the emergence of the social state. The social policy environment was one of emergent priorities and competing interests. New prosperity among a new middle class and ideas of enlightenment meant voluntary organizations to campaign on behalf of children and young people were fast being established (such as Dr Barnado's). Voluntary organizations were the early instigators of institutions such as schools, and industrial and reformatory schools (residential institutions for children without families or who had committed offences), all being

developed and regulated during this era. One effect of this institutionaliza-
tion was to categorize and control children (Rose 1989). Much of the motivation to institutionalize children was a concern with social order and the
potential disorder caused by children apparently without adult authority or
institutions to control their social movements (Walvin 1982). Policy was
directed at regulating the conditions in which children were being reared at
first outside the home, but gradually within the domestic sphere as well.

Debates about women's roles in and out of the family were vigorous in
the 1860s and 1870s, and these shaped the policy environment in which the
Infant Life Protection Act was introduced. For example, questions of women's
suffrage were discussed and a predominant ideology around motherhood
and mothers' roles began to emerge which ideally placed mothers within the
family home and not as full-time workers (Roberts 1986; Arnot 1994). There
was also a perceived split between the responsibilities of the state and those
of families: any increase of the state's powers over the family was considered
an intrusion on the privacy of the family. Women themselves were often
divided on this issue: some feminists objected to state involvement in day
care or childcare, a key area of female responsibility; while others, such as
those involved in philanthropic activity, saw a role for an extension of state
responsibility. However, 'the strongest impetus' for the Infant Life Protection
Act 'came from the medical men' (Arnot 1994: 275).

The Infant Life Protection (ILP) Act 1872 sought to address the problem of
'baby farming', or the practice of paying women to look after infants, while
mothers (who were usually single or widowed) were in paid employment.
Giving their babies to such women was also one option for middle-class
women who had illegitimate babies. Babies could be accommodated temporarily where the mother visited or they could be adopted, in which case
the mother would be unlikely to see the child again. Baby farming was
unhealthy and dangerous: many more infants died in the hands of baby
farmers than did in the Poor Law workhouses of the time. An accumulation
of widely publicized prosecutions in the 1860s together with medical disquiet led to the formation of the Infant Life Protection Society in 1870 and
a House of Commons Select Committee on the subject in 1871 (Cameron
1999).

The chief aim of the Act was regulation of women and premises to ensure
that women who looked after more than one child for the purpose of nursing or maintenance for reward were 'certified as of good character . . . [were]
registered [with the local authority]', and that they were 'able to maintain
such infants'. In addition, houses were to be 'suitable for the purpose'. Failure
to register or, if registered, failure to provide the infant with 'proper food and
attention', or if a house became 'unfit for the reception of infants' would
constitute grounds for de-registration, and being guilty of an offence under
the Act.

However, the Act contained significant loopholes, such as the limitation to
houses with more than one child, an absence of arrangements for inspection
of women or houses, and the lack of an appropriate administrative board to

oversee its implementation. As a result registration barely occurred and baby farming continued virtually unabated. The 1872 Act was amended in 1897 (and again in 1908) to provide local authorities with proactive powers to seek out abusive practice and remove children where their health or proper care and maintenance were endangered or abused. The Act set out to offer protection for infants, through a regulatory framework for childcare or day care, elements of which can still be seen in legislation today.

Arnot (1994) argued that the leading proponents of regulation, medical men and some women philanthropists, supported the legislation in the interests of both improving infant survival and promoting their view that children were 'naturally' and best cared for by mothers and should not be in day care. Indeed a central thread in the contemporary debates was the promotion of middle-class ideals about mothering among the working class: the baby farming debate was used as a vehicle for condemnation of the irresponsibility of those who made a trade out of mothers unable to care for their children at home or to employ servants to do so (Arnot 1994: 278).

The fact that the law attempted to address widespread neglect of children and even infanticide under the guise of 'day care' and those being 'adopted' suggests that there was some recognition of the problem. In particular representatives of the medical profession and philanthropists 'cared about' the survival of young children of illegitimate birth and disposal at the hands of baby farmers. But the extent to which responsibility ('caring for') was taken for the problem was very limited. Suffrage groups raised objections to the regulation of day care on the grounds that efforts to make childcare arrangements more difficult would be detrimental to employed mothers. Further objections by the Committee for Amending the Law in Points where it is Injurious to Women to the regulation of day care were made on the principle that family life was private and therefore out of reach of legislation (see Cameron 1999). Compromises reached during the law-making phases ensured that the remit of the ILP Act 1872 was limited to women who looked after more than one infant under the age of 1 and for more than 24 hours, and who were not relatives or guardians of the infant. Given the scale of the problem,[3] the measures in force applied to only a small minority of baby farmers.

However, the ILP Act was inadequate even by its own limited standards. As stated, the lack of a system of inspection of premises, nor of a dedicated administrative department to oversee the system, and resulted in few registrations. The terms used in the Act to describe care were also limited. A person of 'good character' suggests someone with public decency or a good reputation, not necessarily in relation to childcare, so that no dimension of competence was prescribed in law. The task to be completed is limited to 'maintaining' infants, or ensuring their survival. The phrase 'proper food and attention' (s. 7) is the nearest the Act gets to specifying what is meant by satisfactory care of infants.

The focus on baby farming and the ILP Act served at the time to make visible women's responsibility for children and to open up a tension between paternalist arguments about the privacy of the family and professional interventionists such as doctors, who argued that women could benefit from their involvement in motherhood duties (Arnot 1994; Cameron 1999). These debates arguably took centre stage in the legislation while the concept of care was not much extended beyond attentiveness to the problem and limited responsibility undertaken to deal with it. However, the concepts used to define adequate carers and their premises, 'good character' and 'suitable premises', survive in present-day legislation for childcare regulation.

Children Act 1908

The political space acquired by children as a 'special category' grew during the later years of the nineteenth century and the early years of the twentieth century. An emerging eugenics movement capitalized on the already articulated motherhood ideal and urged women to see their motherhood as a national responsibility focusing attention on the production of healthy children (Davin 1978). The early twentieth century was an era of considerable legislative and policy activity in the arena of public health (1904), education (1907) and welfare (for example, Midwives Act 1902). This activity arose through a concern with both the national interest and social order.

There was considerable disquiet about the health of children as future citizens and future soldiers to fight wars overseas. Measures to improve children's health and welfare were seen to be in the national interest. The late Victorian concern with social order also persisted, and the legislative concern with institutions and individuals' behaviour demonstrates this. Overall, the emphasis was on regularizing parenting and particularly motherhood in order to improve the national standing (see Cameron 1999).

The Children Act 1908 is an example of the consolidation of existing welfare legislation and an extension of protective responsibilities for 'troubled' and 'troublesome' children. In five parts covering infant life protection, the prevention of cruelty, juvenile smoking, reformatory and industrial schools and juvenile offenders, the Act set out a clear moral position on how children and young people should be accommodated within society.

The Act extended the infant life protection legislation to cover all 'nursing or maintenance' for children under the age of 7 for reward. It gave a duty to local authorities to appoint infant life protection visitors for the purposes of registration and inspection of premises and persons. The circumstances where persons were prohibited from receiving children for reward were premises that would endanger a child's health, such as 'unsanitary', 'dangerous' or 'overcrowded', or a person who was 'negligent', 'ignorant', 'inebriated', 'immoral', 'criminal' or in another 'similar way is unfit' (Part I, 5 (1)). Six months' imprisonment was promised for those guilty of such an offence.

There were still exemptions: for relatives, legal guardians, any person nursing for the relief of the poor, hospitals, convalescent homes, institutions established for the care and protection of infants by religious or charitable bodies and boarding schools providing 'efficient elementary education' (Part I, 11 (1)). Part I clearly attends to the problem of regulating the behaviour of those offering day care. It sets out minimum standards reflecting public issues of the day around the physical environment in premises, and the expectation that those who care for children are able to attend to their needs. But the list of exemptions suggests that an assumption was made that the care service provided by extended families and institutions either did not need regulation or would be offended by regulatory legislation (some mothers were subject to other forms of scrutiny, through the establishment of health visitors and Schools for Mothers: see Cameron 1999). Arguably, the legislation is still attentive but takes only partial responsibility for meeting the needs of infants in childcare.

Part II dealt with the prevention of cruelty to children by parents or other adults in private homes or public spaces. It used terminology that showed a clear recognition of the problem of potential cruelty to children: any person who 'wilfully assaults, ill-treats, neglects, abandons or exposes such child or young person or causes or procures such child to be assaulted . . . in a manner likely to cause . . . unnecessary suffering or injury to his [*sic*] health . . . shall be guilty' with a possible fine and two years' imprisonment (Part II, 12 (1)). Further evidence of the Act's remit of care is contained in the definition of neglect: 'if he [sic] fails to provide adequate food, clothing, medical aid or lodging for the child or young person . . . or fails to take steps to procure the same' the person shall also be guilty of an offence (Part II, 12 (1)). The emphasis is on the provision of basic requirements of food and shelter rather than a child's rights to nurturance, warmth or other relational or educational aspects of care.

The Act goes on to list various risks and activities of the day that children should be excluded from such as suffocation, begging, exposure to burning, visiting brothels and prostitution and prescribes various punishments for adults who allow such exposure. Thus formal obligations with police responsibility for enforcement were stated in the legislation.

In terms of care as defined in terms of competence and responsiveness, it is clear that the legislation is concerned with regulating social behaviour within a largely middle-class ideal. For example, it prohibits disorderliness in public spaces (the street) and sanctions confining children and young people to institutions on the grounds of association with improper or unfit adults. Parton (1994) argued that a key theme in the law-making phases of welfare legislation of this era was a predominant concern with the privacy of (middle-class) family life, so legislation had to identify some children for whom 'protection' or 'care' was appropriate without opening up all families to the scrutiny of the state. This approach sees the state's ability to care and the family's ability to care as mutually exclusive rather than complementary and arguably limits the potential for legislation to include within its remit attempts at offering children any more than minimal protection. For example, any concern with competence or the quality of care and responsiveness or the ability to recognize the other's standpoint is absent from the legislation.

Children Act 1948

By the time of the 1948 Act, the social state was still in evidence but the policy environment had shifted. Postwar reconstruction in many areas of social policy combined with the influence of child psychology, for example through the influence of Bowlby and Winnicott on the importance of child–mother emotional attachment for a child's 'normal' development. This provided an opportunity for refinement of legislative concepts of care and their interpretation in practice. The growth of professional 'expertise' gave rise to a renewed confidence in welfare professionals to resolve social difficulties or parenting problems in families (Rose 1989). There was a political will to act on behalf of children, many of whom had been displaced during the Second World War, and a professional confidence in the methods available to do so.

The Children Act 1948 represented a much more inclusive approach to care in child care legislation. The Act followed an inquiry into the death of a child while in foster care (Monckton 1945) and the subsequent Curtis Report into the lives of children 'deprived of a normal home life' (Ministry of Health 1946), in which 124,900 children living away from their parents were identified. Unsurprisingly, parental care was emphasized as offering the best form of care for children. But a widening understanding of care as a public responsibility was implied when Curtis gave the following statement of children's needs: 'some at least of a child's needs (for affection, personal interest, stability, opportunity, homely environment) are supplied by the child's own home even if it is not in all respects a good one' (Ministry of Health 1946: 427).

The Children Act 1948 built on the Curtis Report. It made clear that although it was preferable for children to be brought up by their parents or relatives, where this was not possible through abandonment, death, disease or other circumstances, they would be given the 'care or welfare' of the local authority. In some cases, such as a child's parents being dead or having a permanent disability and having no guardian, the local authority could assume 'all the rights and powers' of parents over children (Children Act 1948, s. 2 (1)). Childhood care would be extended to be available until the young person was 18 years old, and would be available through boarding out with foster families, a local authority or voluntary children's home, or a residential nursery for children under the age of 3 (Children Act 1948, s. 13 (1), (2)).

Included within 'care or welfare' was 'accommodation, maintenance and upbringing'. The local authority was under a duty to 'exercise their powers' with respect to a child in their care so as to 'further his [sic] best interests, and to afford him opportunity for the proper development of this character and abilities' (Children Act 1948, s. 12 (1)). Furthermore, children could attend local facilities and services (Children Act 1948, s. 12 (2)).

There is a twofold shift in perspective in this Act. First, local authorities were seen as offering a positive care service, which could replace and, in terms of quality, equate with parental care. Second, the children who required such a service were seen as in unfortunate circumstances that were not of their own making. The state had a duty therefore to help these children and not view them as requiring punishment of any kind.

With the Children Act 1948 the term 'care' came fully to the fore in legislation for children. However, there was not universal usage of the term. Legislation passed in the same year to update the system of regulation for childcare such as day nurseries and childminders did not use the term 'care', but referred to 'nurseries and . . . persons who for reward receive children into their homes to look after them' (Nurseries and Child-Minders Regulation Act 1948, preamble).

The Children Act 1948 went further than previous legislation in addressing comprehensive ideas about care. By delineating circumstances where children may 'need' the support of the state, the legislation recognizes the needs of others; by spelling out specific local authority duties it shows itself to be 'responsible'. By identifying the elements of care and the physical locations where care takes place it attempted to be 'competent' to supply care. Arguably, by supporting the use of foster care as an equivalent to birth families and in articulating children's needs (in the Curtis Report) the legislation recognized the needs of others – children in this instance. The Act did not give children rights that might safeguard the quality and delivery of services to meet these needs but it did introduce local authority children's officers, posts designed to ensure independent contact with children cared for under the Act. It represented a clear break with the past and a determination to see children in the public care as individuals with needs rather than as agents of social disorder. In its turn the local authority was seen as a 'good parent' with a duty to act 'reasonably' and ensure a child's best interests were met, rather than offering only a very minimal standard of food and shelter.

In a sense the 1948 legislation represents the high point for care in British childcare policy. There is optimism about what the social state can achieve through legislation to provide for children without families, or without adequate families of their own. Care was seen as a synonym for welfare and saw as its legitimate aim the development of character and abilities: such care should preferably occur within a family, where affective relations could best be achieved, but could also occur in institutional settings on a larger scale such as a children's home.

Children Act 1989

The fourth piece of legislation marks a shift in the wider policy environment, from a belief in the state as having the potential to assume parental roles on behalf of some children, to a more circumscribed role for the state. In contrast to much policy making of the time, the Children Act 1989 was remarkably consensual: there was cross-party support for change in the law. Criticism of the quality and cost of public care, together with concern at the evidence of rising numbers of children in care, had been raised during the preceding decade (Parton 1991). The therapeutic and preventive approaches to child care favoured in the postwar years were seen to be discredited and displaced in favour of a new legalistic approach in which the focus was child protection (rather than care), and for which the chief source of 'evidence' was the measurement of risk (Parton et al. 1997). Even the terminology of 'care' in conjunction with local authority parenting was out of favour and considered stigmatizing (Department of Health and Social Security (DHSS) 1985).

A central theme of the Children Act 1989 was the idea of a 'balance' of responsibilities for children between parents and the state. Children in public care were no longer referred to as 'in care'; they were 'looked after', in order to emphasize the fact that local authorities were providing a service which was preferably temporary, and did not take over responsibility on a long-term basis.

The Children Act 1989 was wide-ranging, covering nearly all aspects of children's welfare, including the regulation of a largely private market of childcare services. It aimed to provide a coherent legal framework applicable in private and public law cases. It aimed to be child-centred: the welfare of the child would be the court's 'paramount consideration' upon which cases before it would be decided (Children Act 1989, s. 1). However, the local authority duty to safeguard and promote the welfare of the child was not a general duty applicable to all children, but only to specific groups of children, such as those 'in need', and not those attending childcare services (Cameron and Moss 1995). The Act refined the protection available to children through the range of orders available to courts; it gave weight to the concept of prevention through the duty on local authorities to identify children in need and supply services to them (s. 17), and it reasserted parental rights through a new concept of 'parental responsibility' (s. 1.4).

The term 'care' is retained in this Act in relation to legal intervention: a Care Order and an Interim Care Order. The main grounds for a Care Order are that a child is suffering or is likely to suffer significant harm, and it will be granted only following the application of general principles governing decision-making under the Act.[4] A Care Order gives a local authority parental responsibility for a child, alongside any other persons such as parents or relatives who may have parental responsibility.

The duties of local authorities towards children in their care, whether on a Care Order or voluntarily 'looked after', were made more specific in the Children Act 1989 compared to the 1948 Act. For example, the local authority is required to 'safeguard and promote the welfare of each child they look after' (Department of Health (DH) 1989: 5.9), and to take account of the wishes and feelings of the child, and all those who are important to a child, when making decisions about him or her (DH 1989: 5.10). Due consideration must also be given to the child's religious persuasion, racial origin and cultural and linguistic background (DH 1989: 5.11).

As with the 1948 Act, the Children Act 1989 specified where children looked after should be accommodated. This could be in a family placement such as a foster family or with a relative or with his or her own parents, in a children's home, or in other appropriate arrangements such as a hostel or rented accommodation (DH 1989: 5.14; 5.13).

So far as childcare services were concerned, the Children Act 1989 was primarily focused on the regulation of services in the private and voluntary sectors. Local authorities had to provide childcare services for children 'in need', not for all children, and these services were seen as part of family support for children whose families were in difficulties. They thus often had a specific focus: family centres were particularly recommended in the Act (DH 1991). The only reference in the Act that links the regulation of childcare services to children's welfare or care is that which says 'any person entering premises may inspect . . . the arrangements made for children's welfare' (s. 76(3)(c)) (Cameron and Moss 1995).

Despite the fact that the language of 'care' has largely disappeared in this Act, it goes considerably further than previous legislation both in expressing the quality of the care the state could offer and in recognizing the needs of children. This can be seen in the attention to individuality expressed in taking account of a child's background, wishes and feelings, and in working with parents or others with parental responsibility. There is also the specific objective of working in the 'child's best interests' through the welfare principle, and these 'best interests' are seen in terms of both current conditions and future plans for the child (DH 1989: 3.18). Guidance accompanying the Act confirmed this ambition to view both public and parental care as of a high quality: it stated 'the phrase "parental responsibility" . . . emphasises that the duty to care for the child and to raise him [sic] to moral, physical and emotional health is the fundamental task of parenthood' (DH 1989: 1.4).

Discussion

Over the period under consideration the term 'care' has come to equate with 'welfare', and the scope of care has widened, from food and shelter (1908), to maintenance, accommodation and proper development (1948), and finally to include at least a partial sense of the child and their family as co-participants in care, through the 'wishes and feelings' and 'partnership' dimensions of the welfare principle in the Children Act 1989. The main themes in the deployment of the term 'care' have been whether, when and how the state should adopt *responsibility* for children, who are seen as essentially the province of private families. Responsibility has consistently been framed in terms of offering *protection*. Relatively little has been developed in terms of the affectional content of care within public care, nor of the concept of children's rights to good quality care.

Since 1989, public policy on the meaning of care has evolved further. Several trends are worth noting. First, in a move away from the bureaucratic and professional systems approach evident from the 1948 Act onwards, government appears to favour a managerial role (Parton 1996). Target setting has become a principal means by which the success of public care can be measured. For example, there is a target on the stability of looked-after children's placements, and targets exist to improve the level of employment, training and education of young people leaving care. Successful achievement of these targets is assumed to indicate an improved quality of care. Rather than professional judgement and expertise exercised within a bureaucracy, national targets imply that governments know best what outcomes suit children in public care: and potentially reduce public care to addressing these targets rather than an holistic care relationship with a young person.

Second, the provision of care is being distanced from the state, with care increasingly provided by private and voluntary sector agencies. To an extent this has always been the case, certainly in childcare for young children and fostering, but the proportion of day nursery places provided by the state decreased by 35 per cent between 1990 and 2001 (DfES 2001). The difference now is the degree of distance, with the state role being centred around inspection, curriculum and the setting of standards rather than providing support to those who care.

Third, the public image of social care and social work services is at best ambivalent and often negative, particularly for child care services (Eborall and Garmeson 2001). A series of malpractice cases in residential care and in social work have further dented the confidence and reputation of public care authorities (for example, Waterhouse 2000). A lack of confidence in public care arguably limits the opportunity of professionals to develop the meaning and potential of care within public care, as does poor administrative structures. The Climbié Inquiry, for example, found a chaotic administration with staff shortages and inadequate management and supervision of staff (Revans and Gillen 2001) suggesting an increasingly limited capacity to offer care to vulnerable children.

Last, while the Children Act 1989 promised to keep children from coming into public care, this has worked only in part. A long-term decline in the numbers of children being looked after came to an end in 1993–94, some three years after the implementation of the Children Act. The numbers of children looked after began to increase in 1995 and have done each year since. A total of 92,400 children were looked after at some point during 1999–2000, a 7 per cent increase on 1993–94 (DH 2001). It is clear that legislative meanings of care provide only a framework and much more is required to address needs for non-parental care.

In sum, since the implementation of the Children Act 1989, despite a renewed focus on family support as a means of offering care through the state in the mid-1990s, the concept of care within public care for children has been rarely seen as visible and independent in its own right. Poor outcomes, lack of investment in staff training, increased pressure to privatize and marketize care services have all contributed to a narrowing of what we mean by care, a lowering of expectations of what the state can offer in terms of care. Of particular note is the marked contrast between the potential for care within families as centring on control and love, and the optimum expected from state care, which is around safekeeping. Care as used in legislation seems to have been emptied of its potential, a dried up expression for how to manage an underclass of disadvantage.

In these circumstances public care is more likely to be seen as a stigmatized form of state responsibility than a positive option for enhancing the life chances of disadvantaged young people. This present fragmentation of care, in its sources, definition and supply, compared to vision of the 1948 Act, reflects the decline of the social state and the rise of advanced liberalism with its valorization of the individual, 'linked into a society through acts of socially sanctioned consumption and responsible choice' (Rose 1999: 166). In this policy environment the idea of a positive construction of care as contributing to collective and individual human flourishing, has little political space; it is more clearly negatively construed, as standing in the way of the achievement of an autonomous life (Sevenhuijsen 1999).

If the term 'care' as used in children's legislation cannot now produce the ideal of normative care in families, so rendering those young people whose lives are judged by legal care standards to be less advantaged by the state to further disadvantage, it is possibly timely to consider whether and how to revive the concept of care in public child care policy.

Tronto (1993) argued that all members of society require care. How that care is provided presents a set of moral choices for members of a society: 'for a society to be judged as a morally admirable society it must, among other things, adequately provide for care of its members' (Tronto 1993: 126). This 'ethic of care' has a broad remit, as care is defined as 'everything that we do to maintain, continue and repair our "world" so that we can live in it as well as possible' (Fisher and Tronto 1991). In terms of Tronto's four elements of care, the analysis of care within children's legislation presented here has shown that British legislation as it has evolved has been attentive to the problem of public care, and has assumed the first element of responsibility, but only for defined groups of children. It has been less good at the second element, competence, or ensuring the adequacy or quality of care, and third, at responsiveness, that is recognizing others' standpoints and that caring relationships are often unequal relationships. Good care, argued Tronto, is that which combines intentions, 'deep and thoughtful knowledge' of the situation, and 'judgements about needs, conflicts, strategies and consequences' (Tronto 1993: 136–7).

As law can provide only a framework for practice, arguably achieving this 'good care' is beyond the scope of law and lies with professional practice. But could the framework be improved by taking into account such a broad concept of care? One way of reviving care might be to examine the implicit social relations between the law and children and young people. For example a focus on 'best interests' and 'taking into account wishes and feelings' might imply not only that adults are the experts who can make correct decisions but also that young people's responsive capacity is limited.

However, the study by Brannen et al. (2000) of children's caring work found that children can actively contribute to different dimensions of care (see Chapter 11). A cross-national comparison may be useful here. The equivalent German law (Kinder und Jugend Hilfe Gesetz 1991), for example, emphasizes young people's rights to assistance and upbringing, their involvement in decision-making, and the integration of young people into society. While parents retain their rights and duty to parenting, the emphasis suggests a more active relationship between children and young people and the state than is present in the Children Act 1989.

Conclusion

Tronto's ethic of care offers a way forward for conceptualizing care within public law. It enables us to think about the multidimensional, dynamic nature of care relationships: not only caring about or taking care of, but also being competent to ensure the adequacy of care and responding to vulnerable others by taking their perspective. It enables a focus on process and content rather than a preoccupation with targets and outcomes. Interestingly, Tronto (1993) makes a distinction between 'protection', which is limited to a presumption of bad intentions and harm that is likely to arise, and care which is defined by starting with the other's needs and seeing what can be done to meet them. The latter used to be the starting point for much professional training in social work while the former has overtaken much of social work child care practice. This situation needs to be reversed.

Notes

1 Child care (two words) is used here to refer to social work, residential and other social welfare provisions for children who are 'in need' or 'looked after' and policy for these groups. Childcare (one word) is used (as well as by others such as the DfES) to refer to nurseries, childminders and similar provision for children used mainly while parents are at work, and policy for this type of care service. In legislation, the term 'day care' has been used to refer to childcare provisions.
2 This chapter discusses legislation enacted in England and which applies in England and Wales. The first three pieces of legislation also apply in Scotland, but the fourth, the Children Act 1989, applies only in England and Wales. Scotland has its own legislation.
3 Evidence to the Select Committee of the House of Commons from the Infant Life Protection Society stated that according to the returns of the Registrar General, about 50,000–60,000 illegitimate children were born each year, the majority of whom were placed with baby farmers (see Cameron 1999).
4 The general principles are first, that the welfare of the child is paramount (s. 1), second, that delay in decision-making should be avoided (s. 1 (2)) and third, that of 'non-intervention', that the court had to be satisfied that making an order was better for the child than not making an order (s. 1 (5)).

References

Arnot, M. (1994) Infant death, child care and the state: the baby-farming scandal and the first infant life protection legislation of 1872, *Continuity and Change*, 9(2): 271–311.

Brannen, J., Heptinstall, E. and Bhopal, K. (2000) *Connecting Children: Care and Family Life in Later Childhood*. London: RoutledgeFalmer.

Butler-Sloss, E. (1988) *Report of the Inquiry into Child Abuse in Cleveland 1987*. London: HMSO.

Cameron, C. (1999) Child protection and independent day care services: examining the interface of policy and practice. Unpublished PhD thesis, Institute of Education, University of London.

Cameron, C. and Moss, P. (1995) The Children Act 1989 and early childhood services, *Journal of Social Welfare and Family Law*, 17(4): 417–30.

Davin, A. (1978) Imperialism and motherhood, *History Workshop Journal*, 5: 9–65.

Department for Education and Skills (DfES) (2001) *Statistics of Education: Children's Day Care Facilities at 31 March 2001 England*. London: DfES. http://www.dfes.gov.uk/statistics/DB/SBV/bo293/sb08–2001.pdf

Department of Health (DH) (1989) *An Introduction to the Children Act 1989*. London: HMSO.

Department of Health (DH) (1991) *The Children Act 1989 Guidance and Regulations, Vol. 2: Family Support, Day Care and Educational Provision for Young Children*. London: HMSO.

Department of Health (DH) (2001) *Commentary: Numbers of Looked After Children in England*. www.doh.gov.uk

Department of Health and Social Security (DHSS) (1985) *Review of Child Care Law: Report to Ministers of an Interdepartmental Working Party*. London: HMSO.

Deven, F., Inglis, S., Moss, P. and Petrie, P. (1998) *State of the Art Review in the Reconciliation of Work and Family Life and the Quality of Care Services*, DfEE research report no. 44. London: DfEE.

Eborall, C. and Garmeson, K. (2001) *Desk Research on Recruitment and Retention in Social Care and Social Work*, COI communications for the Department of Health. www.doh.gov.uk/scg/workforce/coidesk.pdf

Fisher, B. and Tronto, J. (1991) Towards a feminist theory of caring, in E. Abel and M. Nelson (eds) *Circles of Care: Work and Identity in Women's Lives*. New York: State University of New York Press.

Fox Harding, L. (1991) *Perspectives in Child Care Policy*. London: Longman.

Hansard (1908) Vol. 186, col. 1252. London: House of Commons.

London Borough of Brent (1985) *A Child in Trust: Report of the Panel of Inquiry Investigating the Circumstances Surrounding the Death of Jasmine Beckford*. London: London Borough of Brent.

London Borough of Greenwich (1987) *A Child in Mind: Protection of Children in a Responsible Society: Report of the Commission of Inquiry into the Circumstances Surrounding the Death of Kimberley Carlile*. London: London Borough of Greenwich.

Mason, J. (1996) Gender, care and sensibility, in J. Holland and L. Adkins (eds) *Sex, Sensibility and the Gendered Body*. London: Macmillan.

Ministry of Health (1946) *Report of the Children in Care Committee (Curtis)*, Cmnd 6922. London: HMSO.

Monckton, Sir W. (1945) *Report by Sir Walter Monckton on the Circumstances which Led to the Boarding out of Dennis and Terence O'Neill at Bank Farm, Minsterley and the Steps Taken to Supervise their Welfare*. Cmnd 6636. London: HMSO.

Parton, N. (1991) *Governing the Family: Child Care, Child Protection and the State*. London: Macmillan.

Parton, N. (1994) Problematics of government, (post) modernity and social work, *British Journal of Social Work*, 24: 9–32.

Parton, N. (ed.) (1996) *Social Theory, Social Change and Social Work*. London: Routledge.

Parton, N., Thorpe, D. and Wattam, C. (1997) *Child Protection, Risk and the Moral Order*. London: Macmillan.

Pollock, L. (1983) *Forgotten Children*. Cambridge: Cambridge University Press.

Revans, L. and Gillen, S. (2001) New concerns over Haringey Office, *Community Care*, 13 December 2001–9 January 2002.

Roberts, E. (1986) Women's Strategies, 1890–1940, in J. Lewis (ed.) *Labour and Love: Women's Experience of Home and Families, 1850–1940*. Oxford: Basil Blackwell.

Rose, N. (1989) *Governing the Soul: The Shaping of the Private Self*. London: Routledge.

Rose, N. (1999) *Powers of Freedom: Reframing Political Thought*. Cambridge: Cambridge University Press.

Sevenhuijsen, S. (1999) *Caring in the Third Way*, working paper no. 12. Leeds: Centre for Research on Family, Kinship and Childhood, University of Leeds.

Stow, D. (1834) *Moral Training, Infant and Juvenile, as Applicable to the Condition of the Population of Large Towns*, 2nd edn. Glasgow.

Tronto, J. (1993) *Moral Boundaries: A Political Argument for an Ethic of Care*. New York: Routledge.

Walvin, J. (1982) *A Child's World: A Social History of English Childhood 1800–1914*. Harmondsworth: Penguin.

Waterhouse, Sir R. (2000) *Lost in Care* (Waterhouse Report). Cardiff: Stationery Office.

Explorations in formal care

Men in the nursery

CHARLIE OWEN

Introduction

Care is gendered, in that it tends to be seen as women's responsibility (for example Finch & Groves 1983), nowhere more so than in the care of children (for example Yeandle 1984). And nowhere more so than in the care of children as a job (Cameron et al. 1999). This is recognized by the government Green Paper *Meeting the Childcare Challenge* (DfEE et al. 1998) where it says: 'Working with children is seen as a predominantly female occupation. Yet male carers have much to offer, including acting as positive role models for boys – especially from families where the father is absent' (para. 2.25).

The extent of the gender polarization in childcare work is shown in figures from the UK census for 1991. The census classified occupations using the Standard Occupational Classification (SOC: Office of Population Censuses and Surveys 1990). This classification has four occupations that are grouped together as 'childcare and related occupations'. These are nursery nurses, playgroup leaders, educational assistants and other childcare workers: this last group would include childminders, nannies, crèche workers and some play leaders. Table 6.1 shows the numbers of men and women estimated to be in each occupation in 1991. There were thought to be almost 57,000 nursery nurses, and just 600 of these were men: a little over 1 per cent. (More recent data from the Labour Force Survey confirm that the position has not changed since 1991.)

There is an official commitment to increasing the number of male childcare workers, as shown by the target for Early Years Development and Childcare Partnerships of 6 per cent male childcare workers by 2004 (Department for Education and Skills 2001). However, changing the gender mix of childcare

Table 6.1 Childcare occupations by gender, 1991 census

SOC	Occupation	Male	Female	Male %
650	Nursery nurses	600	56,380	1.1
651	Playgroup leaders	56	18,430	0.3
652	Educational assistants	1,070	40,690	2.6
659	Other childcare workers	1,640	184,140	0.9

Source: Office of Population Censuses and Surveys (1994)

staff is more than a question of setting targets. To change the gender mix requires understanding why childcare work is as gendered as it is.

The fact that those employed in childcare are almost exclusively women serves to highlight the gendered nature of care in general and childcare in particular. While it is generally accepted that men should play a greater part in the care of their own children, men being employed to care for other people's children is much more controversial. When men enter this most archetypal female occupation, their motives may be thought suspect and their sexuality called into question. This chapter will draw on research carried out at Thomas Coram Research Unit with both male and female nursery workers and with the parents of the children in their care.

Issues

Before looking at the research on nursery workers, I want to give a bit of context, by highlighting a number of issues that all have implications for men in the nursery. They are the issues of gender equality, the labour market, the needs of the children, and the issues of risk and child protection.

Gender equality

More equal sharing of childcare between men and women for their own children has become part of the ideological consensus. As women – and mothers especially – are increasingly likely to be in paid jobs (Brannen et al. 1997), there is an anticipated quid pro quo that fathers will take on greater domestic responsibilities, especially for childcare. However, Gardiner (1997) has reviewed a number of studies to show that even when men do take a greater share, it is still seen as predominantly the woman's responsibility, and that they are just helping out. As she put it, 'Men perceive themselves as a back-up for their wives' (Gardiner 1997: 192). For example, one father in Backett's study (1982: 80) said, 'I don't recognise the things that have to be done'. However, even the expectation that men will take care of their children in the home is not translated into an expectation that men will care for other people's children, as a job. The expectation is still largely that childcare – as a job – is women's work. It is the absence or presence of men in early childhood services that contributes to or challenges the dominant ideologies about gender roles and relationships in the wider community.

Labour market

The occupational segregation by gender has been increasingly challenged as women move into traditionally male occupations. However, there has been less movement the other way, with men moving into traditionally female occupations. This is easy to understand, because the traditionally male-dominated occupations tend to be those with more status, power and pay. Female-dominated occupations, on the other hand, are more likely to be low status, lacking in power and poorly paid. It is sometimes argued that the only way to raise the status and pay of these occupations is for more men to be recruited. This may be insulting to the women who carry out these jobs – such as childcare – with little reward or recognition, yet there is a vicious circle whereby the work that women do is seen as low status because women do it.

However, what happens when men enter female-dominated occupations? There is not some miraculous reassessment of the status of the occupation and a rapid increase in pay. Nursing is a case in point: traditionally seen as part of women's caring work, there have been sustained efforts to increase the number of men in the profession. But as more men did become nurses, there were new concerns that they were 'taking over' or taking all the top jobs, and still leaving women at the bottom of the career ladder (Robinson 1998). The recruitment of men is not a solution to occupational inequalities, but it may be a necessary step (Crompton 1997).

Needs of the children

A completely different set of arguments concerns the needs of the children. The need for male role models is emphasized, especially for boys and for children with no father in the family – as, for example, in the government's *Meeting the Childcare Challenge* (DfEE et al. 1998).

It is often argued that children need 'role models' of both male and female behaviour. As far as childcare is concerned, it is argued that children need to see both men and women in caring roles – to challenge the stereotype that caring is women's work. Another reason given is the widespread absence of fathers in families. This is partly due to the growth of lone-mother families (through women having children alone or through divorce and separation), but also the absence of fathers at work. Fathers with young children work longer hours (on average) than any other group (Brannen et al. 1997). So even when there is a father in the family, they may be 'absent' for much of the child's life.

The idea of men providing role models, simply by their presence in the nursery, is a common one. However, it is not always clear what role models men are meant to be. Is it that they are meant to counteract the stereotypic male, by showing that men have a caring side? Or is it that men are meant to counterpose more stereotypically masculine characteristics in an almost exclusively female environment? In a study of male workers in family centres, Ruxton (1992: 25) noted that, 'the vast majority of the staff recognised the importance of positive male role models which help to challenge the stereo-typical view of men as "breadwinners" alone, and to validate their role as "carers"'. On the other hand, Murray (1996: 374), in a study of childcare staff, found that 'in the childcare environment men are often sought after as workers because of the perceived need to have male role models for children', models which were seen as 'doing truck play with the boys'. In both cases, a single man was seen as able to represent 'men' as a category, and to simultaneously represent and challenge traditional masculinity.

An idea particularly stressed by the Scandinavians is that boys and girls and men and women behave in different ways, and that all children should have experience of both male and female ways of caring and of behaving more generally. More especially, they argue for a 'gender pedagogy' that takes into account these differences. Jensen (1996) has argued that gender pedagogy emphasizes 'that specific gender behaviour [of children] must be reflected in pedagogic work' and that while these considerations apply 'irrespective of the gender mix of the staff group', they are probably more easily fulfilled where men are employed (Jensen 1996: 20–1). This may look like adapting to gender stereotypes, but the argument of gender pedagogy is that a gender-blind approach, which claims to treat all children 'the same', is actually ignoring important differences that the nurseries should be cater-ing for.

Risk and child protection

The main argument against employing men as carers of young children is that men are potentially sexual abusers. Dominant media images of men are as dangerous to children. These are images of violent partners and fathers, sinister residential care workers and predatory strangers. These images reinforce the prejudice that men are dangerous to children – as well as to women and to each other. Associated with the concern over paedophiles is a homo-phobia which questions the sexuality of any man who wants to work in childcare. The message is that men who want to look after children must be gay and that gay men will abuse children.

There has been a lot of media attention on paedophiles and concern that they may target places such as nurseries where they can have access to children and the children are unlikely to make any complaints, because of their age. However, very few cases of sexual abuse in day nurseries have ever been exposed in Britain. Of course, absence of evidence is not evidence of absence: it may be that there are many cases that are not known about. The most extensive research on sexual abuse in children's day care was conducted in the United States of America by Finkelhor et al. (1988), who examined all cases known to official agencies over a five-year period. They found that 40 per cent of known abusers in childcare were women. Of course, the other 60 per cent came from the tiny minority of men who worked in the nurseries or from other men: only two-thirds of the male abusers were workers – either childcare workers or peripheral workers, such as drivers or cleaners – the rest were predominantly young male relatives of family day carers (what in Britain would be called childminders).

There are two clear messages from this research: first, most men who work in childcare are not involved in abuse, and second, not all the abusers are men. It is clear from this study that eliminating all men from childcare work would not eliminate the risk, but would deny the children contact with men as nursery workers. Nurseries need procedures to protect children, and not just from men. As Pringle (1998) has argued,

> Public policy on men's involvement in professional childcare may well be at a crossroads. Unfortunately, that debate might develop into a polarized argument on whether more or fewer men should be in childcare work. That is, however, the wrong question. Instead, the real question is: what strategies can we devise to involve men in childcare in ways that will maximize the safety of children, and indeed women?
>
> (Pringle 1998: 331)

Men in the nursery

To study the experience of that small minority of men who do work in the nursery, we (Claire Cameron, Peter Moss and myself) identified ten nurseries where at least one man was working. We chose these institutions so that they were a good cross-section. All cared for children under the age of 3; three were local authority run nurseries, and one a local authority children's centre; two were private sector nurseries and one a Montessori nursery school; three were voluntary sector children's centres. (More detail about the sample and the procedures are given in the full report of the study: Cameron et al. 1999.)

One aim was to compare the experiences of the men with those of women in a similar position. So we also interviewed a female nursery worker with a similar length of experience. We tried to get a mix of new and more experienced staff. In the end, the sample consisted of eleven men and ten women, because in one nursery there were two men with the same level of experience and we could not choose between them. Four of the men and four of the women had worked in the nursery for under two years, five of the men and four of the women had worked there more than five years. The men were, on average, slightly older than the women.

The sample of staff was each interviewed face-to-face. The interview questions were structured to explore three main concerns. First, the focus was to be on gender as a feature of childcare work, and not just on the 'odd' men who work there. This meant looking at how gender structured the work in the nursery. Second, we had a concern over men in non-traditional occupations, to see whether they saw themselves as pioneers, or role models for other men. Third, there was the issue of gender pedagogy: did the men and the women think that they behaved differently, did they 'care' differently, did they respond differently to boys and to girls and did boys and girls respond differently to them?

We knew that in some other countries, such as Denmark, men working in childcare enjoyed popular parental support, so we wanted to know if the parents in the sample of nurseries were also supportive. In each nursery we telephoned the parent or parents of five children for an interview. We achieved 77 interviews with 50 households, 52 with mothers (or co-mothers) and 25 with fathers. In 16 families the mother was the sole carer, but even the other fathers were more difficult to contact and interview.

Deciding on childcare work

What makes anyone – man or woman – choose to become a nursery worker? Do men and women have different reasons? This was a question we raised in the interviews. Half of the women had grown up with the idea that they would work with children, and had decided to enter childcare work while still at school; a sixth woman decided while at university. Typical comments were, 'I always knew I wanted to work with children' and 'I think it was children or animals'. Two of the women gave up careers after some time and decided to retrain in childcare.

None of the men grew up with the idea of wanting to work with children. Two knew they were interested while at school, but never had an opportunity to do childcare courses: 'They had a childcare course at school . . . but it was open to like the girls basically'. Six men decided to try childcare while they were unemployed. Three men had worked in related areas – one residential social worker and two teachers. Two of the men had been primary school teachers, but wanted to work with younger children.

Men, more than women, were likely to enter childcare as a 'second chance career', but not exclusively so. The choice was also related to education and qualifications, to the support of family and friends, and to personal ambition.

Qualifications

All the workers we interviewed had some form of childcare or related qualification (for example teaching or social work). However, the men who know they wanted to work with young children tended to obtain a teaching qualification rather than an NNEB or BTEC qualification, which were the standard professional nursery qualifications. The difference is that NNEB and BTEC are available at 16 with few GCSEs, whereas a teaching qualification requires A levels for entry. None of the men had begun an NNEB or BTEC on leaving

school and entered childcare in the way that women did. A teaching qualification gives access to higher paid and higher status jobs than the nursery
qualifications.

Support

The degree of support that the nursery workers received from their
friends and family when they decided to take up the work varied very much
between men and women. The women all got strong approval for choosing
childcare. For the men, support was patchy. None of the men entered the
field with the committed backing of parents, partners and friends that the
women had.

The terms used by the women to describe the response from their families
about their work choices included 'pleased', 'proud', 'happy', 'appropriate
for a girl', 'supportive' and 'completely behind me'. There was a strong sense
that childcare was an obvious and appropriate choice for women, even if
they had done something else first.

For men, the reaction was more likely to be one of surprise. As one
man said, 'My mother was surprised when I gave up acting. She very much
felt that's what she wanted me to do and couldn't really understand it.'
Another said, 'My mum was fine, she knows how good I am with children
... My dad, I still don't really get on with him ... He's the sort, "go out
and get a proper job." He thinks we sit around all day ... I get so frustrated.'
The idea that childcare was not a 'proper job' for a man came up several
times. One man, who began his teaching career in a children's centre, said
he was 'not taken seriously' by his family, as the work 'wasn't a proper
teaching job'.

The pattern of reactions from friends was similar to that from families.
Women workers all reported encouragement from their friends about the
choice of childcare work. The reaction from the men's friends ranged from
support, through surprise, confusion and ridicule. One man reported his
friends gave him 'a bit of stick when I first started ... a lot of my friends
are like builders and plumbers ... it's like "oh, it must be a really easy job
where I reckon you just sit around all day and get paid for it". It wasn't
done in a horrible way. It's more joking around.' Another man found that
women friends were more likely to question why a man 'would want to work
with children'. Confusion over 'nursery' was reported by two of the men:
'you say you work in a nursery and they assume it's something to do with
plants!'

The consistent support that women get with their choice of childcare work
helps them to feel comfortable with it. The men, on the other hand, lack
that support and can feel isolated and uneasy. However, the effects of any
lack of family or peer support seem to diminish with time and experience. So
the responses of family and friends could be an effective inhibiting factor
in men taking up childcare work, but this becomes less important over time
– at least for those who stick with it.

The future

We were interested in how settled the nursery workers were and what career ambitions they had, so we asked them what they thought they would be doing in five years' time. Seven of the women and four of the men saw themselves doing much the same as their present job. Six men and three women, on the other hand, saw themselves as moving into more specialist posts, becoming nursery managers or owners, or qualifying for a higher status profession (for example social work or psychotherapy). Contentment and ambition thus had gendered aspects: overall, the women were more likely to be content and the men to talk of ambition. The expectation that men, in traditionally female occupations, will tend to take the senior posts or move out is a common finding (Williams 1993). It is also one of the complaints that the women have about the men.

Even so, some women also expressed the intention to move out of childcare altogether and into related fields, such as social work. However, ambition needs to be seen in the context of the workers' lives, rather than just their work. In particular, their domestic and family commitments continue to be more salient for women than for men (Deven et al. 1998).

The nursery

Gender is produced within all workplaces, but is particularly salient in nurseries, where the whole institution seems predicated on the gendered nature of the work. Hearn and Parkin (1992) have argued that gender in organizations is about the structuring of the experience of work along gendered lines. In the nurseries, it was clear that the activities were structured along gender lines: as one father described it, 'Women spend more time and are more in-depth in caring . . . Men are used in different roles as well. They didn't seem to change nappies much. It's more physical things and going out and playing football.'

Men and women had different perceptions of the division of labour in the nurseries. All but one of the women believed that jobs were shared out equally. Men, on the other hand, knew that they were asked and expected to do practical jobs about the building, such as fixing things and changing light bulbs. This was one area of experience that some of the men regarded as their 'natural' role. This discrepancy – between the female workers' belief about the absence of a gender division of labour in the nursery and the men's experience of it – says something about the gendered construction of childcare work. It may be that the women are not aware that men are doing these practical tasks, because that has traditionally been their role in domestic settings (Brannen and Moss 1991). And this is taking place in an environment where women are engaged in their traditional role of caring for children. In this way, the nursery environment tends to reflect the domestic one.

Studies of conversation in single-sex and mixed groups have suggested that men have different styles of communication:

> The same general findings emerge across many different subject popula-
> tions, settings and research methodologies. Men show a greater task
> orientation in groups, women a greater social-emotional orientation;
> men emerge more often as leaders in initially leaderless groups; men
> interrupt more; women pay more attention to the face needs of their
> conversational partners; women talk more personally with their close
> friends . . . Many people feel these depictions of men and women capture
> their own experience; the research findings mirror gender differences
> they see in their daily lives.
>
> (Aries 1996: 189)

This same pattern was noted by the nursery staff. They reported that women's experiences, as mothers and as workers, formed topics of conversation from which men were frequently excluded. Staff rooms as a site of gendered discussions were noted by four men and two women: these discussions were described as 'women's talk' or 'intimate conversations' from which the men were generally left out. Some women were aware of the difference it made to their conversation of having a man around. One said, 'you get less personal with a man sitting there.'

Since all but one of the nurseries had just one male worker, there was almost no chance to assess the effect on the women and their conversations of men talking together. We know, though, from other studies that men's different ways of talking and acting tend to dominate mixed groups (Aries 1996). Jensen (1996) reported the Scandinavian experience of more mixed-gender childcare working. Men were seen as introducing a new directness into the communications, which was not always comfortable for the women. One of the men we interviewed, for example, complained how staff meetings often failed to get things done because of a perceived lack of directness: people 'say nothing in the meeting, but go back to their rooms and the door shuts . . . You think, "well why didn't they say it?"' In a discussion of social workers, where there are more men, but still a minority, Hicks (2001) noted that,

> Within social work teams, and especially in meetings, men may dominate
> the agenda, space and time, using the justification of 'professionalism'
> and 'having your say'. This is often part of a masculinist work culture, in
> which men must prove themselves by what they say in public rather
> than what they do in their everyday practice.
>
> (Hicks 2001: 52)

Male workers reported ways in which female staff acted which effectively excluded them: for example, one reported being 'cut off' by a female member of staff when he was talking to parents. He said that she would interrupt him and repeat what he had said, leaving him feeling embarrassed. Two men reported that they felt their women colleagues were needlessly over-protective.

They would 'jump in before a possible problem could occur', or would assume that they couldn't do some things with the children properly. Interestingly, no woman reported anything other than feeling at home in her nursery. Women, in fact, were more likely to say there were no gender-based differences between the men and the women in the ways they communicated or acted with the children, and that any differences were due to personality.

Role models

As we have seen, one of the arguments for recruiting more men into childcare is that they provide 'role models', but that there is some ambiguity about what type of role model the men are supposed to be, either conforming to male stereotypes in an otherwise female environment or challenging them. The importance of role models also came up in our interviews. Mostly the men saw themselves as challenging the male stereotype: after all, they were working in a uniquely non-stereotypically male occupation. As one man said,

> *I don't know if it's important what sort of role model you are . . . often I don't come across as a role model that some of the children, boys in particular, would . . . 'cos if I wear pink or something . . . my clothes are sometimes quite bright . . . and . . . their mothers wouldn't put them in that and they'll say, 'Oh you can't wear that 'cos you're . . . boys can't wear that' sort of thing.*
>
> *I'd like to think that I'm a role model that questions the way men have to be . . . but I don't consciously go out to do that, maybe I'm rejecting the old sort of stereotypes and role models that I had . . . by default that means I'm something else . . . and their role models sometimes . . . they might want a guy to play football.*
>
> *[So you think they, the children, families, perhaps other staff, are looking for a kind of fairly traditional male role model?]*
>
> *I think that's their expectation when they come here, but then they don't find that . . . they see me cooking and washing, then that's their role model and . . . so many times they say 'Oh men can't . . .' and talk about men and things . . . I challenge them every time they say it.*

However, the children may want to engage with the men differently, just because they are men:

> *I've never been asked to do these things . . . I sometimes find myself doing them . . . getting myself engaged in rough play . . . that's simply because I'm always down . . . I sometimes put myself on the floor and that's like an open invitation to anybody to jump on you . . . Or if I'm out in the garden and there are footballs out there . . . I think sometimes the children have a tendency of coming to me to play those things . . . They invariably draw me into their game with them.*

The men accept that, merely on the grounds of their gender, they have a particular role to play with the children and families, but that role is not clear. Their gender, in the particular context of the nursery setting, is a constant challenge to predominant ideas about what men do. The role is apparently to embody notions of masculinity, as well as to challenge those notions. There is the additional burden, as most of these men were the only man in their nursery, of one man representing all men, when there are many ways of 'doing' masculinity.

The parents

Having had some experience of their children attending nurseries where men were employed, by far the majority of parents said they were in favour of men workers: 86 per cent of mothers and 85 per cent of fathers. One clear reason why parents supported men working with young children was concern for the boys: for example, one mother of a 6-month-old said she 'was keen for there to be a male role model . . . I felt strongly there should be a male contact for him as he got older.' This view was expressed especially for lone mothers. A father noted, 'It can help with certain stereotypes about men and childcare. And boys think men shouldn't do that work.' A mother of three sons added, 'I like my boys to have male role models. They don't get men in nursery or primary usually until comprehensive and that's a bit late. It was one of the positive things about the nursery, for my boys to be able to interact with men and women.'

There was less agreement about the advantages of male workers to daughters. Only two mothers and one father referred to positive benefits for their daughters of being cared for by a man. Most were more neutral, but three mothers expressed some caution. One said, 'I was worried about a man with my daughter because of my [own childhood] experience.' However, for both sons and daughters, there were seen to be advantages to having both men and women working in the nursery.

The advantages of having male workers were usually put in terms of role models, both for boys and girls, of men's behaviour and to counter the gender division of labour at home and at work. One mother said, 'It's important to get a male role model for children outside the home. Men should do everything . . . children should see it's the same in both worlds [home and work].' Another mother extended the argument: '[It's] important for men to be there as a role model and that it is seen as an acceptable career for men and important as children get older. An all female environment is not representative of the world. There needs to be a balance.'

However, when asked how the male and female nursery workers differed in their behaviour with the children, most parents tended to say there was no difference. One parent said that the childcare workers were just 'different people working in different ways', another that 'a voice is a voice telling the kids to do something. It's just the same if it's a man or a woman.' Comments about differences were usually about individuals, not about their gender: one mother saw that

> *one worker is probably more of an entertainer, it's part of his role. He is funny and making up songs. His approach is less cuddly and caring but very beneficial. I wouldn't want to generalise. It's down to the individual. The men are as interested in the children, it's not necessarily a matter of gender.*

Where parents noted differences between men and women staff, their descriptions tended to follow fairly stereotypical gendered lines. Men, it was said, were more likely to play football, to do things outside and to 'muck about'. They 'let the kids get on with it' and 'are not inhibited by risk'. One mother remarked that, when the man worker first started, 'I saw him cuddling the babies [and] I thought that was different. It was nice. I wouldn't have noticed it if a woman had been doing it.' Women, on the other hand, were seen by parents as providing the substantive, consistent parts of caring. Women workers were referred to as providing a 'maternal role', 'more in-depth caring and nurturing'. In this way, the differences noted by the parents reflect the observation that men in the home do the 'fun' childcare and women do the routine nurturing: the women are described as providing the essential care while the men are 'helping' (Clarke and Popay 1998).

Risk and protection

The question of the perceived association between sexual abuse of young children and men workers was addressed. Both parents and staff were aware of the debate about sexual abuse and men workers. Parents trusted the managers to recruit suitable workers, regardless of gender, and saw this as an essential safeguard. As one mother said,

> *When he turned up I was a bit surprised but I thought, 'Good, why not?' It's great that a guy should want to work with children, to see that it's not just women looking after children, to see that men have a caring side and to see both sides of the population. The one fleeting thought I had was you hear so many horrible things, you know, the sexual things. But I trust the nursery and once I met him I trusted him. I don't think I've thought about it since.*

As might be expected, the risk was not seen as equally involving men and women, but was seen as almost exclusively coming from the men. Differences were seen in what is thought appropriate for men and women to do with the children in their care. Take, for instance, touching and cuddling. One woman nursery worker said, 'If they fall over and hurt themselves . . . I mean you know I cuddle a child if they come up to me or if they come and try to give me a kiss . . . I feel fine about that.' Some men workers had experience of being told not to touch children, or felt their position was vulnerable to accusations of misusing touch. One man reported that, in a previous nursery, he was told not to cuddle the children, as that was not 'expected' of a man. He said, 'The other carers, it wasn't a problem, they'd all cuddle and that sort of thing . . . I kicked up quite a stink about it . . . and in the end they changed the whole ruling and they said they didn't want anybody to cuddle the children.'

Most nurseries had policies for intimate care. Nappy changing tended to be the one part of personal care that was marked out for policy attention. The assumption here is that nappy changing is a discrete area of childcare practice, which potentially offers opportunities for intimacy and privacy with children, and so opportunities for sexual abuse or misinterpretation of staff behaviour. Some centres explicitly excluded men from personal care. For example, in one family centre where many of the women attending had themselves had difficult experiences with men, it was decided that excluding men from intimate care simultaneously protected the children from abuse, protected the men from accusations and reassured the mothers. However, the male workers were not all happy with such policies: as one said, 'everyone accepts a woman . . . an actual issue [is] made about having a man' changing nappies.

Conclusion

We began the chapter by considering the very small number of men working in childcare and the government target of increasing the current 1 per cent to 6 per cent by 2004. A consideration of the issues around men in the nursery showed that the gendered nature of childcare work put it at the intersection of a number of major social currents: of gender equality, the labour market, the needs of the children, and the issues of risk and child protection. Clearly, increasing the number of men working in the nursery has ramifications beyond the nursery itself. Considering the data provided by interviews with 10 female nursery workers, 11 male nursery workers and 77 parents from 10 nurseries helped to throw light on all the issues, but also served to highlight the fact that the gendered nature of childcare work is not simply a question of the number of men working in nurseries. Gender structures the nursery and the experiences of the men *and* women who work there, of the children who attend and of the parents who use the nursery.

The experience of being a male nursery worker was very different from that of being a female nursery worker. First of all, the men had all had other careers before turning to childcare, whereas many of the women had childcare as their first career choice from an early age. So from the very point of entry there is a gendered difference. While young women, still at school might see childcare as an attractive career, consistent with their femininity (Walkerdine et al. 2001), it is unlikely that teenage boys' concerns about their masculinity are going to be consistent with seeing childcare as a career choice at that point (Frosh et al. 2001).

At work, in the nursery, women claim to see very little difference between men and women, yet the men feel that they are positioned and constrained by the women's – and the children's – expectations of them. They feel excluded by the women's talk, embarrassed by their intimacy (with each other) and frustrated at their lack of directness. In this way, the informal structures of the nursery serve to reinforce and maintain its gendered nature. This story is more familiar in reverse, where women entering traditionally male occupations are excluded by the men's informal structures. The men feel that they are expected to behave in certain ways – practical help and rough play – both by the women and the children, and that they are not expected to do certain things – cuddling and nappy changing. Similarly, parents claim there is no difference between the men and the women, yet are surprised and sometimes suspicious to find a man in the nursery.

The men are expected to be role models, but there is ambivalence about what that role should be. Is it to show that men – like women – have a caring side? Or is it to be more rough and forthright, in contrast to the women? The position is made more difficult for the men, because they are usually a lone man in a staff otherwise solely of women. There has to be a recognition that there is not a single masculinity that each man can model in its entirety, but that there are multiple masculinities and that men will vary in how they perform their masculinity (Connell 1995). Having men in the nursery will not, in and of itself, dismantle the gendered nature of childcare.

References

Aries, E. (1996) *Men and Women in Interaction*. Oxford: Oxford University Press.

Backett, K.C. (1982) *Mothers and Fathers: A Study of the Development and Negotiation of Parental Behaviour*. London: Macmillan.

Brannen, J. and Moss, P. (1991) *Managing Mothers: Dual Earner Households after Maternity Leave*. London: Unwin Hyman.

Brannen, J., Moss, P., Owen, C. and Wale, C. (1997) *Mothers, Fathers and Employment: Parents and the Labour Market in Britain 1984–1994*. London: DfEE.

Cameron, C., Moss, P. and Owen, C. (1999) *Men in the Nursery: Gender and Caring Work*. London: Paul Chapman.

Clarke, S. and Popay, J. (1998) 'I'm just a bloke who's had kids': men and women on parenthood, in J. Popay, J. Hearn and J. Edwards (eds) *Men, Gender Divisions and Welfare*. London: Routledge.

Connell, R.W. (1995) *Masculinities*. Cambridge: Polity.

Crompton, R. (1997) *Women and Work in Modern Britain*. Oxford: Oxford University Press.

Department for Education and Skills (2001) *EYDCP Planning Guidance 2001–2002*. London: DfES.

Deven, F., Inglis, S., Moss, P. and Petrie, P. (1998) *State of the Art Review on the Reconciliation of Work and Family Life and the Quality of Care Services*, Research Report no. 44. London: DfEE.

DfEE, DSS and Ministers for Women (1998) *Meeting the Childcare Challenge: A Framework and Consultation Document*. London: Stationery Office.

Finch, J. and Groves, D. (eds) (1983) *A Labour of Love: Women, Work and Caring.* London: Routledge and Kegan Paul.

Finkelhor, D., Williams, L.M. and Burns, N. (1988) *Nursery Crimes: Sexual Abuse in Day Care.* Newbury Park, CA: Sage.

Frosh, S., Phoenix, A. and Pattman, R. (2001) *Young Masculinities.* Basingstoke: Palgrave.

Gardiner, J. (1997) *Gender, Care and Economics.* London: Macmillan.

Hearn, J. and Parkin, W. (1992) Gender and organizations: a selective review and a critique of a neglected area, in A.J. Mills and P. Tancred (eds) *Gendering Organizational Analysis.* Oxford: Pergamon.

Hicks, S. (2001) Men social workers in children's services: 'Will the *real man* please stand up?', in A. Christie (ed.) *Men and Social Work: Theories and Practices.* Basingstoke: Palgrave.

Jensen, J.J. (1996) *Men as Workers in Childcare Services: A Discussion Paper.* Brussels: European Equal Opportunities Unit.

Murray, S.B. (1996) 'We all love Charles': men in child care and the social construction of gender, *Gender and Society*, 10(4): 368–85.

Office of Population Censuses and Surveys (OPCS) (1990) *Standard Occupational Classification.* London: OPCS.

Office of Population Censuses and Surveys (1994) *1991 Census. Economic Activity.* London: HMSO.

Pringle, K. (1998) Men and childcare: policy and practice, in J. Popay, J. Hearn and J. Edwards (eds) *Men, Gender Divisions and Welfare.* London: Routledge.

Robinson, S. (1998) Mixed gender workforces: issues in nursing, in C. Owen, C. Cameron and P. Moss (eds) *Men as Workers in Services for Young Children.* London: Institute of Education, University of London.

Ruxton, S. (1992) *'What's He Doing at the Family Centre?' The Dilemmas of Men who Care for Children.* London: National Children's Home.

Walkerdine, V., Lucey, H. and Melody, J. (2001) *Growing Up Girl.* Basingstoke: Palgrave.

Williams, C.L. (ed.) (1993) *Doing 'Women's Work': Men in Nontraditional Occupations.* London: Sage.

Yeandle, S. (1984) *Women's Working Lives: Patterns and Strategies.* London: Tavistock.

CHAPTER 7

Caring for children in need: the case of sponsored day care

JUNE STATHAM

Introduction

This chapter explores the notion of 'caring' as seen in the work of independent day care providers (childminders, pre-schools and private day nurseries) and their interaction with welfare agencies who are responsible for promoting and safeguarding children's welfare. It draws on information from a four-year study of the social work practice of purchasing places for a small number of children in voluntary and private day care facilities, commonly known as 'sponsored day care', to explore the constructions of maternal care and day care that underpin the Children Act 1989. The characteristics of sponsored day care provision are analysed in order to illustrate how these constructions of care are reflected in practice, for example in the amount of provision that is offered, the length of placements and the type of care that is seen to be appropriate for children at different ages. The perspectives of the various 'stakeholders' are then described – the officers in local authorities who arrange and purchase sponsored day care, the providers who deliver this service, and the parents who are offered a day care place for their child – and similarities and differences in their understandings of care are explored.

Children Act 1989 and day care services

The Children Act 1989 was the main policy development of the last Conservative administration that affected day care providers (see also Chapters 2 and 5). It introduced the concept of 'children in need', and placed a duty on local authorities to safeguard and promote their welfare through the provision of a range of family support services. In the volume of guidance to the Children Act which deals with children in need and day care, local authorities are explicitly encouraged to meet their statutory duty to provide day care provision for children in need by using the private market:

> Local authorities may discharge their general duty to provide day care for children in need either through their own provision or through making arrangements to use facilities run by independent providers such as voluntary organisations or private firms and individuals. In some cases it will be better for the children and more cost effective to use an independent service.
>
> (Department of Health 1991: para. 3.7)

The use of independent day care services by social workers is not new. Local authorities had previously purchased places for children in vulnerable families under section 1 of the Child Care Act 1980, which required them to diminish the need to receive children into, or keep them in, local authority care. Often day care had been provided for single parents to enable them to take up employment or training. However, the Children Act 1989 gave increased prominence to the use of day care to support families, while at the same time linking such support more closely to the concept of 'children in need'.

Children are 'in need' according to the Act if they require local authority services to achieve or maintain a reasonable standard of health or development, to prevent significant or further impairment of their health and development, or if they are disabled. The guidance to the Children Act clarifies that the purpose of day care (and other family support services) is 'to promote the upbringing of such children by their families'. The intention is to normalize such children (by ensuring their development is realized and not impaired), as well as the family situation, since 'in general families have the capacity to cope with their own problems' (Department of Health 1991: para. 2.14). The normal young child is assumed to develop naturally if in the family, without the need for external experiences or relationships, and if external agencies have to intervene, the purpose should be to reprivatize and thereby normalize child-rearing.

In respect to day care services, the Children Act 1989 was thus an essentially conservative measure. It restated and reinforced the limitation of the state's duty to provide to a small group of children deemed to be 'in need'; it reaffirmed the responsibility of parents to make provision for children who do not fall into this category; it tightened the existing state role of regulating the private day care market; and it retained responsibility for day care services within the welfare system (although the change of government to a Labour administration brought a number of changes). In this chapter, we focus on the way in which local authorities have carried out their duty to support children in need through the provision of day care services, and in particular on the use of voluntary and private providers for this purpose, in order to show how the constructions of maternal care and day care that underpin the Children Act 1989 are played out in practice.

The 'mixed economy' and day care for children in need

Sponsored day care is an example of the 'mixed economy' of welfare provision, in which social services departments purchase services from the voluntary and private sector to meet families' needs. However, there are some features of the private market that are unique to sponsored day care and which are not readily comparable to other market-orientated welfare services. For example, sponsored day care is often offered by childminders, who usually work on an individual basis rather than in a formal group setting. Instead of working for an agency such as a day nursery – which operates in a purpose-built or adapted building with staff with professional qualifications in childcare – childminders work in their own homes and are reliant to a large extent on their own resources, with limited access to training and support.

Second, sponsored day care often forms an adjunct to the main area of day care providers' work, again particularly for childminders, because their main 'business' is to provide childcare for working parents. Here the relationship is essentially a private one between parents and provider, whereas with sponsored day care placements the childcare provider may be required to work with other agencies including social services, health and the courts. They are therefore in the position of having both private paying parents and the statutory sector as their 'customers'. The kinds of tension this can create are not unique to day care services: private homes for elderly people, for example, may need to accommodate both private and local authority placements. But whereas 'customers' for nursing homes are likely to have similar needs however they arrive at the service, local authorities may require day care providers to offer a particular service for children in need (for example, providing support to their parents or monitoring the child's well-being) which differs from the service required by the majority of parents who purchase places themselves. The tensions that this can create are explored later in this chapter.

The research study

The sponsored day care study was commissioned by the Department of Health to investigate the use of independent day care services for children in need, and was carried out between 1996 and 2000. It had three stages, beginning with a national overview, followed by study of selected day care schemes in twelve local authorities and ending with a detailed study of childminding placements in two authorities. The study drew on a range of methods including secondary analysis of statistics and documentation, postal surveys, in-depth interviews and observation. This chapter draws on information from all stages of the study, but in particular on:

- a survey of all English social services departments in October 1996 (response rate 83 per cent)
- a postal survey of over 400 day care providers with experience of taking children placed with them by social workers (response rate 50 per cent)
- an analysis of statistics on the characteristics of sponsored day care placements in 12 selected authorities
- interviews with key officers in 12 local authority social services departments
- interviews with 17 childminders and 23 parents of children who had been offered a free childminding place.

The full findings from the study have been reported elsewhere (Statham et al. 2001).

Producing practice: the nature of the sponsored day care service

The way that independent day care services were used by local authorities – the children who were seen as eligible for funding, the hours of care that were offered, the duration of service, the age at which children received different types of care, the characteristics of those providing the service – revealed particular assumptions on the part of the state about the nature of maternal care and day care. First, those receiving the service. The study found that publicly funded day care places were generally provided only for children who were assessed as being 'in need' under the Children Act 1989 (see also Chapter 2). Although almost all local authorities did purchase at least some places from independent day care providers, such provision was very limited and nationally less than 2 per cent of children under 5 received such provision. In addition, local authorities reported that access to sponsored day care had become more restricted in recent years, with almost two-thirds saying that the service had become more closely targeted and was now focused on families categorized as not functioning properly because of individual problems, mainly at the expense of low income families. This response from one local authority officer was typical:

In the late 80s as child protection work became more dominant and demands on these budgets grew, the criteria were tightened so day care became more targeted and low income alone was no longer a sufficient reason for a paid place.

This was confirmed in the case-study part of the project, which included an analysis of the circumstances of 86 children for whom a sponsored day care place was requested over a three-month period. Two-thirds came from families where neither parent was in paid employment. Requests for a sponsored place were generally refused if the main reason was to enable a mother to work, even if this would have improved the situation for the child. For example one social worker described how 'my heart sank when she [mother] said she was considering work. I had to clarify that this was not the reason she was asking for day care because she wouldn't have got it for that reason'. Ironically, when this mother's care of her two children deteriorated so that the older child was removed and placed with his aunt, a full-time child-minding place had to be provided so that the aunt could continue to work full-time.

Second, analysis of the hours and duration of care purchased by local authorities showed that sponsored day care was primarily used to provide short-term crisis support. The majority of placements were offered on a part-time and short-term basis, typically two or three (part-time) sessions a week for a maximum of six months. The explanations provided by local author-ity officers clarified that day care was not intended to provide an ongoing service, and this was rationalized in terms of the responsibilities of mothers and the needs of children (see pp. 119–20).

Third, the ages of children placed in different types of day care also reflected particular views about young children's developmental needs. Sponsored day care predominantly involved children aged under 3 years, and most of these very young children were placed with childminders. Older children were transferred to day care in group settings (in particular playgroups) or moved out of the day care system altogether on admission to the school system, namely nursery or reception class. This predominance of childminding for very young children was partly due to the relatively low level of centre-based services for this age group. But the practice also reflected the view that very young children were best cared for in a one-to-one relationship in a home-based setting, a view explicitly supported in the guidance to the Children Act 1989:

> It is for each local authority to decide on their policy about using day nurseries for children in need who are under two. In many if not all cases it may be considered that childminding is more appropriate because a childminder provides care on an individual basis in a domestic setting.
>
> (Department of Health 1991: para. 3.8)

Finally, the characteristics of the day care providers offering this service also reflected a particular view of the qualities needed to provide care for children in need. Almost without exception the carers were female, and nearly a half (rising to over two-thirds of childminders) had no formal childcare qualifica-tion. Despite the increasing use of independent day care services to provide care for children with a relatively high level of need, training and support appeared to be very limited. The study found that half of day care providers with experience of taking referred children had not been provided with any extra support by their local authority, and two-thirds had not received any special training for this work.

Payment rates were also low. Despite the fact that children placed by the authority often had additional needs, most nurseries and playgroups simply received their normal fee, although sometimes local authorities paid a supplement to take account of the additional one-to-one support such children might require. Various systems of payment operated for childminders, including market rates, fixed hourly rates (usually higher but occasionally lower than the average fee charged to parents by local childminders) and enhancement mechanisms which were often discretionary. Hourly pay ranged from £1.20 to £3.50 per hour (in 1997) and childminders were often not paid if a child did not attend, even though a place had been set aside for them.

These factors could be linked one way by saying that poor pay and conditions are the cause of the gendered and poorly trained workforce. Alternatively it could be argued that the gendered workforce comes first – that day care is understood as substitute mothering, an extension of something women do in the home and something that comes naturally to women, requires little training and is of intrinsically low economic value (Cameron et al. 1999).

Similar findings about poor pay and conditions were reached in a study of children's day care and welfare markets in the north of England (Novak et al. 1997). This study also suggested that an additional reason for low levels of payment for children placed in independent day care services was a fear within some local authorities that they would be 'jeopardising a child's welfare by putting, in effect, too high a price on their head. The concept of providers making a profit was frequently viewed with suspicion' (Novak et al. 1997: 11).

Understandings of care: the local authority perspective on sponsored day care

The social constructions of care suggested by the preceding analysis of the practice of sponsored day care were reinforced by the explanations put forward by local authority officers in their accounts of how and why sponsored day care places were used. Information was obtained from responses to a postal survey of managers responsible for services for children in need in all authorities in England, interviews with key officers responsible for organizing sponsored day care schemes in twelve selected authorities, and information from social workers and health visitors who had requested day care for individual children in two case-study authorities.

The main function of sponsored day care, according to service managers, was to meet a particular need which often involved working with parents, after which sponsorship would be withdrawn. Full-time care was rarely offered, because the primary aim in many cases was to rectify family functioning so that full parental responsibility – perceived normality – could be resumed, either through maternal care or parents paying for day care (although in practice, those who were eligible for a sponsored place were rarely in a position to afford to pay for day care privately once local authority funding ended). Some managers expressed fears that if day care placements were permitted to continue for too long, these norms would be put at risk:

> *Experience has shown that if anything [placements] goes on longer than six months parents become used to it and start abdicating responsibility and expect it to continue until the child is 18.*

> *Sponsored day care is part-time and short-term to help families cope with specific family crises . . . if it's longer parents get used to it and expect it to continue . . . if we offer more than two days a week, it takes the problem away from the parent.*

> *We are dealing with expectations that once a child is in some form of day care then they will have started a career that will continue without interruption until school . . . We are providing a service to address an identified need and only provide the service when we are satisfied the need is there and the service is going to help address the need.*

Social workers, day care officers and health visitors who worked directly with families needing day care help were more likely to say that they would like the authority to continue funding the place, but were constrained by budget pressures. However, these practitioners, too, sometimes expressed the view that day care should be limited in order not to undermine the concept of maternal responsibility. For example, one social worker explained why she had requested only two sessions of care a week in the following terms:

> *I didn't want to give mum total freedom from caring for the child because she has to take responsibility for the child, and she also has a family centre place one day a week.*

Similar assumptions presumably lay behind the instructions which one of the childminders we interviewed reported receiving when a day care officer placed a child with her:

> *I was told don't support the mother too much . . . what does that mean? I would like to know.*

The preference for using childminders to care for children under the age of 3 was also the product of a normative view that care of young children should be by mothers – in whose absence, a home-based, individual female carer was seen to provide the best substitute. As a children's services manager and a day care officer explained:

> *With younger children, one of the things we struggle with is that our professional instincts are to steer towards childminders, but parents can find that hard if they feel another adult is usurping their position . . . I think it is a much more normal experience and meets the needs of the child for attachment to a limited number of adults.*

> *Childminders can provide a normal family experience. However good a nursery, it can't be that.*

Understandings of care: providers' perspectives on sponsored day care

Various different, and sometimes conflicting, understandings of the care they provided for sponsored children were evident in the accounts given by childminders, both in the in-depth interviews and in their responses to the postal questionnaire. These included care as substitute mothering, care as family support, care as a community service, care as child protection and care as work.

Care as substitute mothering

The local authority officers' perception of childminding as the most appropriate form of substitute care for very young children was to a large extent shared by childminders themselves. Other research (Ferri 1992; Nelson 1994; Mooney et al. 2001) has documented how childminders perceive a key strength of their service to be the provision of a homely environment and one-to-one care which mirrors that of mothers. However, for childminders caring for sponsored children, creating this 'home-from-home' had an added dimension, since it was often because of difficulties in the child's home environment that the family had been offered childminding support. In this sense, childminders saw themselves as providing a substitute for care which the children should have been getting at home, but weren't. Some talked about providing children with 'a normal family environment' or 'some proper parenting'. For example one childminder whose husband was at home for part of the day told how she thought they benefited from his presence:

> *The children I look after come 80 per cent from single parent families,*
> *so I provide a lovely caring family atmosphere. My husband works in*
> *a restaurant and is here between 3 and 6 p.m. The children I look after*
> *are very attached to him and get him to do things with them.*

Another described the difficult home circumstances of a child placed with her by the local authority and concluded that 'I feel we are the only normality in his life', while a third childminder noted that she was 'there for the child in a way her mum can't always be at the moment'.

Clearly, this construction of care as compensating for inadequacies in the child's own family life presents a challenge to parents' – especially mothers' – own identities, and was one factor in the reluctance of some parents to accept the offer of a childminding place, discussed further below.

Margaret Nelson (1994), in an analysis of the ambiguous location of childminding between public and private spheres, describes a number of dilemmas that childminders face in their daily practice. These include the need to cultivate a 'detached attachment', because their relationship with other people's children cannot be the same as with their own, and an acceptance of the limits of responsibility – that they cannot ensure that the child is being adequately looked after once they leave the childminder's care. The same dilemmas were present for childminders caring for children placed with them by the local authority, and in some ways were magnified by their inability to influence many aspects of the lives of the children they cared for, or how long the care could continue – a situation summed up by one day care provider as 'responsibility without power'. One childminder described how:

> In some cases you can get too involved with a child's family situation. I got involved with a family of young boys, who stayed with me on many occasions. I wanted to give them a stable life which they were not used to. It really upset me the children going to different foster parents through their young life and how this would affect them in their older life. It really upset me emotionally.

Care as family support

Some childminders became involved with a child's family situation through providing support to mothers as well as caring for their children. More than one-third of survey childminders with experience of taking children referred by social workers or health visitors, said that they had been asked to work with parents as well as children in these sponsored placements. They had provided advice on parenting skills; reminded mothers about appointments; accompanied them to the doctor, therapy group or parent and toddler session; and helped them to complete forms. Other childminders reported providing such additional support even when it was not requested by the local authority:

> It happens informally anyway. I delouse and bath children. I take parents to the welfare rights office. I provide second-hand clothing and furniture. I provide coffee and chat and other things, but social workers have never expected it.

The interviews and observation of childminders in the final part of the study provided a more detailed picture of the nature of such support, and how it operated. There were examples of childminders helping to build up mothers' confidence and self-esteem, offering friendship and support ('It's like a family thing now: she comes over here, we go out there, she knows all my family') and making suggestions for dealing with children's behaviour ('She is taking me up on ideas, not immediately but then suddenly she does it').

Care as a community service

The satisfaction of helping disadvantaged children and families was an important element in many providers' understandings of the care work they undertook for the local authority. When asked about the positive and negative aspects of providing care for children placed with them by the local authority, a key motivation among all types of day care provider was the satisfaction that they derived from feeling that they were providing a useful service, and from seeing disadvantaged children making progress in their care.

You are able to help the children who need you most.

(Playgroup leader)

It's providing a worthwhile service in the community to children and their families.

(Day nursery manager)

I feel I am doing something for a family that really needs help.

(Childminder)

In some cases, this concept of care as a community service appeared to take precedence over the need to earn an income. One childminder described how she wanted to take children referred by the local authority but could lose out financially when no referrals were forthcoming:

Sometimes I refuse private work in the hope that I will get sponsored work, so I go without money while I wait for work to be offered me.

Related to the notion of sponsored day care as a community service was the distinction some childminders made between 'deserving' and 'undeserving' recipients of sponsored places. This assumed that mothers should be provided with publicly funded day care only if they were really unable to cope, not to relieve the mother of her parental duties:

Some parents try to abuse the system. I had one parent who really just wanted someone else to look after her child the whole time.

Childminders accepted that some mothers 'needed a break' in order to be able to care adequately for their children, but some were critical of those whom they perceived as abdicating their responsibilities:

She [mother of a sponsored child] *seemed quite glad to get rid of him. She's at home, the older child is at school. She is not on her own, there are lots of people around and dad is there too and I don't think social services know that. I don't understand why I'm having him.*

Care as child protection

In a national survey carried out at the beginning of the study, most local authorities described using sponsored places as part of a child protection plan: 27 per cent said they did this frequently and 62 per cent occasionally. From the providers' perspective, the need to report back to social workers on the child's welfare could interfere with the relationship of trust that they felt they needed to create with parents.

I do write down what mum tells me and she knows it gets passed on, but it is hard. If you said what was the worst thing about this job, I would say having to pass on information, things mum tells me. I feel like a terrible tittle-tattle.

A related issue was the extent to which social workers shared 'confidential' information about the family with the day care provider. A common complaint from providers who accepted children placed by the local authority was that they received insufficient information about the family background and the reasons why the child was judged to need a sponsored place. This left them feeling unable to meet the child's needs properly, and also that they were not being treated as 'professionals' by the local authority:

We are always being told what to do, but not given the respect of being properly briefed about the child's needs. If we are good enough to take the child, we are good enough to be told what the problem is.

However, an alternative view was that it was better not to know too much, because this knowledge interfered in the process of establishing a relationship of trust with the parents. One childminder described how she thought it was 'good that we do not know too much. It keeps you on a level with the parents better, it doesn't colour your picture of them'. Other day care providers expressed the opinion that they should be told only as much as they needed to know to meet the child's specific needs. The rest was 'private', 'family business', which parents could tell them themselves if they chose to do so (and some had).

Care as work

For all types of day care provider, but especially for childminders, one of the attractions of offering sponsored places was that it provided a source of children to care for, and hence an income, with hours that could be fitted around family and other commitments. Over one-third of childminders in our postal survey said that one of the reasons for accepting local authority referrals was that it helped them to get a regular supply of children to care for, and some specifically mentioned that the hours suited their own circumstances, since sponsored places were generally part-time and children would often be collected by their non-working parents at the end of the school day rather than at 6 p.m.

However, the practice in most local authorities of funding sponsored places for a short initial period, followed by a review to determine whether or not it should be extended, created difficulties for the provision of 'care as work'. Childminders described how they could not rely on the local authority to keep them in work, and the tensions created by trying to keep places available for referred children yet needing to fill places in order to earn an income. This could also lead to a lack of continuity for the children they cared for, as in the following case where a childminder had arranged to care for a privately placed child because a sponsored placement for twin babies had been due to end:

I have taken on a baby in November and it turns out the twins will be long-term. So their time with me will have to be cut down or they'll go to someone else. If I'd known, I wouldn't have taken the other baby on.

For some childminders, one of the attractions of sponsored work was the additional status and sense of teamwork that came from working alongside social workers and day care officers in the local authority. Over a quarter cited this as an advantage of providing sponsored places, and described how it helped them to view themselves as professional workers:

The contact with professionals is interesting and gives me status. I feel like a semi-professional – even though we are at the bottom of the hierarchy in Social Services.

However, the conditions of work – the low pay, late payments and lack of retainer fees to keep places open when they were not needed by the authority, as well as the lack of sharing of 'confidential' information – all made it difficult for childminders to perceive themselves as professional workers.

Understandings of care: maternal perspectives on sponsored day care

For parents, and especially mothers, accepting a sponsored place with a childminder could create feelings of ambivalence and inadequacy. Whereas a group day care service such as a pre-school playgroup or nursery could be rationalized as meeting their child's needs for learning opportunities and contact with peers, the offer of home-based day care was sometimes seen as a threat and criticism of their parenting abilities, especially when they had not requested the care themselves. Most childminders were aware of the need for tact and sensitivity in negotiating the care relationship with parents when the placement had been arranged by the local authority and had developed strategies for dealing with this:

I wouldn't say to them [parents] that their child had been wonderful because they could feel undermined. A different kind of reassurance is needed.

Only half of the childminding places offered over a three-month period during the study were actually taken up, and this was partly because needing a childminder for reasons other than to provide childcare while they worked was seen by some parents as reflecting badly on their own parenting abilities.

I hated it. I still do. I never had help with the other children. I felt really bad not being able to cope.

I wanted a nursery . . . I felt that whatever she [childminder] could do, I could do.

A nursery or playgroup was more acceptable because it was seen to offer a different kind of 'professional' care focused on the needs of the child rather than as a replacement for what mothers should be able to provide themselves. It was not only mothers who espoused this view: one father was happy to accept a paid childminding place while his wife was hospitalized, but asked for it to end as soon as she returned home even though her circumstances still required a great deal of support. A grandfather was similarly unwilling to agree to social services providing a childminder to support his wife who was struggling to care for their grandchild, because he did not think it appropriate for someone outside the family to look after the child. This perceived 'normality' of maternal care for young children was underlined by the allocation of a sponsored childminding place to a father so that he could continue in employment when his wife was in hospital with severe depression, despite the fact that the eligibility criteria for sponsored day care excluded cases where it was primarily needed to provide childcare.

The circumstances in which care was offered appeared to make a difference to how it was perceived. It was easier for mothers to accept a childminding place when it was seen as supporting rather than challenging her ability to care for her own children. For example, a local authority paid for a 1-year-old child to go to a childminder for several sessions a week so that his mother could spend time with her older child who was terminally ill and take him to hospital appointments. This mother was happy with the arrangement and felt in control:

> I liked the way she looked after him. We discussed his needs. I could say he doesn't need that, or would you not do that. After a couple of weeks we were on the same wavelength.

Another mother, a single parent with triplets aged 11 and a 1-year-old boy, was suffering from depression and was offered a childminding place so that she could attend a mental health support group. However, she found it hard to leave her child and to accept help:

> I felt I'd given up on him. I felt bad because I wasn't coping. I managed the others without help.

The offer of substitute care was simply seen as inappropriate by one mother, who was seeking asylum in Britain. She declined the offer of a place for her twin babies (which had been offered because of social services' concerns about the safety of her five young children in an overcrowded flat), on the grounds that what she needed was financial support, not for someone else to care for the children:

> My children don't trouble me. In Africa we look after our own children. I said give me the money you would pay the childminder. But no, they would not do that.

'Care' not 'education'

A number of mothers who had accepted the offer of a childminding place had conflicting views about whether such care had been the best choice for their child. On the one hand, almost all were positive about the particular childminder provided by the authority to care for their child. They described the carer in terms that suggested they particularly valued the qualities of emotional involvement, flexibility and a non-judgemental approach. It was important to them that their child liked the childminder (although some were worried that they would become too attached), that the child was made to feel special and was treated like the childminder's own children. As one childminder put it, 'They want to know that you care'.

For some mothers, especially young single mothers, it was the childminder's ability to 'mother' themselves as well as their child that had been particularly appreciated:

She was sort of like a grandmother really. You could sit down and have a cup of tea with her if you're really down.

I could still go round there if I wanted support. I haven't spoken to her for about six months, but if I was to phone her and say, 'Sue, I'm having troubles', she would be there. She showed me how to be a mum, I've got a lot to thank her for.

However, there was also a perception that childminders, by the very fact that they operated as 'substitute mothers', were less able than other types of day care service to meet children's educational needs. As two mothers explained,

I still feel I would rather have had a nursery. If you leave a child at home with a childminder she has activities: cooking, cleaning, ironing. She does not have time to teach the children.

I liked the way she [childminder] looked after him. But you could see the changes in him when he went to the [local authority] nursery. No way a childminder could be able to make those changes. It's the other children too, and the back-up of other staff. And the training.

Discussion

For most parents, childcare is a private arrangement between themselves and a service provider. Children are parents' 'private responsibilities' and childcare is an issue of 'parental choice' (Brannen 1999). The involvement of the local authority in the relationship between day care provider and parent creates a new set of expectations about the nature and purpose of the care that is being offered, described by one childminder as 'a third party in between'. As we have shown, some day care providers were expected by the local authority to work more closely with parents and to provide some level of informal parent education. Others were expected to observe and record parenting behaviour. Another significant difference between private and local authority placements was that the local authority determined when the placement should end and the amount of care that should be provided. All these factors could alter the nature of the care relationship and create tensions between the needs and expectations of the different parties.

Sponsored childminders were caught in the middle of different understandings of their role – as substitute mothers, as professionals working with the local authority to promote and safeguard the welfare of vulnerable children, as providers of a worthwhile service to support families in their local community, as small businesses needing to earn an income. How did they reconcile these different constructions of care?

One strategy was to extend the 'substitute mothering' role to encompass the child's family as well as the child. This was exemplified by those childminders who kept up a relationship with the family even after the local authority had ceased paying for the place and the child no longer attended, and who encouraged mothers to get in touch if they needed advice or support. Such childminders had often been prepared to negotiate with the local authority on the parents' behalf, for example to extend the hours of care, to obtain additional services such as counselling for the parent, or to arrange nursery education for the child. It was apparent from the case-study phase of the research project that much of what these childminders did was on their own initiative, rather than part of an agreed plan with social services. As one childminder put it,

> It's what you do over and above what you are supposed to do that makes the relationship with these parents work, and it always will be.

A different strategy which some childminders adopted was to focus on the relationship with the child, and regard interaction with parents as a less desirable part of the job. Childminders who took this approach commonly cited the need to negotiate with the parents of sponsored children as one of the disadvantages of doing this work, and made comments such as 'It's not the children that are the problem, it's the parents'. While they accepted the need to sometimes provide additional support for families as part of the agreement with the local authority, they saw their primary focus as the child and found these extra demands of sponsored placements onerous:

> Sometimes you feel you shoulder the whole family's problems on yourself when you are only there for the child.

A third strategy for reconciling their different roles was for childminders to understand the care they provided to sponsored children as part of a professional relationship with the local authority. This allowed them to negotiate the dilemma of sometimes needing to report on children's well-being and parental behaviour in order to protect children from possible harm, while being entrusted by parents with the care of their child. This strategy was noticeably more prevalent in one of the two case-study authorities, where childminders with referred children generally felt that they were given sufficient information about the children's backgrounds to enable them to meet their needs. In the other authority, childminders were more likely to report feeling ill informed and not treated as partners by the authority, and in these circumstances they fell back on describing the care they were offering as 'just looking after' children. In this authority, when asked what they thought social workers hoped to achieve through a particular sponsored placement, typical responses were: 'No idea. I just look after him the best I can' and 'Don't know. I'm only the childminder. I know I have to look after her well'.

But although day care providers were able to adopt a variety of strategies to negotiate the different social constructions of care involved in providing a service for children placed and paid for by the local authority, the practice of sponsored day care described in this chapter highlights a number of more fundamental issues. One is the impact on children of such short-term, crisis-orientated periods of care. There was often little preparation of children for such placements, and the limited hours frequently reflected their parents' needs (for example, to attend hospital appointments or have a short 'break' from childcare) rather than their own. Placements generally ended when a particular crisis had passed, even though the family circumstances were often still difficult and care could be needed again in the future – with no guarantee that the same carer would be available. In these circumstances, it is hard to argue that the child's needs for continuity and a stimulating, secure environment were being put first. As one childminder put it, 'The children just get used to you and start to make progress and then they are taken away'.

The construction of family-based care as the most suitable form of care for very young children also leads to a situation where poorly trained and paid childminders, seen as substitute mothers, are understood as appropriate carers for children with additional needs. The study raised a number of concerns about the ability of independent day care services to provide high-quality care to such children, as well as the tighter targeting of sponsored places, one consequence of which was that children living in low income families were increasingly excluded from receiving such state-funded care.

Conclusion

Sponsored day care provision represents the point at which the state assumes responsibility for arranging and paying for day care services that are generally seen as the private responsibility of parents. The way in which this family support service is organized, the characteristics of those receiving it and the nature of the service provided, reveal a number of implicit assumptions about the concept of 'care'. These include the notion that home-based care is best for young children; that the responsibility of the state should be limited to short-term crisis interventions to help families care for their children when they are temporarily unable to do so; and that the 'care' provided in these circumstances is separate – conceptually and administratively – from arrangements to promote children's learning and education.

This practice is produced by the particular construction of care contained in the Children Act 1989, which itself reflects the dominant discourse in the

UK concerning the respective roles of parents, children and the state (Moss et al. 2000). However, other constructions of care and childhood are equally possible. Other European countries such as Sweden, France and Denmark accept greater collective responsibility for the well-being and upbringing of children, which in turn are reflected in different models of early childhood provision that start from the assumption that all children have an entitlement to good quality care and education services, rather than this being dependent on whether or not their parents need to work or the child is judged to be 'in need' (Moss 2001). Indeed the notion of early childhood services, with its connotation of passive recipients who are provided with 'care' or 'education', is also rejected in the practice of working with young children that has been adopted in the early childhood centres in Reggio Emilia in Italy. There, all children are understood as being 'rich in potential, strong, powerful, competent and, most of all, connected to adults and other children' (Malaguzzi 1993: 10). The practice of sponsored day care in the UK, while it undoubtedly provides valued support to children and parents who are experiencing particular difficulties in their lives, is based on a much more restricted view of the nature of childhood and the duty of the state to provide care for children.

References

Brannen, J. (1999) Caring for children, in S. Walby (ed.) *New Agendas for Women*. London: Macmillan.

Cameron, C., Moss, P. and Owen, C. (1999) *Men in the Nursery: Gender and Caring Work*. London: Paul Chapman.

Department of Health (1991) *The Children Act Guidance and Regulations, Vol. 2: Family Support, Day Care and Educational Provision for Young Children*. London: HMSO.

Ferri, E. (1992) *What Makes Childminding Work?* London: National Children's Bureau.

Malaguzzi, L. (1993) History, ideas and basic philosophy, in C. Edwards, L. Gandini and G. Forman (eds) *The Hundred Languages of Children*. Norwood, NJ: Ablex.

Mooney, A., Knight, A., Moss, P. and Owen, C. (2001) *Who Cares? Childminding in the 1990s*. York: Joseph Rowntree Foundation.

Moss, P. (2001) *The UK at the Crossroads: Towards an Early Years European Partnership*. London: Daycare Trust.

Moss, P., Dillon, J. and Statham, J. (2000) The 'child in need' and 'the rich child': discourses, constructions and practice, *Critical Social Policy*, 20(2), 233–54.

Nelson, M.K. (1994) 'Family day care providers: dilemmas of daily practice', in E. Nakano (ed.) *Mothering: Ideology, Experience, Agency*. New York: Routledge.

Novak, T., Owen, S., Petrie, S. and Sennett, H. (1997) *Children's Day Care and Welfare Markets*. Kingston upon Hull: School of Policy Studies, University of Lincolnshire and Humberside.

Statham, J., Dillon, J. and Moss, P. (2001) *Placed and Paid for: Supporting Families through Sponsored Day Care*. London: Stationery Office.

C H A P T E R   **8**

Mother, teacher, nurse?
How childminders
define their role

ANN MOONEY

Introduction

In recognizing the need for more childcare provision, the National Childcare Strategy was launched in Britain in 1998. The overall aim of the strategy is 'to ensure good quality, affordable childcare for children aged 0–14 in every neighbourhood, including both formal childcare and support for informal arrangements' (DfEE 1998: 6). A key factor in achieving this aim is the recruitment and retention of a well-motivated, well-trained workforce. This chapter focuses on one group of this workforce, childminders. Childminders are self-employed, working in their own homes looking after other people's children. The chapter looks at how childminders understand their work and at how their understanding affects attitudes towards training, the work itself and relationships with parents using their service.

The demand for childcare has been increasing over recent years as more women return to the labour market when their children are young. Between 1984 and 2000, the employment rate for women with a child under 5 rose from 27 per cent to 54 per cent, with the growth in full-time employment recently outstripping part-time growth (Twomey 2001). The strongest growth in employment has been among women with higher qualifications and who are married with employed partners (Brannen et al. 1997; Holtermann et al. 1999). It is this group of parents – couples working full-time and with higher incomes – who are more likely to use formal childcare, such as childminders and nurseries, rather than informal care such as relatives (Mooney et al. 2001a; DfES 2002).

Although informal care is the most common form of childcare for working parents in Britain today, childminders are one of the major providers of formal childcare (Mooney et al. 2001a). In analysis of the Family Resources Survey, an annual UK government survey, for the years 1993–96, 22 per cent of children under 5 were with childminders compared with 19 per cent in nurseries and playgroups. A recent survey of parents childcare use found that among two parent households where both parents work full-time the use of childminders and nurseries/crèches was the same at 17 per cent respectively, whereas lone parents working full-time were more likely to use childminders rather than nurseries/crèches (DfES 2002). Childminding therefore plays an important role, not only in providing a service for working parents, but also providing employment for those choosing to become childminders.

Prior to the implementation of the Children Act in 1991, childminding was subject to minimal regulation. Now, anyone caring for a child under the age of 8 for more than two hours a day for reward must be registered. Childminders are annually inspected and must meet national standards introduced in 2001 (DfES 2001). Health, safety and police checks on all household members over the age of 16 are carried out. Conditions of registration include limits on the numbers and ages of children who may be looked after. For example, childminders can care for no more than three children under the age of 5 including their own children. Although a childcare qualification is not mandatory for registration, all childminders must attend an approved training course within six months of registration. This training is usually no more than six to twelve hours and covers topics such as health and safety, child development, and childminding as a business.

Despite greater regulation, the arrangement between childminder and parent remains a largely private one. It is left to them to decide what their respective role and relationship will be. There are a number of reasons why providing childcare in one's own home is different from childcare provided in an institution such as a crèche or nursery (Saggers and Grant 1999). Not only is there less visibility, but also the public and private domains of work and home are blurred. Unlike childminders, other care workers, such as nurses and nursery workers, can achieve a physical if not emotional separation between their private lives and their paid employment (Nelson 1994). Furthermore, childminders are often caring for their own children while at the same time caring for other people's children. What they do for their own children, which is unpaid, is similar to what they do for other children in their care for which they are paid. The roles of mother and childcare provider are therefore closely intertwined. This chapter considers how these distinct features of this type of childcare may affect how childminders come to understand their work and the implications of the social construction of care.

The chapter is based on data from a study of childminding undertaken at Thomas Coram Research Unit between January 1999 and November 2000 (Mooney et al. 2001a). The study was part of the Joseph Rowntree Foundation's Work and Family Life Programme. The purpose of the study was to look at childminders as a distinct occupational group within the childcare workforce. It included a large postal survey and 30 case studies. The survey involved a representative national sample of 1050 childminders in England. A response rate of 62 per cent was achieved although of these nearly a quarter were not childminding at the time. They had either stopped childminding altogether or were taking a break from this work. This left 497 childminders who both responded and were currently working as childminders. The survey collected information about education, training, past employment, working conditions, commitment to childminding, a childminder's role and views about employed parents and the care needs of young children. The case studies were drawn from an inner London and outer London suburban area and included new childminders, established childminders, and childminders who had recently stopped childminding. Each childminder was interviewed using a semi-structured interview schedule, which covered similar topics as in the survey. In addition, shorter telephone interviews were conducted with 21 parents of children cared for by new and established childminders.

Social constructions of care work

The influence of attachment pedagogy

The normative expectation that young children should be in the exclusive care of their mothers has for many years had a major influence on ideas about what care is appropriate for children (Mooney and Munton 1997). In the context of normative expectations that mothers should be home-based, full-time carers, the purpose of childcare work has been to provide 'substitute mothering'. Singer (1992) has described the idea that mother care is needed for secure development and that, in its absence, non-maternal care needs to be based on a dyadic mother–child relationship as 'attachment pedagogy'. She argues that such ideas have had a powerful influence on the practice of bringing up children both in the context of home and childcare.

   The belief that young children need exclusive maternal care remains influential in the UK despite increasing numbers of mothers with young children in the workforce. In 1994, only 5 per cent of female respondents in the British Social Attitudes Survey thought it acceptable for mothers to work full-time with a child under 5 (Thomson 1996). Childcare workers also express a widespread belief that mothers should be available to children and that children should not be cared for by others (Cameron et al. 2001). Although one-half of the childminders we surveyed accepted mothers with a child under 1 working either full-time or part-time and two-thirds thought it acceptable for mothers with a child aged between 1 and 3, the majority had themselves not worked outside the home when they had children. Although expressing some acceptance of working mothers, there was less acceptance of women who worked through choice rather than necessity: 'Fine, I had to do it. It's part of necessity these days . . . And I just thought, you don't have to go back to work . . . To me, people like that don't need to do it.' It would appear that mothers who exercise a choice not to stay at home with their children are not conforming to the normative image of motherhood.

The image of the 'ideal' mother is one where a mother is always available to her children and, being always available, nurtures love and security. This image is articulated in the comments of childminders interviewed in the study. The comments suggest that working mothers are not conforming to this image of motherhood: 'And I think it's very sad, because a child's been sent out to somewhere . . . Mum's out working, and he needs a comfortable environment – to feel he's cared for and loved'. A childminder trying to understand a child's extremely disruptive behaviour said, 'From 3 months old he was in day care. She never had him with her. He's always been looked after by other people, and could it just be a little rebellion against his mum always leaving him? . . . I think he just really needed his mum and lots of love.'

Working mothers were described as 'missing out' on the benefits of being with their child full-time, such as watching their child's growth and development. Distress and misbehaviour were at times interpreted as expressions of children missing their mothers, whereas maternal guilt about working explained why some mothers, in the opinion of their childminder, were too lenient or possessive with their children. Of course, these views were not applied to fathers.

The belief that children need to be in the care of their mothers full-time underlies the reason why many women take up childminding.[1] Most childminders in the study (95 per cent) had children when they started childminding and three-quarters had at least one pre-school child when they began. The main reason they said for becoming a childminder was so that they could stay at home with their own children or work from home. In choosing to work from home and avoid the need for childcare, they are subscribing to the belief that children need to be in the full-time care of their mothers. As one childminder explained: 'I can't hand my child out to somebody else.'

Just as 'attachment pedagogy' influences views about working mothers, it also influences views on what is the best type of care for young children. If mother care is put forward as the 'ideal', then non-parental childcare should be as close as possible to care provided at home by a mother. Consequently, many parents, childcare workers and professional groups favour home-based, individualized care where children are cared for in a home setting by a mother-like figure. Social workers, for example, prefer to use childminders when sponsoring a childcare placement for a child aged under 2 (Statham et al. 2001).

Around one-third of the childminders before taking up childminding had left their children in someone else's care while they were at work. Informal care provided by friends, partners and other relatives was the most common form of childcare (65 per cent) followed by childminders (26 per cent). Very few had used centre-based care for their children. Although availability and affordability of alternative childcare may be influential, it is likely that their choice of childcare reflects a preference for home-based rather than centre-based care.

Perhaps not surprisingly, childminders consider themselves and relatives to be the best non-parental childcare for children under 3. In the interviews, childminders spoke about giving children more individual attention and providing a home-like environment. With higher adult:child ratios and larger groups they failed to see how children in nurseries could get the same level of individual attention. A childminder who had worked in a nursery observed 'it was very hard to comfort a child when there was about four staff to eighteen babies'. Experience as mothers and the commitment to childcare it conferred was also seen as an advantage that childminders offered: 'They get a more motherly attention from someone that has been a mother that's got her own children – rather than someone, say, a young girl that's just gone into doing childcare'. But childminders are not alone among childcare workers in favouring home-based care for young children. A study of childcare students found that home-based care was considered the best form of non-parental childcare for the under-3s, but particularly for children under 1 year old (Cameron et al. 2001).

How childminders understand their work

Given the strong influence of attachment pedagogy on views about the best care for children, what role do childminders see themselves playing and how do they understand the work they do? In the survey, childminders were asked in a pre-coded question what were their main objectives. Most childminders rated safety, affection and child development as very important in their work. Providing a service for families, preparing children for school and allowing mothers to work were seen as less important (see Table 8.1). Three-quarters thought it very important that they provide 'a home away from home'.

Table 8.1 Childminders' ratings on the importance of these goals in their work

Goals		*Important*		
		Not	*Somewhat*	*Very*
	N	%	%	%
Provide safe physical environment	495	0	2	98
Make children feel loved	494	0	7	93
Help children develop and learn	492	0	12	88
Help child like self	488	1	19	80
Provide fun-filled activities	489	0	20	80
Home away from home	487	1	23	76
Social contacts for children	492	2	27	71
Service for families	491	2	42	56
Prepare children for school	489	2	45	53
Allow mothers to work	487	5	47	48

Source: Survey data

Understanding of the work was explored in more depth in the case studies. When questioned about their role, childminders described themselves as substitute or second mums and likened childminding to parenting. Other researchers, both here and in North America, have also found that childminders understand their work as an extension of mothering (for example Nelson 1994; Gelder 1998; Kyle 2000). During the interviews, childminders talked about the many and varied activities they provided for children, but it was the close affective relationship which they emphasized with frequent mention of the love given to children, the hugs and cuddles.

As Kyle (2000) found in her study, childminders drew on their maternal values to guide them in their care of children. They based their ideas of what was good for children in their care on their ideas about what they thought was good for their own children:

The children I look after, I take round to friends' houses, which – I take them as if they were my own . . . all the things that I would do with my own children, I do with child-minded children . . . they all call my mum nanny and my sisters auntie exactly the same as my children do.

The success of the childcare arrangement often seemed to rest on how well the childminder was able to integrate the child into her family. Here a childminder talks about a child who did not settle: 'She wasn't as much family, even though I tried hard to make her part of the family . . . But she just somehow never got the – I never was as relaxed as with [other child].'

As already discussed, one of the main reasons for taking up childminding is because women can work from home and at the same time care for their own children. The fact that childminders are looking after their own children as well as getting paid to look after other people's children, is likely to influence the way in which they understand their work (Nelson 1994). Much of the work they do as a childminder is similar to what they do for their own children. For example, providing a safe environment in which children feel secure, can establish close, warm relationships and wherein a variety of activities are provided both for enjoyment and to facilitate development. This may make it difficult to differentiate between the care provided as a mother and the care provided as a childminder, particularly as both take place in the childminder's home.

Most interviewees stressed how childminded children were treated the same as their own children and as part of their family. Being like a mother and treating children the same were frequent responses when childminders were asked to describe a good childminder, as illustrated by the following quotation:

Someone who's just willing to make the child one of their own. Because our aims for our children are that they get the best possible of your time, your attention, of the things that are out there. And I think, if as a childminder, you keep that attitude with a minded child, that minded child becomes as your flesh. So that's the best thing. That's what will make a good childminder.

Nelson (1994) suggests that childminders in emphasizing the way in which they treat both childminded children and their own children in the same way are in part wanting to imply that an intense bond with their own children will not stand in the way of fairness. In publicly denying that their feelings differ between children of their own and of others they do not have to deal with the way in which childcare is different from mothering. Yet, other children cannot be part of their family in the same way as their own. Although close relationships develop, and childminders said how hard it could be when a child left, there are transparent differences. Children go home at the end of the day and at some point leave the childminder's care altogether. A childminder's responsibilities are limited. They have no control over what happens when a child is with their parents. Furthermore, mothering does not involve a financial transaction, nor is it time-limited in the same way as paid childcare.

Some accounts did acknowledge a difference in feeling. There was evidence too that some childminders struggled to define what their role was. Perhaps this is because there is no language available other than that associated with mothering to describe the close emotional ties that develop with the children in their care: 'As a childminder you're like mum. But you're not mum. You're more like an auntie, rather than just the childminder'. The accounts reveal ambiguities about what childminding is. On the one hand, childminders interpret what they do as being close to mothering but, on the other hand, they recognize that what they are doing is not the same as mothering:

> I feel like his second mum. Because he is like having one of mine. You don't feel the same, because they're not yours. But he's very loving. He loves being cuddled and kissed . . . And it just feels like having your own child, but you give him away at the end of the day, and you get paid for it.

Parents have somewhat different views about the role of their children's childminder. When asked why they had chosen this type of care around one-half of the 21 parents interviewed (all mothers) said that it was the individual attention and home setting that childminding offered. Few said that they were looking for a substitute mother – someone to replace them while they were at work. Childminders can be sensitive to mothers feeling threatened if a childminder assumes such a role, as explained by this childminder who draws out the contradictions by referring to her own experience. Asked if she thought that parents wanted her to be a second mum she answers:

> Maybe not. I suppose there's two ways to look at it. In one respect, the parents will be looking for someone who will give them the love and affection that they need. But on the other side – I know when I went back to work I wanted [my son] to know that I was his mum. I'm your mum, I want to do everything for you. But, at the same time, I wouldn't want him to go somewhere where he was treated sternly, or without any affection.

Implications of understanding care as mothering

If childminders construct their work around the ideal of mothering, emphasizing the importance of a home environment and treating children as their own, does this influence the way in which they think about training and being qualified as a childcare worker? Does it affect how they perceive childminding as work and a business? Does such a construction have implications for the relationship between providers and parents?

Training and qualifications

Though childminders wanted to be seen as professional childcare workers, less than one-quarter had a qualification related to childcare. These figures are lower than those from surveys of other childcare workers. In a recent survey, 78 per cent of nursery heads and 67 per cent of other staff had a childcare or early years qualification (Cameron et al. 2001). That care is understood in terms of mother care may explain the greater importance attached by childminders to the experience of parenting over qualifications and training. Over one-half thought it very important that childminders should be parents themselves, while having a childcare qualification and training were rated this highly by one-quarter and one-third respectively. 'Childminding is like – it just needs me being a mother. And I don't really know what sort of qualification you really need'.

Parents hold similar views about the need for childminders to have a childcare qualification. Two-thirds thought a qualification was unimportant, with one-half believing that experience as a mother was more important. The experience of parenting is elevated in importance and value, providing feelings and insights that those who are not mothers are deemed to be lacking as implied by this childminder: 'I think you only can understand children and have any love for children once you're a mum. Because you can read it in a book and learn how to do it . . . But the feeling isn't going to be there.' Suggesting that childminders should be trained or qualified may be understood by childminders to mean that their parenting skills are inadequate. The absence of a registration requirement for childminders to be trained or qualified may also reinforce rather than challenge this emphasis on parenting experience.

Childminding as a career

Childcare is an occupation notable for its extreme gender segregation: less than 2 per cent of the workforce are men (Cameron et al. 2001). That it is a largely female workforce contributes to the low pay found in childcare work, well below national average earnings. Home workers comprise some of the lowest paid workers in the labour force (Felstead and Jewson 2000) and childminders are particularly low paid among the childcare workforce. Childminders' average earnings in 1999 were around £5000 per annum, with an average hourly rate per child of £2. This compares with average earnings in private nurseries in 2000 of £13,400 for managers and £7800 for other workers (Cameron et al. 2001). Moreover, childminders' income is not guaranteed or reliable. When childcare arrangements end, their income is affected. They have no idea when they will find new business and restore income levels.

Poor rates of pay affect how the work is valued. Childminders were most dissatisfied with society's lack of recognition for the work they did. This sense of low status also emerged when childminders were asked what could be done to improve childminding as a job or career. Positive publicity about childminding was placed before better pay and financial support from the government:

So I think just that the whole image of it needs a make-over . . . It needs to be an ongoing thing . . . Just to reinforce the message. Because it's going to take time before the whole culture, the whole way of looking at it is improved . . . where people can walk around and say 'Yeah. Actually, I'm a childminder.' 'Wow! Really? You've such a gift. I couldn't survive without you.' But we're not, as a nation, I don't think we're very good at valuing people that do the most important jobs. Doctors, teachers, nurses, the forces. No one gives two stabs about them.

Poor pay and low status contribute to the way in which childminding is not always regarded as 'real' work: 'It's not that I can't be bothered to go out to work. I couldn't get a job. I really couldn't get a job'. Around two-fifths of survey respondents saw childminding as convenient while their children were young and still at home. Just over one-third saw it as their chosen career. There has been some expansion of employment opportunities in the childcare field as seen, for example, by childminders moving into related careers such as childcare development workers. Nevertheless, it is difficult for childminders to see how their experience can be valued in the wider labour market. Furthermore, because childminding is seen as being very similar to being at home and caring for one's own children it was difficult to see it as a career: 'I suppose it is a career in a way. I don't know. You don't really look at it – when you're doing it, you're just doing it. It's just something you do. I suppose it's like – you know, a mother at home, bringing up their children.'

Yet, despite the poor pay and devaluation of the work childminders express a high level of satisfaction with their work. In fact, among different groups of workers, childcare workers have been found to be the most satisfied with their jobs (Rose 1999). The intrinsic enjoyment of working with children seems to outweigh the negative aspects associated with poor wages and low status work. Childcare workers clearly do enjoy interacting with children and find this aspect of their work meaningful. However, other reasons may be contributing to job satisfaction for childminders. Childminders say the most satisfying aspect of the work is working from home and with children. Childminding offers the opportunity for women to earn an income, but at the same time still be available for their children, which is perceived as an important feature of the ideal mother. Childminders can also exercise some control over how they work and this autonomy may contribute to their levels of satisfaction.

Childminding as a business

Being self-employed means that childminders are in effect running small businesses. In our interviews we asked childminders for their views on this. Interestingly, their accounts reveal tensions between being committed to childcare and wanting to earn a reasonable income from it. While some childminders saw it as a business, others were unable to do so since it seemed to suggest a childminder who was more interested in money than childcare. Although the principle reason for childminding was wanting to stay at home while at the same time earn an income, there was strong disapproval of a financial motivation for childminding. 'Good childminders' were described by childminders and parents alike as entering the occupation because they liked children and wanted to care for them and not for financial reasons: 'A good childminder has to love children, and not just do it for the money.' Criticism was levelled at childminders who appeared to put money before children:

> She's bringing in far too many children to actually be able to look after properly. Just to earn more money. That's wrong. Because then it's not about childcare, is it? It's about the money going in your pocket, and who cares about what's happening to the children.

The authors of another study about parents' childcare arrangements reported how parents spoke disparagingly of childminders who see childminding as just a job and a way of earning money rather than really caring for the children (Vincent and Ball 1999).

Parents look for a childminder who is affectionate, loving and good with children. It is these characteristics which were most frequently mentioned by the parents we interviewed. Around two-fifths of parents in a national survey chose their childcare provider because they showed their child affection, which was a much more common reason where an individual, such as a childminder, was looking after the parent's child (DfES 2002). In turn, childminders in viewing care as an extension of mothering cannot easily equate childminding as a business transaction: 'I don't really treat it as work, as such, to me. It's just they're part of the family unit when they're here. And I just treat them as part of a family.'

Nelson (1989) refers to the cultural taboo against redefining care as a commodity. Suggesting that one is motivated by financial gain rather than caring about children appears to suggest that one cannot care enough. Parents want reassurance that the childminder really does care about their child and is not providing care just for financial reward. Increasing fees, charging for extra services or imposing overtime rates interferes with the notion of 'really' caring. Many childminders left their fees unchanged even with a contract detailing increases. A strong sense of commitment to the child and their family made it difficult to ask for more money. A childminder who felt justified in charging a particular amount for her services, began to have doubts when she became attached to the child: 'Because I think if you ask for less than that [£4.00 an hour], it's kind of saying it's not very good care. I decided I wasn't doing it for any less . . . but then when I got him . . . he's so nice, I started feeling guilty.'

The relationship between childminders and parents

The success of the childcare arrangement hinges on the interpersonal relationships between childminders and parents (Mooney et al. 2001a). Childcare is embedded in personal relationships. Yet, fees, contracts, hours and overtime rates imply a formal business relationship:

> I think you kind of start off more formal than you would. And then you can lighten up . . . But if you were too friendly, it was very hard to go the other way. So I think it was about being quite formal . . . Sometimes you get parents who think that if you're being formal you can't be caring. You're only in it for the money, which nobody going out to work would ever think.

Childminders articulated the difficulties of negotiating a relationship which is governed by both the norms of social exchange and the norms of a business transaction (Nelson 1989; Vincent and Ball 1999). The close interpersonal relationships which develop made it difficult to raise concerns with parents about for example timekeeping or fees. As Ferri (1992: 142) summarizes, 'the complexity lies partly in the conflicting components of a relationship which requires the formality associated with financial and contractual exchanges, and, at the same time, the personal intimate rapport deemed essential in caring for a child'. Likewise, parents too find it difficult to raise concerns (Mooney and Munton 1998). Since childminders appear to model childcare on their parenting, challenging their practices may be tantamount to challenging their parenting abilities.

What makes a childminder's situation unique and distinguishes it from other workers in the childcare field and the broader field of social care is that the transactions occur in the provider's home rather than in an institution or in the home of the client. In the context of group care, for example, the relationship between provider and parent may to some extent be regulated by the institutional context where there is usually a management structure which deals with problems. This can serve to avoid difficult relationships or areas of tension arising between parents and staff working directly with their children.

Between childminder and parent there is mutual dependency because both fear that the other may terminate the arrangement if any concerns are voiced (Mooney and Munton 1998). Thus, despite a contract drawn up between them, neither childminder nor parent has much bargaining power. Childminders, in becoming attached and treating the child in their care as 'one of the family', find it difficult to make demands on parents when they are not meeting contractual agreements. They are afraid that parents may respond by withdrawing their child. Not only are there emotional consequences if the arrangement is ended, but also loss of income. Parents too in raising concerns fear the childminder may refuse to continue providing care. They too know moving their child may not be in the child's best interests. They also know that they will be faced with finding alternative childcare when the demand for affordable, good quality childcare exceeds supply. This is not to say that mutual dependency does not exist within other childcare transactions, but the unique features of childminding means it can be more difficult when problems arise.

Conclusion

The chapter has considered how childminders understand their work as substitute mothering because of the distinct features of this type of provision and the powerful influence of attachment pedagogy. This social construction of their work has a number of implications in terms of attitudes towards training and qualifications, their relationship with parents and the value of the work. Although childminders want to be viewed as professional childcare workers, the need for training and qualification is less strongly felt, with some seeing personal experience of motherhood as the most important requirement. The boundaries between childminder and mother and between home, family and clients can be difficult to determine and maintain. There is a tension between being a carer with its emphasis on commitment and affective engagement with children, and operating as a small business in a private childcare market. The poor pay, low status of the work and close links to mothering at a practical level make it difficult to see childminding as a career. In fact, there is some ambivalence among some childminders as to whether it is an occupation.

Childminders have an important role to play in the expansion of childcare provision under the National Childcare Strategy. By 2004, the government plans to create new childcare places for 1.6 million children with a minimum of 145,000 new places with childminders, including 25,000 places in areas of disadvantage (DfEE 2001a). To meet this expansion in childcare provision, it is estimated that at least 150,000 new people will need to be recruited. Yet between 1996 and 2001 the number of registered childminders fell by 30 per cent to 72,300 (DfEE 2001b). The difficulty in recruiting and retaining childminders threatens the government's plans for expansion.

A number of reasons have been put forward to explain the decline in the numbers of childminders including demographic changes (Mooney et al. 2001b). For many women, childminding is seen as convenient while their children are young. When their children are older and at school, they are likely to look for alternative employment and are unlikely to return to childminding. This situation is sustainable only while there are sufficient numbers of women willing to become childminders while their children are young and replace those that leave. There is evidence to suggest that the pool of women from which childminders have been traditionally drawn is shrinking. In the past, childminders have tended to have lower levels of education and possibly be less well placed to return to work after childbirth. For example, childminders in our study were less likely to be in managerial or professional posts before taking up childminding: a reflection of their lower levels of education. However, the level of education has been rising and women are having fewer children and having them later. Consequently, more women are now in a position to pursue a career and pay for childcare. At the same time, there is increasing competition for female labour. Aternative employment opportunities with greater flexibility in working patterns, which often avoids the need for non-parental childcare, is more common. Childminding, with its low pay and status, may therefore be seen as a less attractive employment option.

The time has come, it has been argued, to transform ideas about work with young children so that the workforce can be drawn from a wider and increasing pool of women and men (Cameron et al. 2002). For childminders, the concept of 'substitute mothering' is becoming increasingly problematic. This is due to a number of factors which are changing the role of childminding. First, childminders are taking on much more of an educational role, although in their work with children aged under and over 3, they have tended to integrate care and informal education.[2] Childminders can now become accredited to provide nursery education for 3–4-year-olds for which they receive a government grant. Second, there is a greater emphasis on their welfare role and providing places sponsored by the local authority for children in need (Statham et al. 2001; see also Chapter 7). Third, childminders are being encouraged to see their work in more professional terms and their service as a small business.

How might childminding be understood in a way that is not substitute mothering and not centre-based? Changes in the role of childminders, as described above, may influence how the work is seen and understood, as may the growth of childminder networks. The establishment of formal local networks of childminders, via an approved scheme organized by the National Childminding Association, is a recent development in Britain. Childminders, who are assessed, recruited and monitored by a network coordinator, enjoy certain benefits for being a network member. They have greater access to training opportunities, the chance to use network resources, the help and advice of the network coordinator and the possibility of becoming accredited to provide nursery education.

More support and training may help towards changing the status of the work and the way it is understood. However, there are other fundamental issues which have to be addressed including low pay, the low status of the work and the tension between intimate, close relationships associated with caregiving on the one hand and operating a small business on the other. Some form of salaried childminding as used in several other European countries with pay and conditions linked to training may be a way forward. Under this system childminders are assessed, recruited, supported and paid by an agency, which might be a local authority or private organization. Parents pay the agency and the agency pays the childminders, usually with a substantial subsidy from public funds. Applied in Britain, this option would involve a shift in public policy from subsidizing some parents through tax credits, to subsidizing all providers through the payment of salaries. Furthermore, such an option would require childminders to cede their independence and assume employee status.

In relation to centre-based care other understandings of early years work have been discussed, for example the 'early years teacher' and the 'pedagogue' (see Chapter 4 for discussion of 'pedagogue'). Both involve work with children under and over 3 and an holistic approach to children (Moss 2000). But are these appropriate for childminding? Perhaps what is needed is a rethinking of *all* work with young children, leading to a reconceptualization which can incorporate the full range of current occupations, including teachers, workers in nurseries and other centres and childminders.

Notes

1 Although there are male childminders, the majority of childminders are women (99 per cent in our study).
2 Publicly funded part-time nursery education begins at the age of 3.

References

Brannen, J., Moss, P., Owen, C. and Wale, C. (1997) *Mothers, Fathers and Employment*, Department for Education and Employment (DfEE) research report no. 10. London: DfEE.

Cameron, C., Moss, P. and Owen, C. (2001) *Entry, Retention and Loss: A Study of Childcare Workers and Students*, Department for Education and Skills (DfES) research report no. 275. London: DfES.

Cameron, C., Mooney, A. and Moss, P. (2002) The childcare workforce: current conditions and future directions, *Critical Social Policy*.

Department for Education and Employment (1998) *Meeting the Childcare Challenge: A Framework and Consultation Document*, Cm 3959. London: DfEE.

Department for Education and Employment (2001a) *Early Years Development and Childcare Partnership Planning Guidance 2001–2002*. London: DfEE.

Department for Education and Employment (2001b) *Statistics of Education: Children's Day Care Facilities at 31 March 2001, England*, DfEE Bulletin 08/01. London: DfEE.

Department for Education and Skills (2001) *National Standards for Day Care and Childminding*. London: DfES.

Department for Education and Skills (2002) *Parents' Demand for Childcare*. London: DfES.

Felstead, A. and Jewson, N. (2000) *In Work at Home: Towards an Understanding of Homeworking*. London: Routledge.

Ferri, E. (1992) *What Makes Childminding Work*. London: National Children's Bureau.

Gelder, U. (1998) Childminding: does it work for women? Paper presented to the Social Policy Association Annual Conference, Lincolnshire, 14–16 July.

Holtermann, S., Brannen, J., Moss, P. and Owen, C. (1999) *Lone Parents and the Labour Market: Results from the 1997 Labour Force Survey and Review of Research* (ESR23). Sheffield: Employment Service.

Kyle, I. (2000) *Quality in Home Child Care Settings: A Critical Review of Current Theory and Research*. Toronto: Family Day Care Services.

Mooney, A. and Munton, A.G. (1997) *Research and Policy in Early Years Services: Time for a New Agenda*. London: Institute of Education, University of London.

Mooney, A. and Munton, A.G. (1998) Quality in early childhood services: parent, provider and policy perspectives, *Children and Society*, 12: 101–12.

Mooney, A., Knight, A., Moss, P. and Owen, C. (2001a) *Who Cares? Childminding in the 1990s*. London: Family Policy Studies Centre for Joseph Rowntree Foundation.

Mooney, A., Moss, P. and Owen, C. (2001b) *A Survey of Former Childminders*, research report no. 300. London: Department for Education and Skills.

Moss, P. (2000) Training of early childhood education and care staff, *International Journal of Educational Research*, 33: 31–53.

Nelson, M.K. (1989) Negotiating care: relationships between family daycare providers and mothers, *Feminist Studies*, 15(1): 7–33.

Nelson, M.K. (1994) Family day care providers: dilemmas of daily practice, in E. Nakano (ed.) *Mothering: Ideology, Experience, Agency*. New York: Routledge.

Rose, M. (1999) *Explaining and Forecasting Job Satisfaction: The Contribution of Occupational Profiling*. Bath: University of Bath.

Saggers, S. and Grant, J. (1999) 'I love children, and four-pence a week is four-pence!' Contradictions of caring in family day care, *Journal of Family Studies*, 5(1): 69–83.

Singer, E. (1992) *Child Care: The Psychology of Development*. London: Routledge.

Statham, J., Dillon, J. and Moss, P. (2001) *Placed and Paid for: Supporting Families through Sponsored Day Care*. London: Stationery Office.

Thomson, K. (1996) Working mothers: choice or circumstance? in R. Jowell, J. Curtice, A. Park, L. Brook, D. Ahrendt and K. Thomson (eds) *British Social Attitudes: The 12th Report*. Aldershot: Dartmouth.

Twomey, B. (2001) Women in the labour market: results from the spring 2000 LFS, *Labour Market Trends*, February: 93–106.

Vincent, C. and Ball, S.J. (1999) A market in love? Choosing pre-school child care. Paper presented to the British Educational Research Association Conference, Sussex, September.

Promoting children's health through nursing care

HELEN CHALMERS and PETER AGGLETON

Introduction

This chapter considers the role of health care and health carers, particularly nurses, in the promotion of children's health. As such, it aims to complement other chapters in this book that focus more specifically upon social care and childcare contexts and settings. Our analysis is set against a background of recent significant change in the way children and their rights are conceptualized, and at a time when the implementation of the *NHS Plan* (DH 2000) in Britain has resulted in the establishment of a National Children's Taskforce. The taskforce aims to establish new and better ways of working with, and for, children that will secure them a healthier future. As chairman of this taskforce, Aynsley-Green (2001) has highlighted the crucial role that nurses play as advocates for children and young people receiving care. This chapter will also have a particular focus on the role that nurses can play in the promotion of children's health, through recognizing the broader importance of children's rights, through advocacy and through direct care.

We shall begin by considering the historical background against which current initiatives in children's nursing care are set, and will explore the importance of developing a clear focus on children's health and well-being rather than on ill-health. Among other international human rights frameworks, the UN Convention on the Rights of the Child (CRC) will be examined for its usefulness as a framework in planning and developing children's nursing care. While not often directly used within the field of children's nursing, the CRC transcends some alternative approaches by focusing on children's *rights* within the care context, rather than upon their 'needs' alone. The relevance of different conceptual models of nursing to a rights-based approach to children's care is subsequently explored, together with their potential applicability to the care of children in hospitals, hospices and in the community. Finally, attention is given to the impact of current health and social services developments for the future well-being of children in the UK. Again, the focus will be upon issues of special relevance to nursing care.

Historical background

Several themes emerge when exploring historical accounts of the health care of children, both before and after the establishment of the UK National Health Service (NHS) in 1948. Of particular importance is the relationship between children and the adults who cared for them and the environment in which care took place.

On many occasions, especially when children experienced a mild degree of ill-health, the adults caring for them were their parents but this was not usually the case if a child was deemed to be very sick. When other adults became involved, and if the child was not orphaned or permanently separated from its parents, there was a new relationship to be negotiated between the designated carers (usually nurses) and the parents. Whatever the authority within these relationships, it rarely if ever rested with the child, who was generally regarded as the passive recipient of a routinized care process. Concern for children's rights was rarely made explicit and in most cases was probably not considered.

Adults, and in particular health care professionals, were regarded as the experts where issues of child care and child health were concerned. Such a view gave little or no power to children and frequently little or no power to their parents. The physical needs of the sick child tended to be the main focus of care and health professionals, among others, failed to give adequate thought to the emotional and social needs, or rights, of the children they encountered. Certainly, until the late 1950s in the UK, many carers believed that whatever they did, they were acting in the best interests of the child. After publication of the Platt Report (Ministry of Health 1959), however, there was a growing acknowledgement that children had important needs beyond the physical ones.[1] Despite more attention then being given to emotional and social concerns, the authority to identify and intervene around a range of needs remained with adults.

It was to be rather longer before the rights of the child per se were seen as important. Indeed before that, the rights of parents to participate in the care of their child in hospital was a hurdle still to be crossed, especially as hospitals were not legally required to implement the Platt Report's proposals. However, groups of parents were formed to put pressure on local hospitals to adopt the recommendations of the report. In 1963 these groups amalgamated and in 1965 became the National Association for the Welfare of Children in Hospital (NAWCH, now Action for Sick Children), with both parents and health professionals as members. Once some progress on unrestricted visiting and parental access to children in hospital had been achieved, NAWCH (1984) published its *Charter for Children*, which began to focus on standard setting for children in health care and was one of the first documents to mention children's and parents' *rights* within a nursing context. Statement 2, for example, stated that:

> Children in hospital shall have the right to have their parents with them at all times provided this is in the best interest of the child.
>
> (cited in Alderson and O'Toole 1988: 32)

Also important was the environment in which care was provided. It is relatively recently, in historical terms, that institutional care, in a variety of forms, has been questioned as the most appropriate environment for childcare outside the family. Indeed, prior to the late twentieth century the term 'hospital' is found not only in descriptions of health care settings, but also in relation to the care of children more generally. For example, in 1739 Thomas Coram established a well-known Foundling Hospital to provide care for 'foundling' and homeless children in London. Other similar hospitals were subsequently established elsewhere in the UK.

The Hospital for Sick Children, Great Ormond Street, was the first specialized hospital for children in Britain, and it opened in 1852. From then until the end of the nineteenth century, parental involvement in the care of hospitalized children was not as limited as it was to become in the early twentieth century and in the years following the setting up of the NHS. Mothers were welcome to visit at specified times, as this was felt to provide an opportunity for nurses to educate them in child care. As early as 1850, according to Kosky (1989), the *Edinburgh Medical and Surgical Journal* was advocating that mothers should be resident with their children in the newly established children's hospitals, although the numbers who were enabled to do this were small.

In the early twentieth century, restrictions on parents visiting began to tighten, in part due to increasing concerns about cross-infection, and in part due to more formal nurse training which made nurses more conscious of their skills and status. The presence of parents was seen as disruptive to the timely completion of routine nursing tasks. There was also anxiety about the perceived adverse effects of parents' visits on their children's well-being. Such concerns generally associated the well-behaved and quiet child with the happy child.

The Platt Report and after

The 1959 Platt Report was one of the first government inquiries to question the restricted and closed environment in which most sick children were cared for. Until then, NHS hospitals either forbade visiting altogether or had extremely restricted visiting times on children's wards, sometimes as little as half-an-hour a week. Rarely was any attempt made to accommodate parents wishing to remain with their child. The work of John Bowlby in particular was key in alerting the more receptive of health professionals to the potential long-term risks of separation (from their mother especially) and the consequences for children's emotional security and well-being (Bowlby 1969). There were other psychologists at this time raising similar concerns about the damaging effects of separation on children, most notably Robertson (1958) and Rutter (1972). Robertson's films *A Two Year Old Goes to Hospital* (1953) and *Going to Hospital with Mother* (1953) were shown widely on television in the 1950s and thus brought the issues to a wider audience.

The Platt Report (Ministry of Health 1959) also highlighted the importance of meeting children's emotional needs and advocated unrestricted visiting for parents (although this was to be at the ward sister's discretion) and the admission of mothers, rather than fathers, to hospital with their young children. At the same time the report stressed that admission of children to hospital should be avoided if possible, with additional services provided to care for them at home. Progress in meeting the report's recommendations was slow, however, and the disadvantages of children being separated from their parents by hospitalization were still of concern when the Court Report, from the Child Health Services Committee, was published in 1976.

Why was change so slow? There are many reasons, but central among these may have been nurses' unwillingness to be convinced by ideas associated with psychoanalysis, and their reluctance to break with past practice (Cleary 1992: 9).

During the 1960s, research studies by health professionals (for example MacCarthy 1962; Mahaffy 1965; Brain and Maclay 1968) began to examine the benefits of having mothers admitted to hospital along with their sick children. With the results of such studies came an increased willingness to view parental, and in particular maternal, involvement in a more positive light. Consequently, pressure on health professionals and health service managers to accommodate mothers and later, parents, with their children grew. However, changes to hospital practice were slow to materialize and, as late as the 1970s, writers such as Hawthorne (1974) identified that too many children were still experiencing long separations from their parents.

Connell and Bradley (2000) cite three particular reasons for the continuation of restricted visiting. First, from a medical model perspective, they identify the supposed increased cross-infection risk to children when people from outside the hospital were allowed in. Second, they argue that contemporary childcare practices both at home and in institutions strongly favoured strict routines including those associated with eating and sleeping. Such routines were easier to achieve in hospital in the absence of parents. Also, nursing staff noted that children appeared less troublesome and quieter if their parents stayed away. Third, they note the belief by some nurses that their workload would increase if parents were more frequently with their children in the ward. Connell and Bradley (2000) also lay considerable responsibility for the reluctance to embrace the recommendations of the Platt Report with nurses. A key factor here was what they call 'professional selfishness'. Nurses may have been reluctant to allow greater parental involvement in care because 'parental participation requires nurses to relinquish control and power, and where the nurse values direct contact and desires a close relationship with the child the parent may be viewed as an intruder' (Connell and Bradley 2000: 34).

Hospitals are not the only environment in which care of the sick child takes place. Increasingly in the late twentieth century, the emotional value to children of being cared for at home has been recognized. As early as 1888, the Hospital for Sick Children, Great Ormond Street, set up a private domiciliary nursing service, not in recognition of the benefit of caring for sick children in their own homes, but to boost the hospital's income (Hunt and Whiting 1999). The service, which involved nurses taking up residence with the family, was dissolved at the inception of the NHS in 1948. In contrast, today's community nursing service for children did grow from a desire to improve the well-being of children receiving health care.

Thus, despite increasing concern about the environment best suited to the care of children, beginning with the Platt Report recommending care at home whenever possible, it is only since the 1980s that a community nursing service for children has been available nationally, and that service provision has begun explicitly to recognize the rights of children. As Gow and Ridgway (1993) put it,

> These developments represent a major step forward in the widely-held belief that children should have the right to be cared for at home by an appropriately trained nurse, thereby ensuring that the individual needs of each child can be met.
>
> (Gow and Ridgway 1993: 270)

At about the same time, in 1982, the first children's hospice opened in Oxford as a specific response to the special needs of children who have a disease with no reasonable expectation of a cure, and concern for their families. The concept of 'need' has been the overt theme in the setting up of children's hospices and for developing this aspect of the concept of care. Less overt has been awareness that dying children have the same rights to all that the hospice movement can offer their adult equivalents.

A rights-based approach to children's care

It will be clear from what has been said that, until relatively recently, the best interests and the rights of the child have scarcely featured in the planning and practice of nursing care. When interest in the child has been expressed, this has usually been within the context of the 'needs' which children were presumed to have. The impact of 1950s and 1960s developmental psychology should not be underemphasized in this respect (see Rose 1985, 1990) and its uncritical application in the hands of health professionals, including nurses, led to emotional and behavioural difficulties both on admission to hospital and afterwards. As recently as 1990, Cross followed up 50 young children (from 2 to 7 years of age) after discharge from hospital and found that 54 per cent experienced difficulties when they returned home. Cross (1990) found evidence of diverse behavioural problems including those to do with sleeping and with family relationships.

An alternative approach would have us understand children not as the subjects of needs but as the bearers of rights. While these two perspectives may not ultimately be mutually exclusive, an emphasis on children's rights can help us think more critically about the nature and quality of nursing care.

In late 1989, the UN General Assembly unanimously adopted the Convention on the Rights of the Child. The CRC is a universally agreed set of non-negotiable standards and obligations that spell out children's basic human rights. Children's rights highlighted by the Convention include the right to survival; the right to develop to the fullest; the right to protection from harmful influences, abuse and exploitation; and the right to participate fully in family, cultural and social life. A series of underlying values – sometimes described as 'guiding principles' – exist to guide the way each right is fulfilled and respected. The Convention's four guiding principles are those of non-discrimination (Article 2), the best interests of the child (Article 3), survival and development (Article 6) and participation (Article 12). Each one is detailed below with brief examples of how it might impact on children's health care delivery.

Four guiding principles

Non-discrimination
Article 2 of the CRC requires that the rights of all children be protected and promoted. It clearly prohibits discrimination against children based on their or their parents' or legal guardians' actual or perceived 'race, colour, sex, language, religion, political or other opinion, national, ethnic or social origin, property, disability, birth or other status.' An important part of this for health professionals, for example, is to ensure that written information about service and treatment options is available in a variety of languages so that parents and guardians can make truly informed choices. In addition, in many parts of the UK, health care workers need easy access to translators if they are to be confident that they have understood the wishes of those who speak on behalf of young children, and indeed the wishes expressed by young children themselves.

Best interests of the child
Article 3 of the CRC requires that the best interests of the child be a primary consideration when decisions are made which concern the child. The interests of the child are therefore put on equal footing with the interests of all others including parents, families, communities and the state.[2] A major challenge here, for all those involved in children's health care, is to establish channels of communication and forums for discussion that do not

disadvantage those who are not professionals. For some, this might include thinking carefully about ways of talking with and listening to children and their parents so that their views can be taken into account. Health professionals have already taken some simple steps toward this, for example by avoiding wearing uniforms or making them look less 'clinical'.

Survival and development

Article 6 of the CRC emphasizes children's right to benefit from economic and social policies, which allow them to survive into adulthood and to develop in the broadest sense of the word. It thereby allows the child to benefit from all other rights outlined in the Convention. There is a particular role in this regard for those who work with children from families experiencing poverty. Very often parents are unaware of the welfare benefits to which they and their children are entitled and/or they find the methods of claiming benefit difficult to use. A sensitive health or social care worker should be able to act in an advisory capacity or, in some instances, act for a family. Orem's (1985) model of nursing, mentioned later in this chapter, describes nurses having an educative/supportive role in some circumstances and at times sees nurses acting for others.

Participation

Article 12 of the CRC highlights the child's right to express an opinion and have it listened to and taken into account in all matters concerning the child. Promoting children's right to participation, and creating opportunities for their voices to be heard, is of crucial significance. In hospital and hospice care for children, there is a special need for health carers to develop ways of enabling children to contribute to decisions about their care. Tools need to take many factors into account including a child's ethnicity, age and competencies. For example, pain assessment tools sometimes feature facial expressions so that even very young children can contribute to the management of their pain and to the evaluation of pain-relieving interventions.

Article 24 of the CRC specifically recognizes the right of the child to the enjoyment of the highest attainable standard of health, and to facilities for the treatment of illness and the rehabilitation of health. Beyond this can be discerned three clusters of children's rights, which between them provide the basis for organizing and planning nursing care. First, there is a set of rights relevant to what might loosely be called the 'preventive' aspects of health promotion. Then there is a set of rights relevant to protection and adequate care. A third set of rights relates to especially vulnerable children.

Rights to prevention

Several articles within the CRC recognize the child's right to the education and information that will allow them to make health-related choices. Article 13, for example, recognizes children's right to seek, receive and impart information and ideas of all kinds, regardless of frontiers, either orally, in writing or in print. Articles 17 and 28 establish the grounds for a child's access to scientifically accurate and impartial information about health matters, including health protection. Article 17, for example, recognizes the importance of the mass media and the child's right of access to information and material from a diversity of national and international sources, especially those aimed at the promotion of the child's social, spiritual and moral well-being and physical and mental health. Article 28 of the CRC recognizes the child's rights to education and the importance of international cooperation in eliminating ignorance and illiteracy and facilitating access to scientific and technical knowledge. Between them, these rights lay the foundations for children's access to relevant knowledge and understanding, as well as the development of the life skills and dispositions that will enable them to lead healthy lives.

For many children, learning about health-related information takes place in school, and teachers and health professionals can work together to develop programmes and activities to suit various age groups. A useful workbook for young children to help them learn about which adults to trust has been developed by Lenderyou (1993). For older children, Fitzsimmins et al. (1999), working at the Royal Belfast Hospital for Sick Children, set up a project, in response to the DHSS *Charter Standards for Children and Young People* (1997), to produce an information pack focusing on the rights of young people in hospital.

Right to protection and adequate care

Article 9 of the CRC seeks to ensure that children will not be separated from their parents against their will except in accordance with applicable law. Article 16 provides the child with protection against arbitrary or unlawful interference with their privacy, family or home. Article 19 of the CRC seeks to protect the child against all forms of physical or mental violence, injury or abuse, neglect or negligent treatment, maltreatment or exploitation, while receiving care. Article 31 recognizes the child's right to rest and leisure, and to engage in play and recreational activities appropriate to their age. Article 39 of the CRC calls upon States Parties to take all appropriate measures to promote physical and psychological recovery and social reintegration of a child victim of: any form of neglect, exploitation or abuse; torture or any other form of cruel, inhuman or degrading treatment or punishment; or armed conflicts. As indicated earlier, the National Children's Taskforce aims to secure a healthier future for children and, as part of this, nurses have an important advocacy role to play in ensuring that children are protected from negligent treatment and are cared for in an environment that allows for rest and recreation.

The rights of especially vulnerable children

Beyond the above rights, the CRC recognizes that certain groups of children may be especially vulnerable, and seeks to make provision for their special situation. Article 22 of the CRC, for example, calls upon States Parties to take appropriate measures to ensure that a child who is seeking refugee status or who is considered a refugee shall receive appropriate protection and human- itarian assistance, including help tracing the parents or other members of the family and obtaining information necessary for reunification with his or her family. Article 23 of the CRC recognizes that mentally or physically disabled children have the right to enjoy a full and decent life, in conditions which ensure dignity, promote self-reliance and facilitate the child's active parti- cipation in the community. Together, these two provisions aim to promote and protect the rights of children in especially vulnerable circumstances. Children who are in hospital for long periods may be seen as especially vulnerable. Modern medical techniques mean that some children with malig- nant disease are nursed in isolation for prolonged periods of time, usually to protect them from infection when they are immuno-compromised. There are difficult decisions to be taken in such situations to ensure that restric- tions that are medically advisable take into account the rights of children to enjoy a full and active life.

Models of nursing and their relevance

In the previous section, we identified some current concerns in health care that can be seen to address, in part at least, some of the issues highlighted in the Convention on the Rights of the Child. However, in most cases these ideas and activities demonstrate what might be considered good practice but are not explicitly part of a recognized, rights-based approach to nursing care. Such an approach would have as its ultimate aim the right of children to enjoy the highest standard of health possible so that they can develop into adulthood. In addition, it would advocate care that was inclusive, that pro- tected the child from all forms of abuse, including poor standards of care, and that encouraged children's participation in the care process.

What follows are some ways in which such an approach might be applied within nursing practice. We shall look at how the application of a variety of different conceptual models of nursing to the care of children can help nurses maintain a focus on rights as well as on needs.

So far the terms *care* and *caring* have been used but not defined. *Caring* in nursing has many dimensions and as such it is difficult to produce a satisfactory definition. It is a widely used term and in itself seems to indicate to many something of value. Yet the word is often used loosely, including by nurses, and other health care professionals, to identify what is done in nursing practice. For some, caring encompasses the physical, emotional, social and spiritual needs that people being nursed may have and which nurses attempt to recognize and address. Most nursing models work with this kind of understanding.

The influential US nurse, Patricia Benner, has taken up Skipper's (1965) distinction between the instrumental and expressive roles in nursing care

(Benner 1984). She argues that these two elements are and need to be fused in nursing, and that what nurses do is intimately linked both to meaning and ethics. It is possible to see the beginnings of a more rights-based approach to care when ethical considerations are seen as important although traditional ethical concerns do not focus specifically on human rights. More recently, Brykczynska (1992: 3) has pointed to the fact that 'Nurse theorists and educationalists, even if they have difficulty in defining care, are adamant however, about its intrinsic value and place within the profession of nursing'.

Darbyshire (1990) too has pointed to the importance of caring within nursing, and has advocated for a clearer focus on care within the different frameworks – or models – within which nursing is planned and takes place. To date, most nursing models do not explicitly define caring nor do they take an overtly ethical stance. They do, however, offer a variety of ways in which the practice of nursing can be understood. As we have argued elsewhere (Aggleton and Chalmers 2000) nursing models provide a knowledge base about people (adults or children) from which nurses can develop their professional practice. Implicitly, therefore, a high standard of care is achieved when nursing interventions are in accord with the nature of the people for whom care is provided. So, for example, an understanding that people increasingly live in a multicultural and multi-faith society would lead to the increased development of appropriate care options. Similarly, an understanding that children have specific rights would result in, for example, a focus on ways of determining what treatments are in a child's best interests.

Nursing models first appeared in the nursing literature in the 1980s, although some nurse theorists, such as Hildegarde Peplau and Virginia Henderson, had explored similar ideas somewhat earlier (Peplau 1952; Henderson 1966). In essence, nursing models offer ways of thinking about and delivering care that go beyond a medical model approach. They do this by developing understandings about the nature of individuals that pay careful attention to the contribution of various disciplines such as psychology and sociology, as well as to those that see adults and children simply as made up of anatomical parts and physiological systems.

Most nursing models take a 'needs approach' to the health of adults in particular, and few, if any, have much explicitly to say about children's rights. However, some models are much closer than others to working from a rights-based framework. It is these models that we shall focus on here. First, however, the contribution that nursing models make to the planning and delivery of care and to the care environment will be outlined. The 1980 definition offered by Riehl (later Riehl-Sisca) and Roy remains helpful in explicating the contribution to nursing practice that models can make:

> a systematically, constructed, scientifically based, and logically related set of concepts which identify the essential components of nursing practice together with the theoretical basis of these concepts and values required for their use by the practitioner.
>
> (Riehl and Roy 1980: 6)

Of note in this definition is the *systematic* nature of nursing models, which evolve from nurses' own observations and from existing fields of enquiry that have relevance to care and the care environment. They are intended to *guide* nursing practice and they help to identify the *values* with which nurses should work. Nursing models are not rigid sets of ideas and procedures to which nurses must adhere. Rather, they are philosophical understandings that encourage nurses to think critically and creatively, within a given framework, about the care they offer. In this way, they encourage nurses to incorporate new and important ideas into their practice without the need to abandon a model's main tenets.

So, for example, a clear recognition that children's rights have been underemphasized in nursing practice in the past may not necessitate a new model of nursing. What it may require instead is for nurses and other carers to examine in detail what existing models have to offer, and how they can or cannot easily accommodate a more rights-based approach. Part of this examination will challenge nurses to find ways of reconciling a traditional needs approach to care with an approach that places more emphasis on the rights of the child.

Sometimes, however, nurses develop apparently new models in response to particular concerns. For example, the work of Casey (1988, 1990, 1993) has been notable. As a paediatric nurse at the Hospital for Sick Children, Great Ormond Street, London, she recognized the inadequacies of nurses acting inconsistently because they lacked a common body of understanding (a nursing model) about the care of children. She describes a universal acknowledgement of the desirability of 'family-centred' care, but found its implementation by nurses to be inconsistent.

> In one ward it might mean that parents were allowed to visit all day – the word 'allowed' implying a kind of grudging permission. In the ward next door it might mean that families were welcomed and parents actively encouraged in caring for their child.
>
> (Casey 1993: 184)

Drawing to some extent on the nursing model developed by Orem in 1985, Casey explored the concepts of self-care, nursing agency and nurses' educative role to begin defining the understandings of her partnership model for children's nursing. Largely, she was responding to a variety of accepted 'needs', such as the need for families to remain involved in their child's care, rather than a recognition of any specific children's rights. In addition, needs were still being determined by professional 'experts' and parents, with scant regard for the child's right to participate in care decisions. Indeed, the whole premise of Casey's partnership model is a partnership between nurses and children's families, not between nurses and children. In her later writing, there is an acknowledgement that so far children's views on the partnership model have not been sought (Casey 1993).

Nursing models have a number of key components described and illustrated elsewhere (Aggleton and Chalmers 2000). All have their starting point, however, in what is taken to be true about the nature of people. It is therefore this understanding that needs to be focused upon if we are to see how some nursing models might facilitate a more rights-based approach to child health care in hospitals, in hospices and in the community.

Riehl's model of nursing is unusual in that it emphasizes the capacity of people to give meaning to the situations in which they find themselves, to the events in which they take part, and to their relationships with others (Riehl-Sisca 1989). While Riehl-Sisca does not write specifically about children or their rights, there are clear implications within a symbolic interactionist approach (see for example Mead 1934; Thomas 1967) for thought to be given to the environment of care in which children might find themselves, and for the symbols they might try to understand. To illustrate this, the environment of an Accident and Emergency (A&E) Department will briefly be considered.

Estimates vary as to the number of children who attend A&E Departments annually, but the Royal College of Nursing (RCN 1995) suggests that in some departments children make up over 45 per cent of all attendances. Smith (1997: 22) acknowledges that 'A&E Departments are full of distressing sights and sounds' and children's experiences of such settings can be especially traumatic. By using a model such as that developed by Riehl-Sisca (1989), nurses can be encouraged to consider ways in which the best interests (Article 3 CRC) of the child can be addressed. For example, and in line with government recommendations (Audit Commission 1993), they can be active in ensuring that children have access to designated facilities even when there is not a completely separate department. Such facilities should include waiting, treatment and resuscitation areas designed to minimize the potential for distress. Thought should be given to the symbols present in the environment, including smells and sounds, so that as far as possible children are protected (Article 19 CRC) from the additional anxiety of trying to make sense of the unfamiliar. The use of homely decorations and furnishings and the provision of age-relevant toys and books can all help to render an environment more familiar.

Efforts to construct an environment of care that is supportive of and non-threatening to children and their families have always been a concern of the hospice movement both in the provision of care for adults and for children. Many adult hospices now have designated children's rooms where a less formal environment, devoid of symbols associated with terminal care, can help children to play and to talk about their fears and concerns. Children's hospices try to provide rooms that are as much like a home environment as possible and where families can stay together. Staff may still wear uniforms, but these are usually as informal and non-threatening in appearance as possible.

Riehl-Sisca's model also highlights the importance of the child's relationship with others and what he or she may learn by observing the behaviour of others. Nurses will want to develop their interpersonal skills such that they can gain a child's trust and talk and act in ways that promote dialogue and discussion suitable to a child's level of competence. Article 12 of the CRC talks of making opportunities for the child's voice to be heard, and this presents specific challenges for a sick or unhappy child.

King's (1981) model of nursing focuses specifically on needs: the need for information; the need for preventive care; the need for care from others when unable to cope alone. In a rights-based context, nurses should consider exploring how such a needs-focused approach could be developed to address related children's rights such as those expressed in Article 13 of the CRC among other provisions. Thus, nurses working with King's model might devote time to preparing information in many diverse forms to ensure that children can gain access to it in ways appropriate to their age, competences, gender and ethnicity.

Community children's nurses working with those who are particularly vulnerable might turn to King's model for guidance on how best to offer care to disabled children. Article 23 of the CRC recognizes that mentally or physically disabled children have the right to enjoy a full and decent life including active participation in the community. King's focus on the need for care when unable to cope, could enable nurses trying to incorporate a rights-based approach to care to consider how they can address issues of social exclusion such that the child's own ability to cope is enhanced. At a relatively simple level, nurses can be active in making sure access for disabled children to community facilities is at the forefront of local policy initiatives. More challengingly, however, nurses might involve themselves in helping others work towards greater acceptance of disabled children and young people into community activities and events.

We have written elsewhere about the use of patient controlled analgesia (PCA) for adults being cared for by nurses working with Orem's self-care model (Aggleton and Chalmers 2000). While the challenges of using a self-care model that goes beyond family involvement to more actively involving children themselves in self-care is yet to be fully explored, some early studies have begun. Colwell et al. (1993) report on the use of PCA for selected children, generally 10 years or older, following surgical techniques. From their first pilot studies, they identify two notable outcomes that would find support in Articles 12 and 24 of the CRC. Article 12 highlights children's right to express an opinion and to participate. PCA encourages a child to decide on the need for analgesia and to take control, to some extent, of the analgesia administered. Article 24 explores children's right to treatment facilities. PCA has traditionally been provided for adults but not for children. In their study, Colwell et al. (1993) found that with the use of PCA, the emotional trauma often associated with injections was prevented and the children felt in control of their own pain relief.

A self-care model of nursing such as Orem's (1985) can also be a useful guide for those trying to meet young people's rights to appropriate sexual health services. Children and young people need relevant, sensitive and timely information about their emotional and sexual lives delivered by people they trust and in an environment where confidentiality issues are understood and discussed. Such information enables young people to make their own considered decisions about behaviour. Article 17 of the CRC is of particular relevance here, since it recognizes the child's right of access to information and material from a diversity of national and international sources, especially those aimed at the promotion of their social, spiritual and moral well-being and physical and mental health. All too often, children and young people are denied information about sexual matters in the mistaken belief that this will somehow protect their 'innocence'. There is now abundant evidence to suggest that, contrary to popular belief, good quality education about sex, sexuality and sexual relationships does not encourage young people to become sexually active. Instead, it is much more likely to delay the onset of intercourse and encourage risk reduction among those who are already sexually active (Grunseit 1997).

Conclusion: the nurse as advocate

Associated with all current approaches to nursing practice is a much debated nursing role, and one recognized as especially critical in a care context for children and young people (Aynsley-Green 2001), namely that of advocate. In an interesting article exploring advocacy, ethics and children's rights, Charles-Edwards (2001) points to the complex nature of advocacy for nurses and the challenges to be met if children's voices are to be heard. She concludes:

> The role of the children's nurse acting as an advocate therefore is about upholding the rights of the weak, in this case children, to have a say about the way in which health services are provided: self-advocacy. This is not the same as saying what we think children need or only listening to the views of adult parents or collective advocacy groups.
>
> (Charles-Edwards 2001: 14)

In the future there will be many other ways in which an embracing of the importance of children's rights in the context of health promotion and health care might be manifest. First, and as identified by Charles-Edwards (2001), there is scope for much more involvement of children in the planning and evaluation of services. For this to take place, health professionals will need to acknowledge the legitimacy of children's views and will need to move away from regarding themselves as the only 'experts' in child care issues. Balen et al. (2000–01: 24) argue that for too long research has expected children 'to communicate in an adult frame of reference', and highlight the need for methods that will empower children to take a significant role in research of relevance to their health and health care needs. The authors advocate a raft of research methods including individual and group interviews and expression through play, painting and drawing.

Tessa Woodfield (2001) has also written about involving children in health care decision-making, and as service users across a range of care services. She particularly favours the development of tools suitable to involve children themselves in clinical audit and warns against relying on findings from parents that may not equate with their children's views. Her article challenges the views of those who believe that gaining access to children's views is either too difficult or not worthwhile. Indeed, as Chapter 11 in this book demonstrates, a rich variety of techniques are available which may help to elicit children's perspectives on their lives and well-being. Gradually, the provision of care services for children may better reflect concerns about children's rights. Indeed, several important grassroots developments are already under way. Among these, the Child Friendly Healthcare Initiative (CFHI: Southall et al. 2000) has proposed twelve standards based on the CRC to underpin the care that children and their families should receive as of right. The challenge for nurses and other health care workers lies in working creatively to develop such frameworks for the enhanced well-being of children and young people all over the world.

Notes

1 The Platt Report, *The Welfare of Children in Hospital*, outlined recommendations on the non-medical aspects of care for children in hospital (Ministry of Health 1959). It particularly noted the importance of recognizing and meeting the emotional needs of children and emphasized the role of parents in preparing children for hospital care whenever this was possible.
2 Importantly, the best interest principle (although with less of a rights focus) is reinforced in the Children Act 1989 (DH 1991), which focuses on promoting and safeguarding the welfare of all children.

References

Aggleton, P. and Chalmers, H. (2000) *Nursing Models and Nursing Practice*. Basingstoke: Palgrave.

Alderson, P. and O'Toole, M. (1988) *Your Child in Hospital: A Parent's Handbook*, 4th edn. London: National Association for the Welfare of Children in Hospital.

Audit Commission (1993) *Children First: A Study of Hospital Services*. London: HMSO.

Aynsley-Green, A. (2001) The NHS Children's Taskforce and National Service Framework, *Paediatric Nursing*, 13(4): 10.

Balen, R., Holroyd, C., Mountain, G. and Wood, B. (2000–01) Giving children a voice: methodological and practical implications of research involving children, *Paediatric Nursing*, 12(10): 24–9.

Benner, P. (1984) *From Novice to Expert*. London: Addison-Wesley.

Bowlby, J. (1969) *Attachment and Loss*. New York: Basic Books.

Brain, D.T. and Maclay, I. (1968) Controlled study of mothers and children in hospital, *British Medical Journal*, 1: 278–80.

Brykczynska, G. (1992) Caring – a dying art?, in M. Jolley and G. Brykczynska (1992) *Nursing Care: The Challenge to Change*. London: Edward Arnold.

Casey, A. (1988) A partnership with child and family, *Senior Nurse*, 8(4): 8–9.

Casey, A. (1990) Nursing models in curriculum planning, in S. Pendleton and A. Myles (eds) *Curriculum Planning in Nurse Education*. London: Edward Arnold.

Casey, A. (1993) Development and use of the partnership model of nursing care, in E.A. Glasper and A. Tucker (eds) *Advances in Child Health Nursing*. Oxford: Scutari.

Charles-Edwards, I. (2001) Children's nursing and advocacy: are we in a muddle?, *Paediatric Nursing*, 13(2): 12–16.

Child Health Services Committee (1976) *Fit for the Future* (Court Report). London: DHSS, DES and Welsh Office.

Cleary, J. (1992) *Caring for Children in Hospital*. London: Scutari.

Colwell, V., Fretwell, R.M., Sury, R. et al. (1993) Advances in paediatric surgery, in E.A. Glasper and A. Tucker (eds) *Advances in Child Health Nursing*. London: Scutari.

Connell, J. and Bradley, S. (2000) Visiting children in hospital, *Paediatric Nursing*, 12(3): 33–5.

Cross, C. (1990) Home from hospital, *Nursery World*, 90(3228): 22–3.

Darbyshire, P. (1990) The heart of the matter, *Nursing Times*, 86(47): 63–4.

Department of Health (1991) *The Children Act 1989: An Introductory Guide for the NHS*. London: HMSO.

Department of Health (2000) *NHS Plan*. London: Department of Health.

Department of Health and Social Security (1997) *Charter Standards for Children and Young People*. London: DHSS.

Fitzsimmins, C., Coulter, P. and McDonald, J. (1999) Creating a special information pack for adolescents in hospital, *Nursing Times*, 95(23): 50–2.

Gow, P. and Ridgway, G. (1993) The development of a paediatric community service, in E.A. Glasper and A. Tucker (eds) *Advances in Child Health Nursing*. London: Scutari.

Grunseit, A. (1997) *Impact of HIV and Sexual Health Education on the Sexual Behaviour of Young People: A Review Update*. Geneva: UNAIDS.

Hawthorne, P.J. (1974) *Nurse, I Want my Mummy!* London: Royal College of Nursing.

Henderson, V. (1966) *The Nature of Nursing: A Definition and its Implications for Practice, Research and Education*. New York: Macmillan.

Hunt, J. and Whiting, M. (1999) A re-examination of the history of children's community nursing, *Paediatric Nursing*, 11(4): 33–6.

King, I.M. (1981) *A Theory for Nursing: Systems, Concepts, Process*. New York: John Wiley.

Kosky, J. (1989) *Mutual Friends: Charles Dickens and Great Ormond Street Children's Hospital*. London: Weidenfeld and Nicolson.

Lenderyou, G. (1993) *Primary School Workbook: Teaching Sex Education within the New National Curriculum*. London: FPA.

MacCarthy, D. (1962) Children in hospital with mothers, *Lancet*, 24 March: 603–8.

Mahaffy, P.R. (1965) The effects of hospitalisation on children admitted for tonsillectomy and adenoidectomy, *Nursing Research*, 14: 12–19.

Mead, G.H. (1934) *Mind, Self and Society*. Chicago: University of Chicago Press.

Ministry of Health (1959) *The Welfare of Children in Hospital* (Platt Report). London: HMSO.

National Association for the Welfare of Children in Hospital (NAWCH) (1984) *Charter for Children*. London: NAWCH.

Orem, D. (1985) *Nursing: Concepts of Practice*. New York: McGraw-Hill.

Peplau, H.E. (1952) *Interpersonal Relations in Nursing*. New York: Putnam's Sons.

Riehl, J.P. and Roy, C. (eds) (1980) *Conceptual Models for Nursing Practice*. Norwalk, CT: Appleton-Century-Crofts.

Riehl-Sisca, J.P. (1989) The Riehl interaction model, in J.P. Riehl-Sisca (ed.) *Conceptual Models for Nursing Practice*. Norwalk, CT: Appleton and Lange.

Robertson, J. (1958) *Young Children in Hospital*. London: Tavistock.

Rose, N. (1985) *The Psychological Complex: Psychology, politics and society in England, 1869–1939*. London: Routledge and Kegan Paul.

Rose, N. (1990) *Governing the Soul: The Shaping of the Private Self*. London: Routledge.

Royal College of Nursing (RCN) Children in A&E Special Interest Group (1995) *Facilities for Children in A&E Departments in the UK*. London: Royal College of Nursing.

Rutter, M. (1972) *Maternal Deprivation Reassessed*. Harmondsworth: Penguin.

Skipper, J.K. (1965) The role of the hospital nurse: is it instrumental or expressive?, in J.K. Skipper and R.C. Leonard (eds) *Social Interaction and Patient Care*. Philadelphia, PA: Lippincott.

Smith, F. (1997) Children's rights and A&E services, *Paediatric Nursing*, 9(9): 22–4

Southall, D., Burr, S., Smith, R.D. et al. (2000) The Child Friendly Initiative (CFHI): healthcare provision in accordance with the UN Convention on the Rights of the Child, *Paediatrics*, 106(5): 1054–64.

Thomas, W.I. (1967) *The Unadjusted Girl*. New York: Harper and Row.

Woodfield, T. (2001) Involving children in clinical audit, *Paediatric Nursing*, 13(3): 12–16.

P A R T **III**

Care and family life

Care-giving and independence in four-generation families

JULIA BRANNEN, PETER MOSS and ANN MOONEY

Introduction

Modern welfare states, in their inception, assumed the existence not only of a male breadwinner but also of a female housewife and unpaid carer (Daly and Lewis 1998). Feminist research has made visible, and a subject of debate, the extent and consequences of unpaid care, largely undertaken in families by women. In this chapter we focus on care by women of relatives from their own family of origin and the family of their male partners. We shall refer to this as 'informal care' rather than 'unpaid care', since care of relatives may involve payment or material recompense.

It seems that we usually turn to our kin or give our kin care and assistance when there is deemed to be a 'significant need'. Needs, and therefore the giving and receiving of informal care, are structured by the life course: the transition to adulthood, the life course phases of child-rearing, divorce and other household change, and frail old age. This structuring of care in relation to the life course and its transitions – expected or unexpected – may in part explain why informal care is regarded as a labour of love and duty, not a market exchange: calculating the balance of reciprocity is frowned upon (for example Land and Rose 1985; Finch 1989; Graham 1991).

Yet, as studies increasingly show, family life is in practice actively negotiated rather than being lived according to taken for granted rules or guidelines. The giving of care is carried out by particular individuals (for example by one relative but not another) whose performance of care is part of a web of negotiations (Finch 1989; Finch and Mason 1993). Such processes are not bound by inflexible rules, but rather involve negotiation through practices. As the study by Finch and Mason (1993) suggests, there is a process of legitimation concerning when it is 'right and proper' to give or receive help and which persons are expected to give help and which persons may be excused from helping at any moment in time. Many considerations come into play, not least the matter of balancing dependence and independence, and sensitivities around being dependent: 'since there seems to be an expectation that older generations will give support to younger, and that people in the ascendant generation will continue to be net givers throughout their lifetime, it is a particularly sensitive issue for older people to be in a position of dependency' (Finch 1989: 170).

The preceding discussion highlights the generational nature of much informal care: care flows both across generations (for example from one partner to another), but also between generations (for example from grandparent to grandchild). A key position in intergenerational relations is held by the pivot generation and in particular the women in this generation who occupy the positions of daughter, mother and grandmother at the same time. They may find themselves providing care both to the younger and older generations when the next generation has young children and when the great-grandparent generations are themselves approaching, if not yet at, the upper end of old age. A recent survey of employees and retirees over the age of 50 found that one-fifth had caring responsibilities for both an elderly parent or parent-in-law and grandchildren although the extent and nature of the care varied (Mooney and Statham 2002).

Women in the pivot generation may occupy multiple roles, caught between the competing demands of parent care, childcare and employment (Brody et al. 1983; Stephens et al. 1994). There is little evidence to suggest that labour force participation by grandmothers is a major and consistent influence on involvement in grandparenting (Millward 1997; Attias-Donfut and Wolff 2000; Dench et al. 2000). Many women with a dependent child receive help from their own mothers particularly in the form of domestic tasks and childcare (Grundy et al. 1999). However, grandmothers may not want to be tied to full-time childcare while their daughters (in-law) work. Evidence suggests that they are more likely to provide childcare when their daughters (in-law) work part-time (Dench et al. 2000).

Because of their unique position, there may be an imbalance in the exchange of services between the pivot and other generations (Hagestadt 1985). The pivot generation may provide more support and resources to younger and older generations than it receives back from either. Of course this is at one particular stage in the life course and the 'pivots' may receive resources and support at earlier and later points in time (Finch 1989; Finch and Mason 1993).

Reciprocity is an important aspect of intergenerational relations. Care may typically be provided as if it was a labour of love, given without an overt and calculative expectation of return. However, the ways in which people define the world may not match their practices: some form of reciprocity may be assumed by giver or recipient, and care is, in fact, often reciprocated. Reciprocity may be specific, returned in much the same currency as offered and/or to the person who originally did the caring: for example, the provision of childcare services by one generation is seen as implying a commitment to 'repay' such help with care to the same person at a later point in the life course. Alternatively, the reciprocity may involve different currencies: help may be offered to grandparents in frail old age in exchange for earlier help with housing rather than, say, childcare. Or reciprocity may be more generalized: the expectation of return may be represented by a sense of obligation to help the next generation rather than repay the giver of care from an older generation. The concept of generalized reciprocity denotes circumstances in which a 'fairly immediate counter-gift is not expected, or may not be expected at all. There is simply the expectation that repayment will be made at some point, possibly to the same person but also possibly to a third party' (Finch and Mason 1993: 51). In some cases repayment to a third party is of a similar kind, while in other cases it may be different.

In this chapter, we shall look at the patterning of care over the life course of *women* and between different family generations, with particular reference to the pivot generation. We shall sketch some of the intricacies of informal care, suggesting that, while it is widespread, it may also be variably patterned and less significant in some families. We shall analyse informal care in three families and identify patterns in which care is foregrounded in the life course of some women and not in others and patterns in the giving and receiving of care across family generations. We shall illustrate processes of reciprocity of different kinds across the generations including a case where such reciprocity is high and specific. In another case we have selected a family in which care structures the women's life course very variably, while in the third case care-giving and care-receiving is low and reciprocity more generalized.

The study

The families we draw on in this chapter to analyse informal care are part of a study of twelve four-generation families. Conducted in 1999 and 2000, the focus of the study was care and employment within and across generations. We sought to understand better the extent and nature of change and continuity between different generations within families, in relation to paid and unpaid work, and the relationship between these two areas.

An intensive case-study approach was adopted, the 'case' being each four-generation family. We sought interviews in each family with members of the three older generations: one set of grandparents; one child of the grandparents (with at least one child under 10 years) and his or her partner; and both sets of the grandparents' parents (both the grandfather's and grandmother's parents). We did not try to interview the whole family, for example the other set of grandparents nor other children of the grandparents. Nor did we interview the youngest generation of children. We were left with a potential of 96 interviews across all 12 families. In the event, we interviewed 71 family members: all 24 parents and 24 grandparents, and 23 great-grandparents. Of the 25 'missing' great-grandparents, 20 were dead (6 great-grandmothers and 14 great-grandfathers) while 5 refused.

The families were theoretically sampled. Rather than seeking representativeness, the basis for sampling was to secure a diversity of different employment and occupational statuses among the grandparents, so that we might examine the role of the pivot generation with respect to the twin demands of employment and care. While we achieved a good spread of occupational statuses among grandparents (based on current or main last occupation), it was less easy to find our preferred mix of grandparents' employment statuses. Consequently, our completed sample had more grandparents in paid work than originally intended.

The interviews, which lasted on average around three hours, were influenced by biographical methods and were divided into three parts.[1] In the first, respondents were invited to give an account of their lives from childhood onwards, with a minimum of intervention from the interviewer. This provided an opportunity for the respondent to present their own gestalt. In the second part, the interviewer invited the respondent to elaborate on salient events from the initial narrative. Finally, using a more traditional semi-structured style of interview, the interviewer asked additional questions relating to the specific foci of the study.

Most great-grandparents were born between 1911 and 1921, most grandparents between 1940 and 1948, and most parents between 1965 and 1975. Over the three generations, there was a move to higher levels of education, cohabitation before marriage (in particular among the youngest 'parent' generation) and a longer period between forming partnerships and having children. Members of both older generations became grandparents around the age of 50.

Most fathers in each generation had occupied the role of main bread-winner during child-rearing years. With few exceptions, their employment careers were not obviously affected by parenthood. Women's employment, by contrast, in nearly every case was shaped by motherhood, although the extent and nature changed over the generations. With successive generations, women were less likely to drop out of employment altogether at marriage or parenthood, and more likely to work when children were young and also to work full-time.

Three patterns of care

The Ashton women: care-giving as structuring women's life course

In the accounts of the first two generations of women in this family, the great-grandmother Cynthia and grandmother Janet, care and particularly motherhood are an important structuring feature of their life courses and a central theme in their initial biographical narratives with implications for the construction and representation of their identities. Caring for children, however, was not a full-time activity for the two women: both resumed part-time employment during their years as mothers. In contrast, employment is foregrounded in the account of the youngest generation. Hannah, the current parent generation, was the only woman in the sample whose employment could be said to be uninterrupted by motherhood to the degree she had resumed her full-time job shortly after the birth of both children.

The identity of Cynthia, the great-grandmother, was however largely shaped by care-giving. As a mother to three children she worked part-time and only intermittently. As a grandmother to eight grandchildren, she helped look after them, especially one born with a disability. When her children were young she shared the care of her bedridden grandmother with her sisters. As a daughter (in-law), she looked after her mother and mother-in-law when they were unable to care for themselves and had both to live with her and her husband at different times. As a sibling, Cynthia helped look after her sister when she was dying of cancer, and soon afterwards cared for her husband during the short illness before his death. Cynthia's rationale for care-giving refers to a strong belief that families should help each other and to the close-knit character of her own family. Her rationale for being so 'pivotal' in the care of family members relates to both structure and agency: her position as the eldest of three sisters, the skills she gained as a nurse, and her concern to care for others.

Born in 1921 and having her first child in 1948, Cynthia's career as a mother and as a worker reflects those of many working-class women of her generation. Nursing was clearly one of the great loves of Cynthia's life. She noted early on in her life story that she had rebelled against her mother's and society's expectations by training as a nursing auxiliary in 1945. Yet, Cynthia stopped nursing four months after marriage, when she found she was pregnant. From then on, her role as an informal carer assumed much more significance. She did not work again until her youngest son started school then took a part-time job in a school canteen: she retired at the age of 68, never working full-time again.

In Cynthia's life story, motherhood and family life are presented as more important than work. Despite her love of nursing, she did not have a 'career' view of her working life, reporting instead a variety of part-time jobs following marriage. The fact that her own mother, who had six children, separated from her husband when Cynthia was 11, later getting a divorce (unusual in the 1930s), and worked when Cynthia was a child, was given as a justification for not wanting to repeat this pattern of family life: '[it] made us more determined to do this differently'. Cynthia sought to 'be there' for her children in the way that her mother had not been able to – even when her children were adolescent.

When her children were at school she worked in a school canteen and then as a playground supervisor so that she would be at home at the same time as her children. When her children were older, Cynthia moved to night work so that she was available for the family during the day. She worked one or two nights a week, first as a nursing assistant, then as a care assistant in a residential home for elderly people, and finally as a wages clerk. Referring to her job as a nursing assistant one night a week, when the children were teenagers, Cynthia emphasized how the job did not interfere with mother-hood: 'I went on Friday night because I still had the two teenagers at school. And it didn't affect them in any way'. Throughout her working life, Cynthia organized her paid work around the family. 'Family came first' not just when she was bringing up children, but also later, when she organized her work around the care of her grandchildren, mother and mother-in-law.

Cynthia's daughter, Janet, was born in 1948 and had her first child in 1966, aged 18. Her life story also suggests the centrality of care and the peripheral place of paid work in her life. Janet did not mention her job in her initial biographical narrative, which took roughly 45 minutes, referring to it only when asked in the semi-structured part of the interview. Her first response to the invitation to narrative referred to getting married young and to having children:

Well, I suppose the most eventful thing in my life was getting married! Um – we were only 17, both of us. I was pregnant. It wasn't planned. Parents were horrified. Didn't want us to get married, even. But, um, we did, and it's worked out all right. We've been married coming up to 34 years. It wasn't too bad. God, I don't know what to talk about! I've got three children.

Work figured more significantly later in her life course when, after a series of low-skilled 'little jobs' (cleaning, warehouse work, shop assistant), which she fitted around the family, Janet went on a government training scheme. Her youngest child, Jane, was at school by then. The following year Janet began working for her current company, first full-time (for ten months), then part-time (for four years) and then again full-time. Like other mothers of this generation (born in the 1940s), Janet developed an employment career only after her children were at school, eventually entering continuous full-time employment when her youngest child was at secondary school, as a sales support manager.

Janet was conscious that, by returning to work when her children were small, she had departed from the model of motherhood preferred by her own mother. This emerges in the guilt she expresses looking back over this period of her life from the vantage point of the present in not always having 'been there' for her children: 'I always had this guilt feeling, I think because my mum was always there, I always felt very, very guilty that I went to work, and I think mum felt I shouldn't have done'. She was clearly aware of her own mother's efforts to be a 'good mother'.

The life story given by the parent generation, Hannah, Janet's daughter-in-law, is more focused around work and much less about care, perhaps in part because it is orientated to present experience and her current situation as a full-time working mother with two young children. Born in 1968, Hannah's first child was born in 1994. In time terms Hannah's life is organized equally around family and work. She and her husband have two young children and both work full-time and try to share the care. After both births, on completion of her maternity leave, Hannah returned to her clerical job in a large bank on a full-time basis.

While Hannah foregrounds work in her life story, the rationale she gives for working suggests a feeling of constraint. She and her husband had been in debt, still paying off negative equity on a flat they bought when they were first a couple. Later they had to keep up the mortgage payments on their new 'family house' by working full-time while bringing up two children. Hannah suggests that without such constraints, she might have 'chosen' a different model of motherhood: 'I would love to have stayed at home with him [Joe], but I didn't have a choice. Money-wise I had to go back'.

Hannah expresses some ambivalence around being employed *full-time* rather than about working per se. Despite conflictual feelings about work and motherhood, Hannah devoted some part of her life story to work ambitions, in particular to her regret that her parents had not 'pushed' her enough as a child. At the same time her two young children are presented as a further 'excuse' for her current rather low commitment to her job. Thus even though Hannah expresses ambivalence about being a full-time employed mother, work appears to structure her identity to a considerable extent. In contrast, the identity and lives of the two older women are structured by care-giving. They seek to justify themselves as 'good mothers': paid work is effectively marginalized in their told stories.

The two older generations in this family, Cynthia and Janet, provide interesting contrasts of how employment may affect the care-giving role of the pivot generation. Cynthia is able to provide childcare for her grandchildren because her part-time employment accommodates her caring role in the family. Janet, on the other hand, although looking after her grandchildren to give Hannah and her husband Rick a break, is unable to provide childcare while Hannah works. While the employment status of the grandmothers did not affect active grandparenting, such as babysitting and having grandchildren to stay, probably because it usually occurs in the evenings and at weekends, employment does have a greater impact on the ability to provide childcare. Although in general most grandmothers in our study looked after their grandchildren few provided childcare while their daughters (in-law) worked and those that did were either not working or working part-time.

The Brand family: care as a set of specific or balanced reciprocities

Among some pairs of mothers and daughters, as well as care structuring the life course of women, there is evidence of strong intergenerational support between women of different generations in which care at one point in the life course is repaid with care by the recipient at a later point in the life course: what we have referred to as specific or balanced reciprocities. The Brand family is a case in point. All the generations lived near one another and there was also a strong culture of family closeness. Grandmothers provided some childcare and support to their daughters in the daughters' child-rearing years, care which was then reciprocated by the daughters when their mothers needed help in old age. As the women's accounts make clear, other kin were potentially available to provide this support in old age. However, in these cases the women we interviewed had clearly been chosen or had chosen themselves as carers.

The Brand family is characterized by specific reciprocities with respect to childcare and eldercare. These are very strictly gendered, with a key role played by women from the pivot generation. The gendered nature of these care reciprocities is paralleled by clear reciprocities between the men in the family related to material transfers, of money and services, involving the family business in which all three generations were involved, and the provision of housing. In their accounts, both the maternal great-grandmother, Dorothy, and her daughter, Valerie, talked about the help each had received from their own mothers when their children were young, how they felt that they had wanted to repay them in their old age, and the impetus this experience gave them to offer help to their own children and grandchildren.

Dorothy, born in 1918 and becoming a mother in 1945, had lived near her parents, both of whom supported her and her husband Dick when they moved into their new council house in the late 1940s with two young children. Dorothy was not employed at that time, but the household work was hard as she had no washing machine: 'I had the two babies . . . Dad used to come up every day with a bucket and pail with a lid on and take the babies' nappies home and wash them and air them and bring them back the next day and that . . . I used to go down [to her parents] every day with the babies and that.'

Later, Dorothy reciprocated this help. Her elderly widowed mother came to live with them for four years. While Dorothy's sisters were also available to care for their mother, Dorothy suggested she was 'marked out' for the job, because of her position as eldest child, her life course phase and her 'specialness': 'I was the eldest and my family had all left home and they'd still got their families at home, you see. And my family all had left home . . . I was always dad's favourite girl and always looked after mum'.

When her own daughters had young children, Dorothy provided them with considerable help. Valerie was born in 1945 and had her first child in 1968. While her children were still under 3, Valerie returned to part-time work as a hairdresser, with Dorothy providing childcare. Later on Dorothy, who lived a bus ride away from Valerie, came over to Valerie's house to look after the children after school. She also looked after the children of her other daughter. In the school holidays, all four grandchildren came to her.

Dorothy explained why she helped her daughters in terms of her positional status (as a mother) and went on to comment on the particular 'needs' of mothers and children at a particular historical moment:

I thought I was a mum I should help them . . . It seemed harder for them I don't know why . . . Well I think it's harder 'cos the children demand so much. You know they're so demanding nowadays. They want this and they want that. They're not content with little things.

The concern about 'making life better' for the next generation is a common theme in the study even when in material terms it was quite clear, as in this instance, that the younger generation was financially better off than their parents.

At the age of 54, Dorothy's daughter Valerie took early retirement. Not only did Valerie retire earlier than Dorothy (who worked in a school canteen until the age of 61), but also she had worked her way up after having children to become the dispensary manager at a local heath centre. Her reason for leaving work was informal care: she wanted to be more able to visit and help her parents whose health was beginning to deteriorate and also help with her grandchildren. In spite of her employ-. ment progression, Valerie expressed no sense of loss or regret in having given up her work.

Valerie's sister was significantly 'excused' by her parents from being involved to a significant extent in their care on the grounds of her own health problem and having limited access to a car. Valerie was moreover seen as the one to whom people in general turned for help; being helpful was described by her mother as an enduring aspect of Valerie's personality. Dorothy and Dick (her husband) regarded Valerie as somehow 'special', just as Dorothy had earlier suggested that she was her own father's 'favourite'. Thus in both cases Dorothy and Valerie seemed to have singled themselves out from their siblings as providers of their parents' care. Valerie saw herself as repaying her mother's help with the same currency as her mother gave her, namely time:

My mother has given me so much when I was young and needed a lot
of help. And I felt I wasn't going to have my mum and dad for ever
and I wanted to look after them ... I can give them something ...
my time which is what I feel they gave me really as a child, especially
my mum.

Valerie also repeated the pattern down the generations. She helped her own children, including care for her grandchildren: at the time of interview she was transporting one of her two grandchildren to and from school and looking after her after school. But Valerie also contrasted the type of help she was able to offer her children with that of her own mother. She saw herself as able to provide a different type of social capital, illustrating how each generation can put its own stamp upon the resources which are passed on (Bertaux and Bertaux-Wiame 1997). Valerie felt that she had been able to offer her family something additional. Her experience of employment contributed to the personal resources she felt she had passed on to her children: 'freedom, encouragement and confidence. I can give [daughter] more than my mother gave me, not that what she gave me, in her special way, wasn't just as important.'

Valerie is one of two women in the pivot generation in our study of twelve families occupying a dual caring role, caring for the older and younger generations. Most women in the pivot generation did, however, care for members of the older generation, usually for their own parents, though three also provided some care for their in-laws as Valerie had done. As recent survey evidence shows, care by the pivot generation takes many forms and its extent can vary considerably (Mooney and Statham 2002). The care provided to parents (in law) was predominately emotional and social, involving visiting and telephoning. Practical help in the form of domestic tasks, shopping and providing lifts, occurred less frequently. Whether women were working or not appeared, again, to have little influence on whether they provided elder care, although those providing practical care like Valerie were more likely to be retired. Perhaps emotional and social care is more easily combined with employment, though much depends on the nature and extent of the care required.

Valerie's daughter-in-law, Jane, was born in 1970 and had her first child in 1995. Jane noted that her mother-in-law's own background was rather similar to her own especially in the sense that both Valerie's parents and Jane's parents had very limited aspirations for their children, all daughters, but were very caring people. But as a working mother and as an aspirant parent, Jane identified more with Valerie than with her own mother, even though her mother was the main source of childcare for her first child. Jane regarded Valerie as much more enterprising than her own mother, a quality which she clearly admired.

Jane was helping her own parents financially because they were 'struggling'. She said she would in the future want to help her parents-in-law if and when they needed it: 'They've helped us out over the years, and, um, that wouldn't even be a consideration in my mind. I would do what I could'.

Dorothy and Valerie, as members of the pivot generation, were repeating similar patterns of specific reciprocity. Moreover both saw themselves as repaying their mothers in old age for the support which they had provided them during the child-rearing life course phase. Compared with her own mother, Valerie was more involved in her paid work; she eventually progressed occupationally and her work career contributed to her broader outlook on life. However, Valerie retired early and her work career gave way to the family project of 'taking care of our own'. Moreover Valerie's daughter-in-law, Jane, appeared to be consciously engaged in a similar pattern, both to repay and to repeat a pattern of caring for kin, while at the same time harbouring work and educational ambitions. Like her mother-in-law, Jane also sought to break out of the mould set by her own mother in which care and family life closely circumscribed her horizons. However, while Jane wants her children to 'get on' in the world and also to do well for herself, by returning to further education, she recognizes in herself a 'conservative tendency' to stick with the status quo, for example staying in the same job (just as her father had done, she notes). Whether her part in the future is to contribute to and maintain this pattern of continuity and the specific reciprocity of care (between mothers and daughters) is as yet unclear, though it seems a possibility.

The Samuels women: care as a peripheral identity and the absence of reciprocity

In the third family, there is little exchange of care intergenerationally between the three women. The key member in the chain of three women, the grandmother, has resisted a caring identity beyond motherhood after which caring played little part in structuring her life course. None of the women is biologically related, which may weaken the intergenerational transfer of care: other research has shown that both men and women are more likely to care for their own parents than their in-laws, but this is particularly marked for women (Mooney and Statham 2002). However, in the Samuels family the ties between biologically related members were not particularly 'close' either.

The leitmotiv of this family is 'independence', both at household and individual level. The Samuels family, unlike the Brand family, has been geographically mobile. Each generation moved to live in a different part of the UK, away from the family of origin. Doris, the great-grandmother, as the oldest surviving member of her family (she was born in 1906), was considered and considered herself to be the matriarch of the family, although the whole family met only very occasionally. She married down the social scale (her husband was a bank clerk) and had never worked. Doris saw herself at the age of 92 as still very independent and not in need of care. The fact that an unmarried daughter lived with her was somewhat discounted by her, emphasizing instead the independent means provided by an inheritance. She spoke of being 'lucky' to receive help, thereby suggesting that she did not expect it; luck was seen to come to the rescue when independence failed. She asserted that if she were to need care 'I'd rather be in a nursing home', a view also expressed by her son, Richard (Sally's husband), who noted that he had 'inherited' from his mother a desire not to be cared for by family.

Sally, Doris's daughter-in-law, born in 1942, came from lower-middle-class origins. She felt a strong need to rebel against her parents, whom she described as 'old', relating that her father had thwarted her ambition to go to art school. Instead, she became a secretary. By the age of 22, in the mid-1960s, she was married with two children and a husband who was still completing his first degree at university and had yet to start his professional training. When he finished his degree, the family moved to the other end of the country away from both families. The accounts of both Sally and her husband suggested an explicit strategy of distancing themselves from kin both geographically and emotionally, though, as Sally noted, this 'made it tougher for ourselves'. Even before moving south, Sally resisted her parents' expectations – 'they wanted us to go round every Sunday for tea' – as she was later to resist expectations of herself when she became a grandmother.

Despite having a young family and no kin available to help, the young couple built up careers in professions within the public sector. Before her youngest child started school, Sally returned to full-time education, went on to take a degree and eventually entered full-time employment and a career in hospital administration. She talked a great deal about 'running to keep up' with her husband and eventually outshone him in the employment stakes. The couple organized childcare when their children were young via au pairs and nurseries.

The theme of children learning to be independent – their 'parenting project' – emerged in both their interviews: 'You know we felt quite strongly that the whole role of the parent is to actually ensure that your children emerge fully fledged and independent and can do what ever they're going to have to do'. The children were expected 'right from the start' to manage their pocket money and also their finances later on at university.

The theme of independence is carried through to grandchildren. For Sally, grandparenthood was personal rather than positional (Bernstein 1975). It depended upon the mutual negotiation of a relationship by grandparents and grandchildren alike: 'I would like to be a friend . . . They have to have a choice as well.' Initially 'appalled' at being a grandmother 'so young' (she had her own children young), Sally was quick to excuse herself from any responsibilities for her grandchildren: '[I said] Don't expect anything. I'm in full-time work and I've every intent – [she broke off here to talk about her very demanding job] . . . we're not going to do standard drop all and look after the kids sort of stuff.' In Sally's view, a key part of being a 'good grandparent' was to refrain from 'interfering'. This meant resisting the assumption of parent-type care responsibilities, as well as the 'indulgent grandparent' role in which grandparents spoiled grandchildren. Just as Sally sought to reinvent motherhood so that she could also pursue a career, so she sought to reject the positionality of grandparenthood.

Sally was not caught between the roles of grandmother and daughter: her mother died the year Sally's first grandchild was born. Following her father's death, Sally's mother had moved into sheltered accommodation with a nursing home attached: 'a perfect place for someone to grow old on their own in and become less able to look after themselves'. Although she visited regularly, Sally's intention was to assist her mother to remain 'independent' and to help her mother to make her own 'choices' about care. Asked whether she felt any obligation to her mother, Sally exempted herself by making reference to the history of their relationship as never being 'close'. When Sally became a mother she rejected her mother's efforts to become closer. When her mother's health deteriorated, Sally never contemplated the possibility of her mother, who had remained in northern England, moving nearer to them, explaining that she had no ties in the south. She also gave the 'legitimate excuse' of her own employment career. In reflecting on her own care in the future, Sally was quite explicit: family would not be part of the solution:

Whatever happens I would expect to manage it . . . We might need some physical care which I would hope to be able to manage ourselves . . . I don't think [family care] works in this culture. I never want to be dependent.

Her vision of old age was to be on 'an equal footing' with those giving the care which, by implication, Sally saw as ruling out family.

Sally and Sarah, her daughter-in-law, offer a series of clear contrasts. These are to do with family background and culture. They are played out in the women's personal aspirations and priorities with respect to work and care. Sarah, born in 1962, was the youngest of five girls; Sally was the elder of two children. Sarah was very close to her mother and not close to her father, whom she found to be a rather frightening person; Sally was not close to her mother but very close to her father. Sarah flourished in the 'golden' childhood of a well-off, large professional middle-class family; she liked her private school, and enjoyed the family's structured lifestyle and clear expectations. Sally's family, by contrast, was lower-middle-class; she hated being sent to a private girls' school and rebelled against her parents. Sarah loved the feeling of her mother's overarching protectiveness; Sally resented her mother not working and had a distant relationship with her.

The contrast continues in employment and parenting. Sarah went straight to university from school and established herself in a career before embarking on motherhood at the age of 28. Sally, a mother at 20, only later embarked on a university education and a career. Sarah repeated some of the features of her own mother's mothering. She and her husband sought to give their children a sense of continuity and security by taking holidays in the same place every year – in fact the same place as her own parents had taken their family on holiday. Sally and her husband sought to provide their children with experience of the unfamiliar by taking them abroad on holiday. Sarah's motherhood practice was to protect children by keeping clear boundaries around their childhood – 'I don't want them to have to think about my life' – replicating her own mother's ability to protect her children from her own distress caused by her husband's 'temper'. While Sally tried to make her children independent and self-reliant, Sarah sought to nurture her children and, in Sally's eyes, to constrain their independence: 'in my eyes, I'm surprised she didn't do more . . . I think her parenting is more about – I saw her as nurturing some sort of dependence on her . . . she needed to be needed.'

In this case, a number of factors work against mutuality of support between the three generations of women. They relate not simply to the women's lack of biological connection. Two other sets of factors are particularly important. The first is the way the historical context shaped the aspirations of the women in each generation. Like many women in the current pivot generation, Sally reached young adulthood in the 1960s. She embraced the cultural changes of the decade, while as a young mother lacked the freedom to enjoy them. She thrived in the expanding opportunities for women in the 1970s and the climate around the growth of the Women's Liberation Movement. While being a mother of two young children she fought for financial independence and opportunities to make her way up the occupational ladder. In contrast, the oldest generation, Doris, grew up in a middle-class environment in a period when women of her class did not harbour employment ambitions. Sarah, the youngest generation, established herself in a profession in the postfeminist late 1980s, a time when women increasingly entered higher education and established themselves in the labour market before childbirth. Sarah returned to her teaching post after the birth of her first child but, following the birth of twins, decided to put her teaching career on hold, opting for part-time work, and prioritized motherhood.

Second, the Samuels can be characterized by a culture of 'independence' which was transmitted across the generations, while taking different material forms and expressions in each generation and being premised on the different social and economic conditions of the periods in which they lived. The source of such independence therefore differs across generations. In the oldest generation it is based on family inheritance accrued by the great-great-grandfather and passed on to his daughter (Doris). The middle generation stands out from the others for growing up during the expansion of the welfare state in the post-war period. Sally and Richard, the grandparents, have drawn considerably upon public resources – their own higher education, their children's education including higher education, and employment opportunities in the expanding public sector providing them with professional careers. These resources have given them a sense of 'independence', which is in effect independence from family.

In the youngest generation, Alex (Sally's son), like his father, was adamant about not depending on family for financial help and sought to repay any loans given by kin. He had 'ditched the rat race', running his own business from home and was aiming to generate his own pension and assets. Sarah, Alex's wife, talked about creating a particular kind of lifestyle and a particular kind of childhood for her children. In the youngest generation, independence was allied to a discourse of individualization and lifestyle choice, emphasizing their own efforts in fashioning a particular (rural) lifestyle – rather than relying upon the resources of the state or resources provided by their parents. Such worldviews and strategies were generated in a period of resurgent liberalism, in the 1980s and 1990s, at a time when the welfare state was in decline and a public ideology of personal responsibility was in the ascendant. (See Brannen and Nilsen 2002 for evidence of similar discourses among particular groups of educated middle-class young people.) The postmodernist emphasis upon lifestyle choice of the youngest generation is set against the modernist discourse of the middle generation who subscribed to notions of progress, notably through the pursuit of higher education and public sector 'careers for life'. The story of the oldest generation (via the account of the paternal great-grandmother) is set in the cement of an entrepreneurial middle-class past which in part resembles the present times in its emphasis upon individual enterprise, but differs greatly in gender role expectations and in women's aspirations and opportunities.

While it is not clear from Doris's account how far, as a past member of the pivot generation, she may have been involved in providing support to her other children and grandchildren (she has several other children) nor does she mention involvement in her own mother's care, it is clear that both Sally and her husband set out to be independent of their kin when they were parents and have so far provided little in the way of grandparenting or elder care. However, Sarah, as the youngest generation, stands out as having already provided some significant support to her elderly mother, who had recently experienced ill-health, together with her other sisters.

Conclusion

In this chapter we have offered some different patterns of informal care – both in terms of the structuring of the life course of women and also in terms of relations between family generations. We have shown both the complexities of these patterns, and given some indication of their variability across and within three families. Indeed, we do not claim to offer a comprehensive account of informal care relations, for example no illustrative case material is provided here for what is termed 'care as a general or imbalanced reciprocity'. Nonetheless a common pattern of generalized reciprocity was identified in the study, especially the provision by parents of material support to their children during the transition to adulthood. Parents did not expect their children to repay them. Rather they expected their children to continue this practice in respect of the next generation of young people.

Moreover, while we may discern different patterns and processes, they are not all mutually exclusive. For example, care as a set of specific or balanced reciprocities is compatible with care-giving structuring women's life course. Yet, at the same time, we have suggested some stark discontinuities between different generations within the same family and between families, notably the centrality of informal care in the Ashton and Brand families, and its peripherality in the Samuels family.

The provision of care – whether informal or formal – remains mainly 'women's work': while it may not be a prescribed norm, it is still a gendered responsibility. These case studies show variable patterns of involvement among women in the pivot generation which are not necessarily repeated across the generations in the families. In the case of Sally in the Samuels family, we have a woman whose life project following motherhood becomes her employment career which effectively takes over from care as a central 'life project'. This case contrasts with Valerie in the Brand family, also of the same generation and a member of the pivot generation. In this case, while Valerie develops an employment career after motherhood, this is eventually displaced by informal care responsibilities. While employment figures significantly pre- and post-motherhood among the youngest generation, it is by no means clear how far this will continue. As the case analysis shows, how far the pivot generation of women is active in care-giving relates to a complex of factors: (inter-)family structures, family relationships, personal identities and preferences. It is also a question of proximity and social and occupational mobility and is shaped by historical context.

The focus on informal care makes very visible two facets of care which are less apparent when the focus is on formal care which have implications for its theorization. First, the interdependency of care relations is clearly revealed, reminding us that care can be understood to consist of several dimensions, including care-giving and care-receiving (Tronto 1993). The potential for reciprocity is more pervasive in informal care, far more limited in formal care since there is less opportunity for continuity in care relations over time: the young child at nursery may give and receive care, to and from nursery workers and other children, but only while she is of nursery age and in the nursery environment. Informal care, as we have shown, often involves reciprocities over time and across generations. Second, when we look at informal family care intergenerationally, it is important to see the links between the care of children and that of dependent adults. This contrasts with the dichotomy frequently found in the literature on formal care (Daly and Lewis 1998) and embodied in public policy and the compartmentalizing language of 'childcare' and 'social care'. In some cases, careers in informal care may span the life course from cradle to grave.

The three examples we have provided have emphasized continuities and discontinuities across generations. There are processes of both transmission and innovation across generations (Bertaux and Thompson 1997), which generate intergenerational ambivalences (Luscher 2000). Discontinuities occur as the conscious or unconscious exercise of agency (for example, people like Cynthia Ashton who react against their own upbringing) but also because of changing times. This is in part a matter of higher educational and employment aspirations and changing practices among women – and is clearly revealed in the case of Sally Samuels, a pivot generation woman who eschews typical forms of engagement in grandparenting and who believes strongly in formal care support in old age. Such change is likely to have more far-reaching implications for care relations among the more educated and employment-orientated women of the pivot generation. Moreover, as far as the youngest generation in concerned, change is likely since most young women today continue their employment careers when they become mothers. However, this is not the end of the story; how such women will negotiate care of their children and elderly relatives in the future is not yet clear.

There are also changes in the 'external' environment of care, currently producing declining expectations of the welfare state and reasserting the virtues of individuals over collectivities, for example the citizen's duty to become an autonomous subject able to take responsibility for managing risk, both at an individual and a family level.

What is striking, though, from a cross-generational perspective is how care relations are *not* diminished by changes in care practices. Older generations, for example, are not overtly critical of their daughters or granddaughters working, and therefore relying more on non-parental childcare, even when they themselves did not work when they had young children. Great-grandmothers (like Dorothy Brand) willingly provided childcare for their daughters, while disagreeing in principle with mothers working. While the former may hold *general* normative beliefs that mothers of young children should not work, they resort to more personalized and complex assessments of their own kin which recognize the changed historical context in which new generations of parents are bringing up their children.

Finally, we can observe that informal care involves relationships not only with other family members, but also with the self. Certainly for many women, a relationship to care forms an important part of the way they see themselves – either seeing themselves as 'caring' or 'helpful' to others or, less commonly, as 'independent'. In this context, Sally Samuels stands out from most other women in the pivot generation (both the grandmother and great-grandmother generations), at least in our study, for foregrounding her professional career and downplaying informal care.

Acknowledgement

Our study was funded under the ESRC Future of Work Programme Award no. L21252027.

Note

1 The biographical methods we adopted drew upon the Biographic-Interpretive Narrative Interviewing approach (Wengraf 2000). However, we adapted the interviewing approach and the mode of analysis to fit our purposes.

References

Attias-Donfut, C. and Wolff, C. (2000) The redistributive effects of generational transfers, in S. Arber and C. Attias-Donfut (eds) *The Myth of Generational Conflict: The Family and the State in Ageing Societies.* London: ESA/Routledge.

Bernstein, B. (1975) *Class, Codes and Control, Vol. 3: Towards a Theory of Educational Transmission.* London: Routledge and Kegan Paul.

Bertaux, D. and Bertaux-Wiame, I. (1997) Heritage and its lineage: a case history of transmission and social mobility over five generations, in D. Bertaux and P. Thompson (eds) *Pathways to Social Class: A Qualitative Approach to Social Mobility.* Oxford: Clarendon.

Bertaux, D. and Thompson, P. (eds) (1997) *Pathways to Social Class: A Qualitative Approach to Social Mobility.* Oxford: Clarendon.

Brannen, J. and Nilsen, A. (2002) Young people's perspectives on the future, in J. Brannen, S. Lewis, A. Nilsen and J. Smithson (eds) *Young Europeans, Work and Family.* London: ESA/Routledge.

Brody, E.M., Johnson, P.T., Fulcomer, M.C. and Lang, A.M. (1983) Women's changing roles and help to elderly parents: attitudes of three generations of women, *Journal of Gerontology: Social Sciences,* 38: 597–607.

Daly, M. and Lewis, J. (1998) Conceptualising social care in the context of welfare state restructuring, in J. Lewis (ed.) *Gender, Social Care and Welfare State Restructuring in Europe.* Aldershot: Ashgate.

Dench, G., Ogg, J. and Thomson, K. (2000) The role of grandparents, in R. Jowell, J. Curtice, A. Park, K. Thomson with L. Jarvis, C. Bromley and N. Stratford (eds) *British Social Attitudes: The 16th Report.* Aldershot: Ashgate.

Finch, J. (1989) *Family Obligations and Social Change.* Cambridge: Polity.

Finch, J. and Mason, J. (1993) *Negotiating Family Obligation.* London: Routledge.

Graham, H. (1991) The concept of caring in feminist research: the case of domestic service, *Sociology*, 25(1): 61–78.

Grundy, E., Murphy, M. and Shelton, N. (1999) Looking beyond the household: intergenerational perspectives on living kin and contacts with kin in Great Britain, *Population Trends 97*, autumn: 19–27.

Hagestadt, C.O. (1985) Parent–child relations in later life: trends and gaps in past research, in J.B. Lancaster, J. Altermann, A.S. Rossi and L.R. Sherrod (eds) *Parenting across the Life Span: Biosocial Dimensions.* New York: Aldine de Gruyter.

Land, K. and Rose, H. (1985) Compulsory altruism for some or an altruistic society for all?, in P. Bean, J. Ferris and D. Whynes (eds) *In Defence of Welfare.* London: Tavistock.

Luscher, K. (2000) Ambivalence: a key concept for the study of inter-generational relations, in S. Trnka (ed.) *Family Issues between Gender and Generations*, Seminar Report. Luxembourg: European Commission European Observatory in Family Matters at the Austrian Institute for Family Studies.

Millward, C. (1997) Effects of gender and paid work on grandparenting, *Family Matters*, 46: 18–21.

Mooney, A. and Statham, J. (2002) *The Pivot Generation: Informal Care and Work After Fifty*, a report for the Joseph Rowntree Foundation. Bristol: Policy Press.

Stephens, M.A.P., Franks, M.M. and Townsend, A.L. (1994) Stress and reward in women's multiple roles: the case of women in the middle, *Psychology and Ageing*, 9: 45–52.

Tronto, J. (1993) *Moral Boundaries: A Political Argument for the Ethics of Care.* London: Routledge.

Wengraf, T. (2000) *Qualitative Research Interviewing: Biographic Narrative and Semi-structured Methods.* London: Sage.

Concepts of care and children's contribution to family life

JULIA BRANNEN and ELLEN HEPTINSTALL

Introduction

Care can be analysed through the prisms of both givers and receivers of care and according to the different strands of activity which the concept implies – the ethical aspects of care as duty, care as work, care as relational, and care as involving the exercise of power. In this chapter we propose to adopt a 'take' on care which focuses upon those who are usually seen as the receivers of care namely children. Rather we shall consider children as the active participants in care as an activity and in care relations.

The concept of care in family life

Care is at the heart of social relationships. It is used in common parlance and in formal languages to describe the processes by which human beings respond to one another's needs. The engine of family life is 'care' – care defined in terms of the practice of caring and care as being cared for. Central to the concept of care are notions of relationship and connectedness and a desire to create a sense of well-being in others. As feminist sociological analysis first identified, care is a form of both labour and love (Finch and Groves 1983; Wærness 1984a, 1984b; Land and Rose 1985; Ungerson 1990; Graham 1991; Thomas 1993).

A fundamental contribution – in terms of theoretical and empirical analysis – was made by feminist sociologists to understanding the work aspect of care in which they explored the consequences of care responsibilities, especially its material and practical aspects (housework and the domestic division of labour), for gender relations and gender inequalities. As Morgan (1996) argued, the emphasis placed on the work aspect of care occurred for very good reasons at the time since there was a need to redress the invisibility of carers. But the main conceptual endeavour has now been extended to a wider examination of the concept with a new focus upon the cared for and the relational aspects. Because of this shift in focus there is now less concern among social policy analysts about the surveillance exercised by professionals who deliver care and who seek to regulate care-givers notably mothers caring for their children. Instead there is a concern about the nature and quality of care which professionals provide notably to children (a change of focus seen in Chapter 5).

As Morgan (1996) suggested, care encompasses a wide range of skills, acts and sentiments. Care cuts across the Cartesian divide of mind and body. Caring is implicated in the conduct and experience of everyday life and is a constituent of cooperation and solidarity in social relations. Care is typically discussed however in the context of a significant need as when a child or frail elderly person requires care but which is often socially constructed in terms of a person's 'age'. Care is less commonly conceptualized as part of the ongoing processes of social relations in which care is reciprocated by all parties in a set of relationships. As Waerness (1984a, 1984b) first argued, caring occurs in different kinds of relations – symmetrical relations as well as between subordinates and superordinates, for example between children and parents. Care is typically discussed in relation to contexts in which there is an asymmetry of power relations which the very process of giving care accentuates. Delivered in the 'best interests' of the child or elderly person, care is represented as 'love' while the power which is exercised is silenced or treated as invisible. Care as a concept is therefore chameleon-like; it carries different meanings and changes meaning depending on the context. It is also a concept with a double character; it not only serves to describe social phenomena but also carries prescriptive messages about how we should behave to others.

However, care need not imply dependency since it may be reciprocated. As studies of intergenerational relationships in families suggest (see Finch 1989), a great deal of care is reciprocated if not at the point of its provision then later in the life course when the balance of need shifts towards the elderly generation (see Chapter 10 in this book). As a study we have conducted on children's contribution to family life in later childhood shows (Brannen et al. 2000) and to which we shall shortly turn, children seek to reciprocate their parents' care.

Care critically raises central questions to do with relationships and their negotiation as Mason (1996) argues, drawing upon the work of Tronto (1993) and Sevenhuijsen (1993). Importantly it implicates concepts of dependency, responsibility, and competence in providing care. Many of these concepts have been developed in relation to care conceptualized as a practical activity; less conceptual emphasis has been placed upon orientations to care which is not to say, as Mason (1996) argues, that care can be divorced from caring activity. Rather than thinking of care as either labour or love, Mason suggests that it is more useful to conceptualize the practical activity of 'caring for' someone as intrinsic to care as 'sentient activity' – 'caring about some one' and being attentive to others' needs. Sentient activity may be thereby transformed into 'active sensibility' in which persons come to feel responsible for and committed to other persons.

Care is a form of ethical activity and moral thinking which is not well captured by the dichotomous approach which has been applied to care as either love or labour. Drawing on the work of Gilligan (1982) and the writing of Benhabib (1992), Smart and Neale (1998) argue that care adds a moral dimension to the avoidance and repair of harm. In creating and maintaining committed and cooperative relations with others, care becomes a central rather than a peripheral moral question. As Finch (1989) has argued and demonstrated (Finch and Mason 1993), in modern British society family obligations no longer are defined in terms of an absolute duty to care nor is there a normative consensus concerning the rules about the provision of kin support. Finch offers a framework for interpreting the ways in which individuals apply moral rules in everyday life concerning the 'proper thing to do'. While people endorse general principles, they make decisions about providing care to others in particular circumstances and with respect to a variety of claims which may also have a moral dimension. Thus, while people may agree with the general principle that they ought to care for kin in the abstract, they may disagree about the 'right thing to do' in a particular circumstance. Thus morality in everyday life is constantly renegotiated in relation to particular situations and social conditions, including the specific history of social relationships and in the context of other, often competing moral claims and social norms.

Care is also central to discourses which define notions of *childhood* and what a child 'is'. Children's need for care is typically related to biological notions of the life span and to the concept of 'age'. But children's care is also generational; each generation of children and adults views itself and the other in relation to their own generational position as a parent or child, and in relation to their respective historical generational positions (Alanen 2000). Such positional or structural relations between generations (in both senses) of adult and child are moreover interactional processes which involve care of different types – moral, practical, material and emotional.

In public policy, the care of those children whose parents are unable or are deemed unable to care for their children is subject to particular discourses of care. These reflect the normative importance placed upon 'the family' as the single 'proper' context in which childcare should take place. They also reveal as much about the care of ordinary children as they do about the care of extraordinary groups of fostered children who, when their parents 'fail' to care sufficiently for them, are taken into the care of the state. The language used to describe such situations has undergone an intriguing transformation (Rhodes 1995). Children are no longer said to be 'in care' as formerly; they are now 'looked after' by the state. Moreover, according to British social policy, the everyday care of foster children is carried out by those who are *not* invested with the daily responsibility for the children, namely foster carers; this responsibility remains with social services and with their birth parents. Foster carers are no longer referred to as foster parents, the underlying assumption being that children's 'proper carers' in Britain are their parents.

Parental responsibility is synonymous with children's care in Britain and implicates power and control, as legislation making parents legally respons- ible for children when they break the law underlines. Care implies the exercise of control but does not necessarily reveal it (Walkerdine and Lucy 1989). Moreover, while in the eye and intention of the care-giver, care is designed to produce positive consequences, from the position and perspective of the cared for, care may also be experienced as constraint. Children may experi- ence their parents' care as both constraint and liberation, as parents seek to foster in children a sense of independence but also to protect them from risk and danger. Yet resentment of care as control within family relations is likely to be offset or balanced out by the perception of care as love. Indeed control within family relations may be understood as an expression of 'caring about'. In short, care is a double-edged concept which overlaps with a variety of other concepts including power and control.

The focus of the chapter

In this chapter, as in the study we carried out at Thomas Coram Research Unit in the late 1990s, children are conceptualized as active agents in their relationships with their carers – parents and foster carers. In the con- ceptualization of care as an activity having a key moral dimension, we first examine children's views of the obligation to care for others and the influ- ences they refer to in seeking to bring an ethical commitment to care into practice. Second, we examine how far children make an active contribution to care. Third and relatedly, following Mason's (1996) helpful conceptual distinctions, we are concerned not only to identify the practical contribu- tions children make (care as work) but also to identify whether and when children engage in sentient activity and provide emotional support to others. If it is the case that children engage in sentient activity, then we may begin to understand the processes by which sentient activity turns into active sensibility. In short, we may begin to understand how children's own caring identities are constructed both through expectations concerning the enact- ment of the ethic of care (through their own agency) and through their experiences of the care which adults provide them with. Fourth, we discuss the ways in which children evaluate the care given to them by parents.

The study

The basis of this examination is a major research study conducted in the late 1990s which was funded by the Department of Health (Brannen et al. 2000).

The London-based study which set out to examine children's concepts of care, and their experience and contribution to family life covered a multi-ethnic sample of nearly 1000 10–12-year-olds who were going through an important transition in their own lives – the transfer from primary school to secondary school. The researchers conducted a questionnaire survey with 10–12-year-olds in school time (in 3 mixed-sex state secondary schools and 12 primary schools) and also 63 interview-based case studies, conducted in home settings, from four different types of families which were drawn from the survey sample: two-parent, lone mother and step-families. A group of children in foster care was found through two social services departments. The survey sample reflected the ethnic composition of the schools which were disproportionately composed of Asian origin and African Caribbean children. While we sought to include equal numbers of boys and girls in the interview study, the occupational statuses of the children's parents were disproportionately low status, itself a reflection of the fact that middle-class parents in London tend to opt out of the state system, especially for their children's secondary education. The study drew upon a variety of methods – self-completion questionnaires, in-depth interviews, vignettes, and visual ways of mapping children's social networks and families (Brannen et al. 2000).

Children and the ethic of care

Care involves the recognition that we depend upon one another and that each of us has a moral commitment to act toward one another in caring ways. Two-thirds of children responded in the questionnaire survey that being concerned about others was 'very important' compared with only 42 per cent who said the same with respect to money. But while they considered this was 'right' in principle, it was not always seen as easy in practice. For example, in discussing a vignette set in a school playground in which a girl was depicted as standing apart from the group, while children generally subscribed to the principle of being caring and acting inclusively towards the isolated girl, many children had doubts about this happening in practice. Children constructed the isolated child as an outsider and emphasized her 'otherness'. Children's positioning of themselves in relation to other children suggests that children may have difficulty in practising the ethic of care; this is because of the cultures and norms guiding the strongly hierarchical relationships which exist in the contexts which children inhabit notably schools. Children also noted the indebtedness created between givers and receivers of care.

In addition, children suggested that adults do not always set children a good example in terms of being caring and considerate to them. For example, children noted that adults in public places expected children to give way to them even though in certain situations, for example queuing to be served in a shop, children held the same status as consumers and had an equal right to be served. In family life, children referred to being excluded from or ignored during important family discussions, notably concerning issues of children's residence after parents divorced.

In terms of their own contribution to care and household work, from a general normative stand point, almost all children agreed that they ought to contribute. The reasons they gave relate to the ethic of care and to family mutuality: 'because it's your own family, you're doing it for your own good'. Instrumental reasons for helping (in terms of payment) received little support. In particular, children from minority ethnic groups regarded payment as transgressing norms of family mutuality. However, children in general thought that their contribution should be modest. Children's responses to a vignette which portrayed parents working in a shop revealed the basis for these claims. Asked whether the girl shown in the vignette ought to help her parents in the shop when she returned from school, children prioritized their commitments in relation to their school work over their family commitments. Most children considered that as school pupils who were expected to do homework, parents ought to exempt them from family work, although some children disagreed.

Children's contribution to household and care work

Despite their reservations about providing help at home, children reported making a considerable contribution in terms of frequency of doing household tasks although they were more likely to help with self-maintenance than with tasks which were other orientated. Between roughly one-third and one-quarter of 11-year-olds in the school survey reported performing self-care tasks such as clearing away their own dirty dishes on a daily basis, while the figure fell to under one-fifth for family care tasks such as making something to eat for someone else and vacuuming/dusting. Around four-fifths reported doing self-care tasks, either everyday or some days in the past week, while two-thirds to three-quarters carried out family care tasks. Reflecting earlier research (Brannen 1985), black children and Asian origin children were more likely than white children to do household tasks while, unlike in other similar studies of older children, gender was not significant.

On the one hand, there was only a small difference between the frequency with which children in the survey reported doing tasks and the frequency with which they said they carried out tasks without being asked, although there was a discernible reduction in the number family care tasks reported when the caveat 'without being asked' was included. In response to an open-ended question in their interviews, however, most children noted only one task for which they were responsible in practice.

Children negotiated their contribution to household work in relation to their understandings of what it means to be a child. As already noted, children considered school work to be the 'proper work' of children at this point in the life course which was seen to be a 'legitimate excuse' exempting them from household work. Also relevant were negotiations among the sibling hierarchy. Children sought to transfer household tasks allocated by parents to their siblings and often used money as a means of bargaining with them. They also sought to contest parents' power to exempt one child rather than another, notably on the grounds of gender and birth order. In effect, as well as being an opportunity for being caring and helpful, household work was a site of contest in which children used their status as children to set limits to taking on responsibilities.

By contrast, children reported in the survey a higher frequency of general caring – both caring for and about other people including mothers, fathers, siblings, classmates, elderly people and pets. On some caring activities, children reported higher frequencies than for household tasks, with half reporting giving help 'every day' to their mothers and over one-third to their fathers. Similarly, over one-third said they were nice to or helped their classmates, and over one-third looked after their pets. Over half said they took care of younger brothers and sisters some days a week and nearly two-thirds reported helping an elderly person (Table 11.1). Caring activities less commonly reported were looking after pets and looking after siblings, mainly because some children either had no younger siblings or had no pets. In fact 39 per cent of eldest children and 35 per cent of middle children in families reported looking after younger children every day and four-fifths at least once a week. In the interviews, children were careful to report they never did so 'on their own'. The kinds of 'legitimate excuses' (the term used by Finch and Mason 1993) which children gave for not taking charge of siblings related to notions of parental authority and parental responsibility: they saw their status as children by definition as ruling them out from taking responsibility considering that they lacked the authority needed to take charge of others.

Contributing to housework was statistically associated with caring work ($r = 0.45$; $p > 0.001$). Unsurprisingly, children living in lone mother households were less likely to report helping their father, stepfather or male foster carer. When birth order was taken into account, Asian origin children who were the oldest or middle children in the family were significantly more likely to

Table 11.1 Children's contribution to general caring by frequency (questionnaire survey)

	Every day (%)	Some days (%)	Not at all (%)	N
Help mother/stepmother/female foster carer	50	47	3	820
Be nice to/help class mates	37	57	6	818
Look after pets	37	21	42	800
Help father/stepfather/male foster carer	36	48	16	800
Be nice to brothers/sisters	26	62	12	815
Take care of younger brothers/sisters	25	30	45	775
Help an elderly person	16	56	28	815

look after siblings every day than other groups, while Asian origin and black children were more likely to report being nice to brothers and sisters every day compared with white children and children from other minority ethnic backgrounds (see also Morrow 1998 for a similar finding). Interestingly in this study gender had no effect in this regard.

Children as providers of emotional support

As noted above, we conceptualized children as sentient beings who had the competence to provide emotional support as well as practical support to others. In their interview accounts, children volunteered many instances of providing unsolicited practical support: doing the shopping, washing the family car, helping with housework, looking after siblings and elderly grand-parents. A number of children referred to buying presents for parents, siblings and other family members.

Children also suggested that they provided emotional support especially to parents though this was typically contextualized in accounts of giving practical help.

Several children said that they wanted to repay their parents for what they had done for them, including a number of Asian origin children who talked in terms of having 'respect' for parents. A girl in the survey wrote about helping her parents with housework: 'It gives me a chance to do something for my parents instead of them doing things for me.' Another wrote: 'I help my parents because I love them and I would do anything for them.' In response to being asked what she did for her mother, Serena simply said: 'I love her and I care for her and I look after her.' As Claudia noted, love was the only means available to her of reciprocating her mother's care: 'I love her, help her and that's it because I can't feed her because I ain't got no money.' Just as mothers talked about 'being there' for their children, so Lee said he would 'be there' for his mother, now and in the future: 'I love her. I'll be there when she's old and that's it.'

Three girls talked about providing their mothers with a listening ear.

LATASHA: *If she [mother] finds she has any problems she'll talk to me a little bit.*

LEILA: *I think I'm her security. I think she can always talk to me and everything. Because my brother isn't around, he's at my dad's.*

ZARINA: *Because sometimes my mum speaks about her problems to me. Her deep inside secrets to me. And I understand them. So all parents should . . . they should inform the children as well, 'cos otherwise they might not know. They might get a shock. The problem is that parents should understand children as well. And children should understand parents. Some parents say it so high that children don't understand it. But some parents say it so softly, in the children's point of view.*

The rationales children gave for providing support reveal their ability to project themselves into the position of their parents. Elliott, who wanted to give financial help to his mother who was a non-employed lone parent, understood his family's poor financial position from his lone mother's perspective: 'If I had a job, I would look after my mum . . . if she needs help with her bills or anything like that, I would be glad to help.' Anna understood how tired her mother was when she arrived home from a long day at work and took her mother's part: 'It's not fair. They go out and work all day, then they have to come home and do everything for you.' Ben, whose mother was convalescing after a major operation, understood the effect of a hysterectomy upon his mother's ability to lift heavy things and wanted to do it for her. 'So Mum don't have to do it.' Several children described not wanting pocket money because their lone mothers could not afford to give them any. Another boy described returning his grandmother's gift of money because he thought she could not afford it. Although Amy was not a very willing carer of her young half-brother, she displayed considerable ability to put herself mentally in her mother's shoes: 'When I get home from school I usually have to look after him [young half-sibling]. Well, I mean fair enough, my mum has had him all day. But it gets a pain because, like, you've been to school all day. You've done this hard work and then you have to come home and look after this screaming baby.'

Several children showed understanding of their parents' disposition to worry about them and sought to dispel their worries. Baldev was mindful that he should telephone his mother or father if he wanted to stay late at his friend's house 'Because you don't want to worry your parents'. He was also mindful of the worry his older sister might cause their parents and had bought her a mobile phone. Two girls described how they had come to realize how much anxiety they had created for their mothers on occasion by not telling them their whereabouts, which they said had since led them to be more considerate.

Mothers confirmed their children's accounts but elaborated on the subject much more than the children did. There are two possible reasons for this. The first is simply that mothers were the grateful recipients of the support provided by their children. Niaz's mother who was a diabetic noted how pleased she felt about her son's response when her blood sugar level rose:

> Like, I'm a diabetic. Sometimes if my sugar level is high, then he knows I'm not feeling well. I say 'Niaz, I don't like noise or something.' Then he will take both [younger] sisters out from the room and say 'You must not make any noise, mummy is not feeling well.' He will go and make a cup of tea for me. He'll bring the tea, sit down next to me and say 'How are you feeling, are you feeling better now?' . . . [How do you feel when Niaz is like that?] He makes you cry, it's really nice.

Jasmine's mother described how her daughter supported and advised her when her marriage broke up.

Yes, when I split up with my second husband Jasmine knew I was upset and she was quite good. Obviously, I didn't want it to be a burden to her, she was only small, she was only 7. But, you know, she went 'Mum don't get upset, everything will be alright, you've got us'. So then I thought maybe I put a bit too much on her . . . I mean, I could tell Jasmine anything now and she would sit down and listen and she would sort of try and advise me even though she's [only] 11, she would. You know, if I moaned about [stepfather] she says 'Well, have it out with him when he gets in then', you know. She is pretty good like that.

Similarly, Daniela's mother was very grateful to her daughter for the support she gave her when she was receiving treatment for cancer:

I mean, yes, the times when I have been ill. She has been there . . . And you know, she was very, very supportive. I mean, when I had radiotherapy and I really wasn't well, I used to flop into bed. And she would come in and she would say things 'Do you want this mum? And do you want that mum?'

The second reason why mothers were so expansive about children's ability to 'read' their feelings and situations is that this contradicted their normative expectations of what it means to be a child. Surprise is clearly evident in the remarks of Barry's mother:

Yes, the funeral of Princess Di, I was sitting there, I was watching it . . . and when Elton John sung I started crying. And then when her brother done that speech . . . I was really upset. And he was sitting there, he was looking at me. I'm going, 'You don't understand Barry, this is a really sad occasion.' Children don't understand this. And then he went up the road to my friend and said, 'Can you come down to my mum, she is crying.' He sent her down, you know. Things like that he does. He is really good. If he feels he has upset you, he'll make you a cup of tea. [How does that make you feel?] To think that he thought about you, run up the road, and you know, done something. It's nice. He is very thoughtful like that.

The basis of such surprise about their children's emotional intelligence emerged in mothers' responses to a question about the appropriateness of revealing their (adult) problems to children. More mothers said that they disagreed with disclosing their problems than agreed or gave a qualified response. In many cases they were highly ambivalent about what they saw as a 'burden'. They saw childhood as a protected time during which children ought not to perform 'proper' work and should be free from stress. They considered that children's 'special' status as children and children's 'sensitivity' needed safeguarding: 'I don't think they should learn too quick. They should still have their childhood.' Others thought that disclosure should depend upon the kind of problem. All three arguments were used by children as well as by mothers. Some children said they were 'not yet old enough' to know adults' problems, while others said that these matters were simply 'confidential'. By contrast, yet other children considered that children needed to know parents' problems in order to be prepared when things went wrong.

In short just as emotional intelligence and support are central components of the care that parents, especially mothers, seek to provide their children, so children also demonstrated that they were capable of providing similar support. Just as children wanted their mothers to 'be there' for them, so children sought to 'be there' for their parents.

Children's assessments of care in the family context

Children applied stringent criteria in judging parental care. They clearly understood that parents were supposed to provide children with care of a particular kind. The criteria they referred to included: care as unconditional love, care as connectedness to others, care as a gender-free activity, and care as a child-centred experience.

First, children considered that their parents' main job was to offer them unconditional love. Children's representations of family life suggest that love and care, provided consistently and on an everyday basis, were far more important to them than family structure; parents were 'people who never ever don't care about you' as one child put it. No matter what family type they lived in, children considered both their birth parents and their siblings to be 'very important' to them. Children described their parents' and carers' importance in a variety of ways, emphasizing the importance of love and affection, although children tended to assume or understate other key aspects of parenting such as security and setting boundaries (control). As for adults who act in loco parentis, for example stepfathers, children suggested that these adults had to earn their importance in children's eyes and lives; for children's part, care and its reciprocity were matters to be worked at.

Like other children, foster children considered their parents to be 'very important' to them even though in some cases they rarely saw them and even though their parents were not able to care for them adequately. However, they did not view parental care in the same way as other children. They attributed their parents' importance to 'positional' ties of biology rather than to 'personal' modes of relationship (Bernstein 1975) or, in the case of the importance of their foster carers, simply to the 'fact' that they 'looked after' them. These discourses draw upon similar distinctions to the social policy language of 'looked after children' in which notions of care and love are reserved for biological parents. On the other hand, in the context of being taken away from their own parents on the grounds that their parents were not 'fit' to take care of them, children were left with few linguistic resources other than to refer to biological ties or the facts of everyday life. Yet, it seems likely that children's silences also concealed unexpressed ambivalences. It was striking how much importance that foster children attached to their siblings especially since many of their siblings had been placed in other families and they rarely saw them. In some cases children had never met some of their siblings; yet they still considered them very important. It was as if siblings, more so than birth parents, symbolized the family they once had. Perhaps some siblings were of particular importance because, unlike birth parents who had often failed them, they reminded them of some positive aspects of their past family lives.

The second criterion according to which children evaluated parental care concerns the notion of connection. While children equated family life with love, they did not seek to limit family boundaries to parents and the household. Both in the focus group discussions which preceded the interview phase of the study and in completing their own maps of significant others, children suggested that those people who were very important to them encompassed a wide range of relationships which, in some cases, extended to friends and family members they had never met or rarely saw.

A third criterion concerned the gendered nature of parenthood. However children largely considered that parenthood ought to be 'gender free'. In the survey they did not consider that mothers were in principle any better at providing love and care than fathers; rather they suggested that both ought to provide children with the same types of care and to be equally involved in family life. By contrast, when asked about parents' labour market participation, children's opinions divided. One-half subscribed to the traditional normative notion of maternal care in terms of the 'at home mother', while the other half expressed a less traditional view, suggesting that *both* mothers and fathers should be employed but only part-time when children were small. Girls, Asian origin children and younger children (those still in primary school) were more traditional in their attitudes. However, boys were equally likely to express a preference for working part-time when they grew up and had small children.

The fourth criterion by which children judged care in family life arises from their generational and life course positions; children considered that family life was centrally about providing love and care to children. (While most considered lone parent and stepfamilies to be 'proper families', few considered a couple without children to be such.) A child-centred perspective is moreover entirely in keeping with the public discourse of 'parental responsibility' which defines children as the recipients of parents' care. As we have noted, children were able to put themselves in the place of the other and understood their parents' feelings and situations but, not surprisingly, they still viewed family life from the position and vantage point of children.

Yet while children applied stringent criteria to judging care in the family context, their investment in being cared for was such that they did not criticize their parents when they found them wanting. It was notable that in talking about family change in the context of parents' divorce, children were reluctant to reveal their feelings, even though it seemed likely from the facts they mentioned and on the basis of their mothers' observations that children were sometimes disappointed in the lack of care shown by a non-resident parent (the father). While none of the children refused to discuss their parents' divorces, their responses were typically brief especially when they were asked about their non-resident birth fathers. Moreover, in line with normative views of parents as equally providing for children's various needs, children were reluctant to differentiate between their mothers and fathers for fear of being 'unfair' to one parent. Yet, in reporting everyday realities, children of lone mothers in particular suggested that their mothers were more involved in their everyday care and, as a consequence, they considered them to be more important in practice. Parental power and control were also areas of silence unless children were asked directly and even then many children represented their parents as 'fair' and 'reasonable' or indicated that they had internalized parents' rules and expectations.

Conclusion

In conclusion, children emerge as active co-participants in care and co-constructors of family life. Like adults, they are moral actors; they make sense of the rules which guide caring behaviour and negotiate family life and family change. In negotiating ethics of care and the conduct of family life, children emerge as strongly child-orientated, asserting the centrality of children to family life, and the need to prioritize the interests, needs and concerns of children. In interpreting what it means to be cared for in a family, however, children showed themselves to be emotional actors who were able to offer parents emotional support: they showed themselves to be capable of taking the perspective of the other and of putting themselves in adults' shoes, notably understanding the needs and feelings of their parents. However congruent with dominant discourses of parental responsibility and childhood, children did not represent themselves as doing much work in their families; the 'proper work' of children was seen to be schoolwork while the 'proper role' of parents was to care for their children.

In terms of the ways in which children as recipients of care portrayed family life, children applied a stringent set of criteria to the way they should be cared for. Children saw love and care as being at the heart of family life, together with a highly inclusive approach to those whom the term 'family' covers. Having a group of foster children in the study served to illuminate the salient meanings and often taken for granted significance of families to children, especially the importance of parents and siblings. In terms of 'focus', family life was considered to be chiefly about children. Children were very little concerned about issues of gender equality and wanted both parents to be equally involved in their care.

In this study we sought to make children authors of their own life stories. Inevitably there were limits to this ambition, however sensitively we as adult researchers tried to pose our questions and devise our methods. Moreover, a methodology which seeks to invoke reflexivity needs to match the inclination of research participants to engage in reflexivity at the moment which the researcher dictates. Children did not generally position themselves as commentators *on* their lives nor did they often engage in detailed narratives of their past experiences. Children were living *in* their lives and getting on with the business of changing schools and negotiating their everyday routines. We tried to create as little disturbance as possible in their rhythms and concerns. Thus the story which we have told of family life as children see it is often a 'between the lines story' based on children's often elliptical reports. Yet, while children may have been less discursive than some adults in speaking about their lives, they none the less emerge as active agents in the giving and receiving of care.

References

Alanen, L. (2000) Explorations in generational analysis, in L. Alanen and B. Mayall (eds) *Conceptualising Child–Adult Relations*. London: RoutledgeFalmer.

Benhabib, S. (1992) *Situating the Self*. Cambridge: Polity.

Bernstein, B. (1975) *Class, Codes and Control, Vol. 3: Towards a Theory of Educational Transmissions*. London: Routledge and Kegan Paul.

Brannen, J. (1985) Young people and household work, *Sociology*, 2: 317–38.

Brannen, J., Heptinstall, E. and Bhopal, K. (2000) *Connecting Children: Care and Family Life in Later Childhood*. London: RoutledgeFalmer.

Finch, J. (1989) *Family Obligations and Social Change*. Cambridge: Polity.

Finch, J. and Groves, D. (eds) (1983) *A Labour of Love: Women, Work and Caring*. London: Routledge and Kegan Paul.

Finch, J. and Mason, J. (1993) *Negotiating Family Obligations*. London: Routledge.

Gilligan, C. (1982) *In a Different Voice*. London: Harvard University Press.

Graham, H. (1991) The concept of caring in feminist research: the case of domestic service, *Sociology*, 25(1): 61–78.

Land, K. and Rose, H. (1985) Compulsory altruism for some or an altruistic society for all?, in P. Bean, J. Ferris and D. Whynes (eds) *In Defence of Welfare*. London: Tavistock.

Mason, J. (1996) Gender, care and sensibility in family and kin relationships, in J. Holland and L. Atkins (eds) *Sex, Sensibility and the Gendered Body*. London: Macmillan.

Morgan, D. (1996) *Family Connections*. Cambridge: Polity.

Morrow, V. (1998) *Understanding Families: Children's Perspectives*. London: National Children's Bureau.

Rhodes, P. (1995) Charitable vocation or 'proper job'? The role of payment in foster care, in J. Brannen and M. O'Brien (eds) *Childhood and Parenthood: Proceedings of the International Sociological Association Committee for Family Research Conference 1994*. London: Institute of Education, University of London.

Sevenhuijsen, S. (1993) Paradoxes of gender: ethical and epistemological perspectives on care in feminist political theory, *Acta Politica*, 2: 131–49.

Smart, C. and Neale, B. (1998) *Family Fragments?* Cambridge: Polity.

Thomas, C. (1993) De-constructing concepts of care, *Sociology*, 27(4): 649–69.

Tronto, J. (1993) *Moral Boundaries: A Political Argument for an Ethic of Care*. London: Routledge.

Ungerson, C. (ed.) (1990) *Gender and Caring: Work and Welfare in Britain and Scandinavia*. Hemel Hempstead: Wheatsheaf.

Wærness, K. (1984a) The rationality of caring, *Economic and Industrial Democracy*, 5: 185–211.

Wærness, K. (1984b) Caring as women's work in the welfare state, in H. Holter (ed.) *Patriarchy in a Welfare Society*. Oslo: Universitetsforlaget.

Walkerdine, V. and Lucey, H. (1989) *Democracy in the Kitchen: Regulating Mothers and Socialising Daughters*. London: Virago.

C H A P T E R   **12**

Some thoughts on rethinking children's care

JULIA BRANNEN and PETER MOSS

Introduction

In this brief concluding chapter, we shall offer some thoughts which have arisen for us from our work at Thomas Coram Research Unit (including editing this book) and which we hope may contribute to the process of rethinking children's care. These are not, however, conclusions, although we identify some positions that we have provisionally adopted. The field is too large, complex and diverse to be able to impose the order and closure that conclusions assume. Much more work also needs to be undertaken which connects different perspectives and understandings, connections which will bring both complementarities and tensions: one obvious connection is between feminist and childhood studies.

Finally, by way of introduction, we feel there is a pressing need for all involved in children's care to have more space – to read, think, discuss, write, problematize and evaluate – about theory, practice, research, the world we live in today and the past from which it comes. We say this not as academics situated above the forces and pressures that close off such space for others, but as researchers subjected to the same forces and pressures in an increasingly marketized research arena. Only by valuing and creating such space can rich and provoking processes of rethinking occur – and without such rethinking, restructuring is simply a superficial exercise.

Blurring boundaries

First, there is the increasing blurring of boundaries between care and care services, and other domains and services. This is a process affecting policy, provision and practice, but which is underpinned by changes in thinking. For children, an important boundary in Britain that is now beginning to blur has been between care and education, but there are also others that are significant: health, social welfare, play and so on. In the case of care for elderly people, this blurring is leading to new relationships between care, housing and health.

At a policy and administrative level, these boundaries are already becoming less clear: childcare in England and Scotland, for instance, is now part of the education regime, while social services and health are forming new relations for the delivery of social care. The time is ripe we think to conceptualize the new territory. Does 'care' remain a distinct policy field, to be 'joined up' with others? Or, as we suggested at the beginning of the book, might it become a way of acting and a habit of mind informing education, health and other domains – the manifestation of a 'caring' society applied across all public services and other human services agencies? Might there be new theories and practices of work with children which weave care, education, health and other fields into new entities – more than and different from the sum of the parts? One example of a new entity (new to Britain, not to much of the rest of Europe) is 'pedagogy' – although our discussion of pedagogy in this book illustrates that it can take many forms. But there could well be others.

The boundary issue is not however only between formal care and other policy domains. It is also about the relationship between formal and informal care. This relationship is, of course, in a constant state of flux, not only as ideas about care, family, gender, market and state fluctuate, but also as conditions change. Large-scale institutions (such as the Foundling Hospital in London) lost their appeal as care regimes in the second half of the twentieth century, but the demand for services dedicated to providing for 'illegitimate' children has fallen as the meaning of birth outside marriage has changed and as it has become increasingly the norm for children born outside marriage to be raised by their mothers (and in some cases by their fathers also). The employment of a servant class to care for the children of the middle classes has come and gone and is, to a limited extent, reappearing as changes occur not only in attitudes, but also in the labour market in general, and women's participation in it in particular.

These economic changes, more generally, have driven the turn to formal childcare in the 1990s (just as the wartime economy produced a temporary turn to formal *public* services in early 1940s), a turn which poses new questions about the concept of care – not only how 'childcare services' relate to education and other services, but also how they relate to care in the home. Is home care normative and 'childcare provision' an attempt to replicate home care – or, at the very least, a way of minimizing the 'harm' to children from not being cared for at home? Is 'childcare' the same whether done at home or outside? Or do nurseries, kindergartens, out-of-school settings and other services offer different opportunities, relationships and practices to children compared with those of parents and the home? Are these second best, or equal but different?

As such questions imply, the changing relationship between formal and informal care, between care outside the home and care by family, is far from simple. It goes well beyond a simple zero-sum game, in which more of one means less of the other. Instead, new forms or dimensions of care may emerge, both in the home and in services. More and better services have their own care identity, connected to their particular context and other purposes. By reducing certain kinds of care in families, in turn they may free parents and other family members to give more time and attention to other dimensions of care.

The field of eldercare offers examples of how the growth of formal services providing care generates new care relationships, rather than simply substitution effects. Norway and Denmark are countries with highly developed welfare states, including services for elderly people, and hence are a good test case. Young and old Norwegians alike set great store on not being a burden to others (Daatland 1990); wide support exists *both* for the idea that families should take care of their members and for the norm of independence. At an aggregate level, rather than public provision replacing private maintenance, the two processes work together (Gulbrandsen and Langsether 2001). Despite well-developed services, informal care continues to be very significant. But, it is suggested, increased public services may contribute to new forms of involvement by families with elderly people, including service promotion, service mediation, service support and mediation between services (Lingsom 1997). In short, rather than providing evidence of a 'crowding out hypothesis' (Becker 1993), formal services increase informal support, and 'may have contributed to re-positioning its role and contribution' (Deven et al. 1998: 11).

Applying such thinking to 'childcare' could be interesting. The present dominant discourse in Britain – which assumes the norm of maternal care, and focuses on the extent to which that norm is transgressed (for example Chapter 7 on sponsored day care for children in need) – might be recast. Instead of framing policy questions thus – 'What are the adverse effects for children of non-parental care?', other questions might come to the fore. What new experiences and relationships do different forms of formal and informal care together provide for children? What possibilities and risks might open up for children as citizens of today as well as citizens of tomorrow? What are the implications of such developments for the ways we think about and practice parental care?

Changes in the wider landscape

At the same time as boundaries between care in different contexts are changing and often blurring, there is a wider transformation of the landscape within which care and care relations are configured and practised. This is occurring at a particular historical moment in Britain. In the policy arena, driven by the current New Labour government's agenda – including Welfare to Work initiatives, the creation of an increasingly competitive workforce and the emphasis it places upon markets – British mothers are in the process of being repositioned as workers rather than carers (Brannen 1999). The increased participation of women in the labour market – in particular mothers and grandmothers, both key resources for the care of children in Britain, is overturning old orthodoxies. However parents (mothers) are constituted as making consumer choices: about whether to support their children through paid work and, if they choose to do so, which choices to make about their children's care. The onus is on mothers individually to modify their employment to fit with their caring responsibilities.

Not only are more women employed today, including women in the parent and pivot generations, but also more do not leave employment when they have children. They are developing employment careers, like men, based on expectations of a pattern of continuous employment. Moreover, young women's educational and employment expectations and aspirations have overtaken those of young men (Brannen et al. 2002) while the evidence of a 'turn to domesticity' among men remains largely anecdotal (Warin et al. 1999).

These changes are not however uniform across all women. Participation in the labour market varies greatly between women, strongly associated as it is with education, class and ethnicity – mothers with 'high educational attainment' are more than twice as likely to be employed as those with 'low educational attainment' (61 per cent compared to 23 per cent in 1997 (Moss and Deven 1999)). Nor is it simply a matter of the latter experiencing difficulties in finding employment. There are major differences here in understandings of what it means to be a 'good mother' and what is 'good childcare', with many women affording high value to 'being there' for their children (Duncan and Edwards 1999). Indeed, one of the ironies of the current situation in Britain is that many women in the childcare workforce (nursery workers and childminders) provide care for the children of other women, but are unwilling themselves to work full-time when they have their own children, viewing this as incompatible with their idea of 'good' mothering (Cameron et al. 2001; Mooney et al. 2001).

The growth in women's employment is accompanied, and indeed is partly generated, by wider changes in employment and the economy, changes which affect everyone, men as well as women. The turn to neo-liberalism during the 1980s and 1990s, combined with the ever-increasing importance of the service sector, has led to new patterns of work and new expectations of the workforce. One consequence, arising from reductions in staffing levels and changes in work organization, is 'that a substantial sector of the workforce has been affected by an intensification of work and by increased levels of stress' (Esping-Andersen et al. 2002: 199). These trends have been accompanied by rises in perceived job insecurity, especially among professional workers (Burchell et al. 1999) and among full-time working parents (Cully et al. 1999).

Another consequence of the turn to a new market-orientated form of capitalism has been discerned by Sennett (1998), Bauman (1998a, 1998b, 2001) and Gray (1998) who have argued that employment in the 'new capitalism' bears values and creates conditions that are at odds with those required for care. For while the 'new capitalism' calls for individualism, instrumental rationality, flexibility, short-term engagement, deregulation and the dissolution of established relationships and practices, caring relationships in informal contexts and in caring services are predicated upon an expressive rather than instrumental relationship to others. They are based on trust, commitment over time and a degree of predictability. While there may be more talk and some increased provision, at public and company policy levels, of 'family friendly policies', not only are these accompanied by a more general increase in work intensification and insecurity, but also they are often treated as individual benefits to reward and retain specific valued employees rather than forming part of collective solutions to endemic issues in the organization of employment and its relationship to care (Brannen 2000). Behind talk of 'work/life' balance lurks an increasing tension between the ethics and values of caring and employment.

Who will do the caring in the future?

Changes in informal and formal care, family life and employment, makes the question 'Who will do the caring in the future?' all the more critical. There is, it might be said, a triple whammy. People are less available to provide informal care; there is a rapidly growing demand for paid care workers, not just for children but also for elderly people, as well as for people to work in schools, hospitals and social services; and educational levels are rising and there are increasing and widening employment opportunities for people in the service sector and the 'knowledge economy'. But formal and informal carers are not just 'workers' or 'people'. Care has mostly fallen on the shoulders of only one-half of the population – women. Yet women's lives and aspirations are undergoing considerable and rapid changes.

Public policy has so far failed to grapple with this 'wicked issue'. Public policy responses are either weak or fragmented. At the time of writing we can see deep concerns about recruitment and retention in various services for children and adults – childcare, social care, health, education. But each concern is addressed separately, as if driven by different dynamics.

One response to the informal care issue (as is currently happening) is to create more services. However, when care is commodified, care work simply transfers from one group of (unpaid) women to another group of (paid) women. At the same time the pool of women from whom paid carers have been drawn – mainly women with low levels of education – is dwindling as well as being drawn into other expanding parts of the service sector (supermarkets, call centres and so forth). One proposed solution is to try to expand the pool. To this end, recent government policy has set targets for increasing the proportion of childcare workers from various underrepresented groups (for example ethnic minorities, over-forties, people with disabilities, men). Work with children is also seen as an important means of moving people from welfare to work, so tapping into the previously nonemployed.

The pool of potential female care workers can be enlarged from national sources – or from global sources. As we described in Chapter 1, there is already a global trade in carers, both privately (nannies and domestic workers) and publicly (in the case of teachers and nurses). This trade might be enlarged, to provide an increased supply of women willing to work for low pay, both with children and elderly people. This is the logic of free market globalization, and a framework for this trade already exists in the Global Agreement on Trade in Services. The import of such solutions to Britain may have frightening consequences (Brannen 2000), and may contribute to the development of an hourglass society composed of the 'care rich' and the 'care deprived' as described by Hochschild (2000) in the USA. 'Work rich' parents may buy out their own time with their children, not only to provide for their care but also to give their children a head start in education and many other pursuits. Rather than the spread of new concepts of care related both to ethics and other domains and the status of care work improving, care may become more firmly embedded in a consumerist culture, unquestioningly treated as a marketized commodity, with increasing numbers of care workers locked into servant class relations. In this scenario, there is an even greater concentration and overload of care work among those who are least economically advantaged, with deleterious implications for the care which these paid carers can provide for their own children and families and for themselves.

An alternative approach envisages new relationships between gender, care and employment, which we come on to discuss at a general level in the next section. More specifically this involves a recognition that paid care work (or rather, given our questioning of 'care work' as a separate domain, paid work involving a strong care dimension) is highly skilled, requiring theoretical understandings and practical competencies acquired through education, training and apprenticeship (Brannen 2000). In this way, the work escapes from its association with unskilled manual labour and mothering.

Good models for the professionalization of work with children exist in countries such as Denmark and Sweden. In Britain, training at a higher education level, matched by pay and conditions similar to those for teachers, would help tap into a new and expanding pool of recruits. It would certainly greatly increase the costs of care. Sweden, for example, spends 2.6 per cent of gross domestic product on its services for children under 6 years of age, a combination of extensive publicly funded provision and a highly trained, relatively well-paid workforce (OECD 2001).

If the professionalization route offers great opportunities, it also carries risks. As many commentators have reminded us (for example Stone 2000), there are dangers to commodifying care. It is not a neutral market process; it structures class relations and international relations. Moreover, the ideals of public care all too easily clash with the ethic of private enterprise. As we have argued, the rationalities of care are very different and ought to be different from the rationalities of bureaucracy and the market.

Transforming gender, the life course and generational relations

We have suggested that one answer to the question 'Who will do the caring?' involves fuller mobilization of the female population, both from home and abroad, to sustain a low-paid care workforce. From our perspective, however, this is deeply problematic. We have instead proposed rethinking paid work, both how it is structured and the level of training and pay. What might emerge from this are new professions educated to work with groups of children across many settings, the pedagogue being one example. This does not mean closing off work with children to people with lower levels of education. There can and should be a considerable amount of work for those without a professional qualification. However, as in Denmark and Sweden, most workers with children would be classified as professional workers on account of higher education.

This is only part of the approach that is needed. What is needed is a wider rethinking of the relationship between gender, care and employment, which addresses the ways in which care not only divides different classes of women but also shapes the life course, the relationships between and the responsibilities of men and women, and the relations between generations. We must also confront the relationship between production and reproduction, and between the values of care and business.

Fraser (1997) sets out some possibilities. She offers three models for postindustrial welfare states, in which unpaid work, paid work and gender are closely related, but with different relationships and borders for each model. In the Universal Breadwinner Model, the aim is to achieve gender equity by promoting women's employment. Women adopt male employment and care roles and the 'bulk of care would be shifted from the family to the market or the state, where it would be performed by employees for pay' (Fraser 1997: 52). The Caregiver Parity Model aims to promote gender equity this time by supporting informal care work: 'the aim is not to make women's lives the same as men's, but rather to make difference costless . . . The caregiver role is to be put on a par with the breadwinner role' (Fraser 1997: 55).

Fraser argues that neither of these models can achieve gender equity. This aim requires a third model: a Universal Caregiver Model, based on making 'women's current life-patterns the norm for everyone . . . all jobs would be designed for workers who are caregivers too'. This approach would 'integrate activities that are currently separated from one another, eliminate their gender-coding and encourage men to perform them too'. Such an approach would be addressed to informal and formal care, care in and outside the home. It would tackle head on the deeply gendered nature of care, acknowledging the unsustainability and undesirability of expecting women to do so much caring when they are also increasingly assuming other responsibilities and identities. It would require a complete redrawing of the gendered borders of care work and a quite new relationship between women, men and care (Fraser 1997: 61).

Fraser's discussion illustrates how any rethinking of children's (and others') care requires going beyond a search for technical solutions, to a political and ethical enquiry into the good life and a society and world which is fit for people to live such a life. For changing gender roles in the way proposed by the Universal Caregiver Model would have major consequences in every aspect of life and society. Some might doubt the feasibility of such fundamental change. Others, however, might question if we can afford not to explore this option seriously.

For at present, the inflexibility of the way we are 'supposed' to live the life course is based on an outdated male model in which employment is the filling in the middle of the sandwich. This model does not lend itself easily to most citizens' lives, with its over-concentration of employment and childcare responsibility in the prime working years. One glaring sign that the present situation is not working is Europe's flagging fertility: the birth rate for years has been below population replacement level, young people postpone parenthood to older ages, more women have no children at all and, overall, citizens have fewer children than they desire or are necessary to sustain a balanced and diverse population (for a fuller discussion see Esping-Andersen et al. 2002). Flagging fertility has knock-on effects throughout the life course: grandparenthood comes later in the life course when grandparents may not have the energy or desire to care for children on an everyday basis (Dench et al. 2000); families are smaller with each of us having fewer relatives as potential carers; and there are fewer people of working age to sustain the costs of the welfare state.

It is not our intention to spread a message of doom and gloom. Rather we want to emphasize that changing fertility, just like increasing female employment and more formal services, creates issues about care that need to be better understood and thought through. For example, as Chapter 10 discusses, a great deal of informal care is provided by family members of different generations. Such transmission of care needs to be examined and understood from policy as well as social scientific perspectives within the wider framework of intergenerational relations which include transfers of money, goods and services as well as care between family members and between family generations. Even as there is greater demand for informal care as people live longer and welfare states restructure, so family members are less available. Yet people's commitment to care for or about their kin remains very strong. More time in the labour market for women means that they have less time to care personally – but they have greater financial resources and an increased sense of economic independence which may lead to a greater transfer of money for goods and services. Such consequences of change have been little explored for care relations.

As we have already suggested from the experience of countries with well-developed services, it is clear that public and private provision, including care, work together. For example, public pensions sustain the power of older generations in relation to younger generations, providing them with material resources to make gifts to their kin (Kohli 1999). We need to understand better how public support can buffer and support informal care. Only in this way is it likely that we shall create the necessary social cement between the generations and generate a sense of reciprocity between family members and between citizens.

Reconceptualizing childhood

Rethinking children's care also means rethinking what it means to be a child and childhood itself. In Britain, a particular conceptualization of childhood has long held sway. This considers childhood as a passive status and a time of dependence. First and foremost, children have been seen as 'adults in the making' who are to be protected and acted upon by adults. The corollary is an image of the child as poor, an unrealized person, needy and weak, dependent and in need of protection and/or control. The concept of the child as an active agent and contributor to society who has interests and rights on the basis of their current status of childhood has been sadly missing (for a fuller discussion of this and other social constructions of childhood, see Moss and Petrie 2002).

As others have commented, no system of domination tells its own story (Tronto 2000). We need to move away from dominant mindsets in which children are seen only as the objects of adult care. Care also has the merit of giving us a new perspective on childhood, removed from seeing children mainly in terms of linear, developmental pathways. For, as research on children and adolescence shows (Brannen et al. 1994; see also Chapter 11), the notion of children's separation from parents is only part of the story; children seek connectedness to, as well as independence from, their families. Children now need to enter the public discussions about care and to be considered as active participants in their own care, rather than dependants to be cared for and products to be worked upon.

Through rethinking children's care and childhood, we may also be able to rethink the place of dependency in society. We have already questioned the value that liberalism attaches to individual responsibility and independence, attainable primarily through adulthood (or, more precisely, economically active adulthood) and paid work. Such rationalities define children as dependent – occupying an incomplete state which precludes being able to make decisions and exercise agency – and excludes them from citizenship. But if we can turn away from the dependent/independent dichotomy, and turn towards a recognition of interdependence and reciprocity within society as well as the family, then citizenship can be redefined to encompass caring and care relationships. And children can be seen as citizens rather than citizens-in-waiting, citizens capable of being active, interdependent members of society.

Towards an ethic of care in public policy

Returning once again to our opening chapter, we want to argue that care is about creating and maintaining committed and cooperative relations with others. This makes it a central moral question (Tronto 1993). We want to suggest that future policy confronts the proposition that 'good care is a moral issue where neither the client nor the care worker can be treated as objects ... [T]here is no way to shield care workers from the burdens connected to providing care in difficult and ambiguous situations'. This suggestion by Wærness (1999: 225) points to the need to rethink care rationalities, care perspectives and care practices. Rather than current instrumental approaches – technical, managerial, normalizing and universalistic – which are under-pinned by market or business ethics, an 'ethics of care' approach would seek ways to work with diversity, complexity and uncertainty.

It would nurture and support care practitioners' ability to make 'careful judgements' about what constitutes good work with children and other 'cared for' groups in particular contexts. It would help practitioners to reflect critic-ally on their practice and evaluate the value of their work, and to respect Otherness and their relation to the Self. Care is not a state but a process in which there can be mutuality if not parity. Practitioners and policy makers need to move away from a linear developmental model of the life course – infant dependence to independence and back again, in frail old age, to dependence – and to think in terms of the complexity of human interdependence.

Care: a political concept

But not only is care a form of ethical activity and moral thinking, but also it has the capacity to become a political concept. Childcare (and child care) involves considerations of equity, rights and power, not only for women but for children too. The ethics of care offers a sound basis for a politics of social inclusion and the renewal of citizenship. It may help us better to connect children's interests as a collectivity, in terms of their current childhoods, with children's individual needs which we, their adult carers, typically define for them.

As children's care has surfaced on the political agenda in Britain, so it is important to keep it there. While care remains a political issue, debates can be conducted between competing groups with different normative views and perspectives concerning: who should care for children, what care involves, what it means for children's lives, the costs of care and how we calculate them. However, once political issues are transformed into policy solutions, political closure takes place and the issues become depoliticized (Haines 1979). In the current context, policy solutions in general hinge upon the 'What works?' approach and are reduced to outcomes and targets. The risk is that care is professionalized and/or subjected to technical discourses and managerialist approaches which are treated as neutral ('evidence based') rather than being positioned within power relations and particular regimes of truth.

Provision and practice as well as policy need to be subject to democratic debate, which can bring critical thinking to bear and make visible our assumptions, understandings and discourses concerning care. Only through such a process is the familiar rendered strange, and the self-evident problematic. Care (and related fields such as education and social work) need to be recognized for the complex, ambiguous and demanding activities that they are, with opportunities for carers to document, discuss and reflect upon their practice. Any care service which does not allow ample opportunity for such reflective practice risks reducing care work to the application of low-level technology by low-skilled technicians.

Conclusion

Now more than ever, there is a need to make space for thinking and rethinking, for struggling with difficult questions and bringing an ethical and political dimension to bear on children and their care. The politics of care – Who will do the caring? How do we understand and practice care? How does care relate to other domains? How do we evaluate 'good' caring and what conditions enable this? – should be at the heart of political endeavour and the renewal of citizenship.

References

Bauman, Z. (1998a) *Globalization: The Human Consequences*. Cambridge: Polity.

Bauman, Z. (1998b) *Work, Consumerism and the New Poor*. Buckingham: Open University Press.

Bauman, Z. (2001) *The Individualized Society*. Cambridge: Polity.

Becker, G.S. (1993) *A Treatise on the Family*. Cambridge, MA: Harvard University Press.

Brannen, J. (1999) Caring for children, in S. Walby (ed.) *New Agendas for Women*. London: Macmillan.

Brannen, J. (2000) *Employment, care and citizenship, 14th Sinclair House Debate: The Silent Revolution – The Change in Gender Roles*. Bad Homburg: Herbert Quandt Foundation.

Brannen, J., Dodd, K., Oakley, A. and Storey, P. (1994) *Young People, Health, and Family Life*. Buckingham: Open University Press.

Brannen, J., Nilsen, A., Lewis, S. and Smithson, J. (eds) (2002) *Young Europeans, Work and Family Life: Futures in Transition*. London: Routledge.

Burchell, B., Day, D., Hudson, M. et al. (1999) *Job Insecurity and Work Intensification*. York: Joseph Rowntree Foundation.

Cameron, C., Owen, C. and Moss, P. (2001) *Entry, Retention and Loss: A Study of Childcare Students and Workers (Research Report RR275)*. London: DfES.

Cully, M., Woodland, S., O'Reilly, A. and Dix, G. (1999) *Britain at Work: As Depicted by the 1998 Workplace Employee Relations Survey*. London: Routledge.

Daatland, S. (1990) What are families for?, *Ageing and Society*, 10: 1–5.

Dench, G., Ogg, J. and Thomson, K. (2000) The role of grand parents, in R. Jowell,

J. Curtice, A. Park, K. Thomson with L. Jarvis, C. Bromley and N. Stratford (eds) *British Social Attitudes: The 16th Report*. Aldershot: Ashgate.

Deven, F., Inglis, S., Moss, P. and Petrie, P. (1998) *An Overview Study on the Reconciliation of Work and Family Life for Men and Women and the Quality of Care Services*. London: Department for Education and Employment.

Duncan, S. and Edwards, R. (1999) *Lone Mothers, Paid Work and Gendered Moral Rationalities*. London: Macmillan.

Esping-Andersen, G., Gallie, D., Hemerijck, A. and Myles, J. (2001) A report submitted to the Belgian Presidency of the European Union.

Fraser, N. (1997) *Justice Interruptus: Critical Reflections on the 'Postsocialist' Condition*. London: Routledge.

Gray, J. (1998) *False Dawn: The Delusions of Global Capitalism*. London: Granta.

Gulbrandsen, L. and Langsether, A. (2001) The elderly: asset management, generational relations and independence. Paper presented at the Fifth Conference of the European Sociological Association, in the Research Network on Ageing in Europe, August.

Haines, H. (1979) Cognitive claims-making: enclosure and the depoliticization of social problems, *Sociological Quarterly*, 20: 119–30.

Hochschild, A. (2000) Global care chains and emotional surplus value, in W. Hutton and A. Giddens (eds) *On the Edge: Living with Global Capitalism*. London: Jonathan Cape.

Kohli, M. (1999) Private and public transfers between generations linking the family and the state, *European Societies*, 1(1): 81–104.

Lingsom, S. (1997) *The Substitution Issue: Care Policies and their Consequences for Family Care*. Oslo: NOVA – Norwegian Social Research.

Mooney, A., Knight, A., Moss, P. and Owen, C. (2001) *Who Cares? Childminding in the 1990s*. London: Family Policy Studies Centre, in association with the Joseph Rowntree Foundation.

Moss, P. and Deven, F. (eds) (1999) *Parental Leave: Progress or Pitfall?* The Hague and Brussels: NIDI CBGS Publications.

Moss, P. and Petrie, P. (2002) *From Children's Services to Children's Spaces*. London: RoutledgeFalmer.

OECD (Organisation for Economic Co-operation and Development) (2001) *Starting Strong: Early Childhood Education and Care*. Paris: OECD.

Sennett, R. (1998) *Corrosion of Character: The Personal Consequences of Work in the New Capitalism*. New York: Norton.

Stone, D. (2000) Can public care-giving fill private needs? Some reflections on the dilemmas of paid caregivers. Paper delivered at international conference, *Work and Family: Expanding the Horizons*, San Francisco, CA, April.

Tronto, J. (1993) *Moral Boundaries: A Political Argument for the Ethics of Care*. London: Routledge.

Tronto, J. (2000) Better care: from the managed household to a caring society. Paper delivered at international conference, *Work and Family: Expanding the Horizons*, San Francisco, CA, April.

Wærness, K. (1999) The changing 'welfare mix' in childcare and care for the frail elderly in Norway, in J. Lewis (ed.) *Gender, Social Care and State Restructuring in Europe*. Aldershot: Ashgate.

Warin, J., Solomon, Y., Lewis, C. and Langford, W. (1999) *Fathers, Work and Family Life*. London: Family Policy Studies Centre and the Joseph Rowntree Foundation.

Index